The Talent Lab

The secret to creating
and sustaining success

**Owen Slot with Simon Timson
and Chelsea Warr**

EBURY
PRESS

1 3 5 7 9 10 8 6 4 2

Ebury Press, an imprint of Ebury Publishing
20 Vauxhall Bridge Road
London SW1V 2SA

Ebury Press is part of the Penguin Random House group of companies whose
addresses can be found at global.penguinrandomhouse.com

Copyright © Owen Slot and UK Sport 2017

Owen Slot and UK Sport have asserted their right to be identified as the authors of
this Work in accordance with the Copyright, Designs and Patents Act 1988

First published by Ebury Press in 2017

www.penguin.co.uk

A CIP catalogue record for this book is available from the British Library

ISBN 9781785031762 (hardback)
ISBN 9781785031779 (trade paperback)

Printed and bound in Great Britain by Clays Ltd, St Ives PLC

Penguin Random House is committed to a sustainable future
for our business, our readers and our planet. This book is made
from Forest Stewardship Council® certified paper.

To the great athletes – past, present and future – who pass through the Talent Lab. You inspire us.

Contents

Prologue

The war-room for the GB Olympic campaign for Rio is an office in Loughborough. It doesn't look much until you slide back the panels that stretch across the whole of one wall to reveal, behind them, staring at you, the exact health of GB's Olympic medal offensive. When a government official from the Department of Culture, Media and Sport saw it, he asked if there was any concern that the Chinese might fly a drone up to the window to take a look.

What you see behind the panels is the Medal Tracker Board. There are 200 individual names or names of teams up on the board. If you get your name up here, you are considered to have a chance of winning a medal. There is such an intricate patchwork of colour-coded information written next to each name, it looks as much like a Jackson Pollock painting as it does a sporting masterplan.

Medal Tracker meetings are convened quarterly and I have been invited to this one, four-and-a-half months before the start of the Rio Games. On the board, you can quickly identify the most crucial piece of information because, of all the detail here, the one that you really want by your name is an H. H stands for 'high' as in high-confidence medal hope. Today there are 44 Hs. There are also 27 Ms. M stands for medium-confidence medal hope.

There are not enough Hs or Ms in front of us. Thus, the tone is set at the start of the day by our group leader who tells us, 'This meeting is myopically focused on what we are going to do in the next four months to get those numbers up.'

The number upon which there has been a myopic focus is 66. Sixty-six has been the target for nearly four years. For four years, though, no one really thought it was possible.

The number is rooted in the London Olympics, four years previously, which had been an astonishing tale of victory for British Olympians. It had delivered the biggest haul of GB medals for over a century, and it was so overwhelming it had sportspeople – competitors, fans, ticket holders, media – shaking heads in disbelief. It was a triumph on a preposterous, rather un-British scale. Great Britain won 65 medals at those Games; they even had the temerity to get into a fight in the medal table with Russia. GB versus an Olympic super-power – and GB won.

Yet it was what followed that was so intriguing. At pretty much the first opportunity, the people who run Olympic sport in the United Kingdom got up and said: 'We're not done yet. At the next Olympics, we're going to win 66.'

They didn't need to do that.

In fact, their pitch was even ballsier than that. A month after the London Olympics, GB finished third on the medal table in the Paralympic Games with 120 medals. And so what did they say they'd do next time round? They said they'd win 121.

The questions, for me, were: how can you know? How can you even have any confidence that you can find 66 potential Olympic or 121 potential Paralympic medallists? How can you be so sure that you can help these people become the top one, two or three in the world? You have just punched massively above your weight, so what makes you think you can win a fight like that again? Success at this level is so unusual, what is it that makes you believe that you can sustain it? Because there is history here: Olympic hosts tend to do well, they tend to peak at their own Games, but after hitting the heights at home, every single host in the modern era has then dipped. That is why the figure, 66, would represent an unprecedented achievement. Why should it be GB that sets the precedent?

And so I asked them these questions and the reply was: 'Come inside and find out.'

That is what this book is about. This is the inside story of how Great Britain became an Olympic super-power.

Twenty years earlier, at the Atlanta Olympics, two British athletes – they were on the diving team – set up shop on the streets of the Olympic city. They had finished competing, they hadn't won a medal, they hadn't been expected to; between them they hadn't actually reached a final, but they were virtually broke and they wanted to raise some money by flogging their GB kit to shoppers passing by. Their pop-up shop quickly made it into the newspapers and it did not go down well with GB team management. Nevertheless, it symbolised rather effectively the fact that GB were paupers in the Olympic world. Success was not the norm. Great Britain finished 36th in the Atlanta medal table, behind the likes of Nigeria, Ireland and North Korea; they were minnows in the Olympic pond.

Any appreciation of the rise of GB as an Olympic power has to be tagged back to those streets of Atlanta. That is why the target of 66 and 121 seemed such a long shot.

The body at the centre of all this is called UK Sport. UK Sport is the funding body – an investment enterprise, if you like. A business. It receives its own income from two sources, the National Lottery and the government, and it invests that money into the sports and athletes it believes can win medals. It then rides those investments hard. So this is a story, too, of how business principles took Olympic and Paralympic sports management to new heights.

It was UK Sport that set the target of 66 and 121. This was the Big, Hairy, Audacious Goal, or BHAG – an acronym well enough established in business to have its own Wikipedia entry; it is a goal that is, by design, so challenging and risky that it stimulates progress. That was exactly what UK Sport wanted to achieve. That was why the numbers 65 and 120 were hung, large, on the wall of the reception of the UK Sport offices. That was the target to beat and the intention was that those numbers, in reception, would drive the organisation's focus every day. Yet, in the lead-up to Rio, those figures looked a long way off.

One of the constant commentaries throughout the build-up to every Olympic Games comes from Holland where a company called Infostrada Sports is based. Infostrada (which later became Gracenote Sports) is arguably the world's leading authority in sports data and analytics and it publishes a regular forecast of how all the Olympic nations are expected to do at the next Olympic Games. Its 500-days-to-go forecast pre-Rio was not a happy one for the GB investors. 'Bad news,' claimed the Infostrada head of analysis. 'GB is not going to perform anything like it did in London. This drop-off – as it stands – is quite large.' The Infostrada forecast had GB to finish in tenth place on the medal table with 45 medals.

Over the middle weekend of the Rio Olympics, though, Infostrada and every other doubter out there started to be proved wrong. That weekend was phenomenally successful for Britain: across seven different sports, British athletes won nine gold medals. Never before in the 120-year history of the Olympic Games had a Briton won a gold medal in gymnastics, yet Max Whitlock won two in two hours. By that Sunday night, GB had gone above not only Russia in the medal table again but China too.

At that point, the rest of the world really took notice. 'Remember the good old days when we used to have fun teasing the Brits about how we beat them in the medal count at the Olympics? Well you can forget it, because those days have gone.' That was how it read in *The Courier-Mail* in Brisbane, Australia. 'We've got four TVs covering four different sports at once in our office and it seems like at least one of them is playing "God Save the Queen" at any given time.'

How have GB done it? What is the secret? That was what the op-position suddenly wanted to know. How do you take on China and beat them? That is what this book is about.

One quick answer is money. Lots of it. The rise of 'Team GB' was mirrored closely by the rise in its funding. For Rio, £274,465,541 was spent over four years on funding and preparing the Olympic team and £72,786,652 was spent on the Paralympic team. Did they just buy their way up the medal table?

Well, not exactly. The Americans, who invest mainly through their college sports system, spend infinitely more than the UK, and invest-ment in Russia and China is completely off the graph. Analysts say that China pumped US$1billion into their elite end for their home Olym-pics in 2008. The Association for Asian Research (2004) estimated that in the four years up to the Athens Games in 2004, China invested US$2.4billion in the China General Administration of Sport. These numbers are astonishing.

This is an arms race and, yes, it is one that many do not believe is worth fighting. The way that GB fights the race, though, is by mak-ing its money go further than much of the opposition. For the build-up to the London Games, South Korea and Japan each spent between three and four times more than GB, yet GB's medal haul pretty much matched theirs put together. For the Rio Games, GB outspent Australia by 37 per cent and beat them on the medal table by 131 per cent. New Zealand run a tight, very targeted programme that sees their money go further, but in cycling, for instance, where GB invests heavily, the cost of success in Rio was £2.5million per British medal, which is around three times a better return than you get for your Kiwi dollar.

So, no, GB did not *just* buy their way up the table.

The penultimate day at the Rio Games was warm, muggy and overcast. For GB, the day started early with Liam Heath, a 31-year-old from Guildford, winning gold in the canoe sprint. The focus then switched to the women's triathlon and a thrilling, desperate head-to-head final sprint for the bronze medal between Vicky Holland, from Gloucester, and her friend and flatmate Non Stanford, from Swansea. Holland won it; the medal was GB's sixty-second.

The 66-medal mark was looming ever closer. Nicola Adams, the boxer from Leeds, took gold in the afternoon and then Bianca Walkden, from Liverpool, won taekwondo bronze in the early evening. That was 63 and 64. The great Mo Farah, in the 5,000m, was the sixty-fifth. And then, shortly after 10pm, in the athletics stadium, in the women's 4x400m relay, the gold was won by the US, silver by Jamaica and in third place, fighting off the challenge of Canada and Ukraine, was GB. That was the sixty-sixth. Just to ram it home, the next day, Joe Joyce, the super-heavyweight from London, took boxing silver.

These people are the talent pool; these are the names that went through the Talent Lab, up onto the Medal Tracker board in Loughborough and then, in Rio, into history.

Yes, we can do it

ADAM PEATY

On 5 August 2013, Fran Halsall, a 23-year-old Merseysider, stood on the block above lane six of the Palau Sant Jordi swimming pool in Barcelona. It was the last day of the World Swimming Championships and Halsall, in the 50 metre freestyle, was Great Britain's final hope. Weighing down upon her in lane six was a double mission. The first was her own ambition: this was a gold medal she thought she could win. The second was to save the GB team from complete humiliation, because when Halsall was standing on that block, that was probably the very moment when British swimming, in the modern, professional era, was at its all-time low.

The Olympics, in London, the previous summer, had been disastrous enough for British swimmers, but Barcelona had now taken them to new depths. At the London Games, it had seemed that GB athletes everywhere, in every sport, rose to the occasion – everyone bar the swimmers, that is. Swimming was GB's embarrassment sport, a single group of athletes who strangely, serially underperformed; they were the black sheep in water-wings. In London, though, they had at least scraped together three medals. Here in Barcelona, before Halsall hit the water, they had won none.

There is a wide assumption in Olympic sports that money equals medals, that if you douse your Olympians in enough funding cash, then the investment will be rewarded, but for over more than a decade the GB swim team had collectively been proving this wrong. If the money-equals-medals equation was so straightforward, then the £52million that had been invested in GB swimmers over the three Olympics up to London would have had them bathing in gold because, by any measure, a £52m Olympic investment is huge. Yet from the Athens Olympics in 2004, to Beijing in 2008 and London in 2012, £52m had bought swimming only 11 medals. There was one genuine, major superstar in the team, Rebecca Adlington, and if you took her out of the equation, then you would have lost four of the 11 and both of the golds. Adlington had single-handedly kept afloat the reputation of the GB swim team. Now, though the baton had been handed to her friend, Fran Halsall, in lane six, the evidence was over-whelming and the swimmers knew it.

If you look at which sports provided the most bang for their buck at London 2012, the GB boxers were top. Do the maths: pounds invested over the four years per medal won and the boxers delivered a medal for every £1.9million of investment. Cycling was second (£2.1m), followed by taekwondo (£2.4m). Bottom was hockey (£15m) – though that is an unfair comparison because you need to fund two full teams to compete for only two available (gold) medals. Swimming, where there are 34 medal events, was the next off the bottom. Each swimming medal had taken funding of £8.4m.

How long can you continue spending so much for so poor a return? How far, and over how many millions, could patience stretch? Invest-ment in swimming wasn't working; was it actually time, now, to start shutting it down? At the very highest level, with three years to go to the Rio Olympics, these were questions that were now being ad-dressed. Over successive Olympiads, GB had consistently proved that it could not compete with the rest of the world. Was it time to start admitting defeat?

In the stands at the Palau Sant Jordi, then, on the last day of those Barcelona Worlds, British swimmers were supporting Halsall in their numbers, desperate for her, desperate for some face-saving success for the team. She was their last hope. It probably didn't help that Halsall had a recent record as a so-near-yet-so-far performer in big events. In the Worlds in Shanghai in 2011, she finished fourth – twice. In the London Olympics, she got a fifth and a sixth. Here, she already had one fourth-place finish in the 50m butterfly. As a sprinter, she knew all too well that if you make one mistake, you will pay for it.

But this final started well for her. She was quick at the start and by the halfway mark she was ahead. With 10m to go, she was still ahead. At that point, though, she started spinning. In layman's terms, spinning is what you do when you want to go faster but you are not catching the water properly. Halsall said later that it was when she realised she was at the front that she started spinning. In those last few yards of spinning, she went from first to third. Britain at least had a medal, but even this one came with a measure of disappointment.

Afterwards, Bill Furniss, the head coach, made himself available for media interviews but he was short in his responses. The Halsall bronze hardly registered as a consolation. Talking of the Barcelona campaign as a whole, he said: 'This has been a huge disappointment. There is going to be a sea-change.' Hard words, but there was no room for debate here. Halsall's bronze was no saviour. Swimming was at a crossroads: sea-change or sink.

Barcelona was therefore the line in the sand. For the next three years, on the road to Rio, swimming would fastidiously pursue sea-change. Just as a failing business can be rescued by intelligent turn-around, swimming aimed to show that a failing sport can turn around too.

When you compete at an Olympics or a World Championships, or whatever is the biggest event of that year, you want to deliver your best performance of the year. Ideally it would be a PB – an all-time 'personal best' – but maybe that is asking too much; those are, by definition, rare occurrences. You cannot expect all competitors in every lane of a swimming final to produce the best swim of their lifetime every year. But if you can produce your best for that one year, then you are likely to be competitive. Producing a 'year's best' on the most important day of the year is what any high-performance organisation would expect and they will normally get exactly that from around 60 per cent of their athletes. One of the reasons that GB swimmers had done so badly at the London 2012 Games was because the number who swam season's best times was 20 per cent.

After London 2012, there was the predictable management clearout: the two top dogs – the performance director and the head coach – both left their jobs. Indeed, there is a pattern here, there was a different PD and head coach for the Beijing Games and the Athens Games before that too. That's three different PDs, three different head coaches all with different philosophies, in three consecutive Olympic cycles. No business would elect to run itself with such frequent regime change. Is it any wonder that swimming kept on lurching forward a bit and back a bit but never made concerted long-term improvement?

When British Swimming was looking for its new PD post-2012, one of the leading candidates, Chris Spice, started looking into the health of the sport. It was this stat, for season's-best performances, that most interested him. How and why did they hit 20 per cent at their home Games?

Spice thought, 'There is no point taking over a sport if you haven't got the raw material. So first I had to assess whether there was talent there and my own research showed that there was. Twenty per cent swimming their season's best at the Olympics themselves? That's a gross underperformance. I would expect 65 per cent; even 50 would be acceptable. But 20? The point was this: it's not that they couldn't swim fast, it was that they weren't swimming fast on the big occasion. They *were* capable of swimming fast, but not of doing it on the right day.'

Across a decade of underperformance, arguably the stand-out, most desperately sad case-study of a British swimmer failing to do it on the day was at the Athens Games in 2004 where Mel Marshall, a 22-year-old from Lincolnshire, was expected to be one of GB's superstars. Before those Games, any newspaper of worth had Marshall down in their 'ones to watch' selection. The year before Athens, she had won the 200m freestyle gold in the European short course championships. In April 2004, at the British Olympic trials four months before the Games, she won the 200m with a PB of 1min57.85, a performance that sent ripples around the world. Anyone who can go under 1min-58sec has to be taken very seriously; only three other women going to Athens had ever been under 1min58sec. Marshall would go to those Athens Games ranked number one in the world, the fastest of them all that year. And not only did she go to Athens ranked number one in the world, but she had the personality to match: effervescent, extrovert, when she won races, she would skip around on the pool deck, shadow-boxing in celebration. She used to say that when she eventually retired from the pool, she would be a firefighter. She wasn't afraid of anything.

Athens, however, was a personal disaster.

How so? Now, over a decade on, she describes British Swimming, back then, as a 'stressful industry rather than an enabling industry'. She says Athens and pre-Athens was 'a stressful situation' and that there was 'no protection' from it. 'On top of the stress of being at an Olympic Games, there was a lot of unnecessary stress and that was all internalised. There was a lot of stress coming from the coaches which came down from the PD and then the national coach. That created a stressful environment for the athletes.' This is her saddest and most shocking observation of all: 'For me, it was game-over by the time I got to the Games. I was knackered, emotionally exhausted. Deep down, I probably knew it was over before I had even arrived in Athens.'

In the heats, she finished tenth overall, which was enough to get her into the semi-final. In the semi, though, she came in last. In neither of the semi-finals or the final did anyone dip below the 1min58sec threshold, but in that semi, Marshall was three seconds off it. 'The biggest high in my career,' she says, 'was becoming the fastest woman in the world in Olympic year; the biggest low was not even making that Olympic final.'

Spice did indeed get the PD job and, eight years on from Athens, he was determined to establish the extent to which this environment, which had poisoned Marshall at the very high point of her career, still existed. He was appointed in March 2013, the same time that Bill Furniss was made head coach. Furniss had been Adlington's coach, so he had proven credentials, but only with individuals, never across a whole programme. However, when they went to the Barcelona World Championships that summer they were so new to their roles that it was too late to have much influence on the outcome: their mission was more to find out what they had inherited.

Spice was not impressed. These are his impressions of how the GB team operated at Barcelona, and they mirror Marshall's experiences a full nine years previously: 'It was too stressful, the athletes were feeling the pressure, the leadership was putting pressure on them. The amount of over-coaching going on before a race was incredible. There were only one or two coaches that were calm under pressure. There wasn't a relaxed, business-as-usual approach. I saw nervous, anxious athletes, anxious coaches, poor coaching, over-coaching during the meet itself. A grossly underperforming team. I said to the coaches: "How do you coach them to swim like that? How do you coach them to choke? Because your coaching is delivering that outcome." They looked at me as if I had two heads. They were stressed, standing on the side of the pool yelling out instructions, white knuckles around their stopwatches, panicking. They thought they weren't, but they were.'

So it was not just Furniss who wanted a sea-change but Spice too.

How do you deal with a failing sport? It was not just Spice and Furniss trying to find an answer, but the source of their funding, UK Sport. UK Sport is like an investment fund, but it is investing in businesses where the rewards are medals rather than dividends and share-price growth. After £52m invested over three Olympics, and such a poor return, any investment fund would be considering taking its money out and UK Sport was no different. After London 2012, it took a deep breath and invested another £21.4m in swimming for the next four years; another huge amount of money. Only four other sports had received more. But the Barcelona World Championships focused minds further: if swimming was simply not going to deliver medals, then maybe it was time to pull the money out for good and invest it in other sports that could.

When managing the investment in a failing sport, there are four options available. One: turn the lights out, pull the plug altogether, just say: 'Thank you, swimming, you've had your go, but it's all over.' Two: cut investment, make life hard, refine the scope of where you are investing and say, for instance, 'OK, we'll cut the sprinting and butterfly programmes because they deliver the least return.' Three: keep the investment as is. Or option four: decide that, to get a return, you actually need to invest more, but with heavy conditions. The fourth choice was never going to happen because there was no spare cash. The first choice, the Armageddon option, just didn't make sense because when there are 34 gold medals, or 102 total medals available, there are just too many opportunities to get a return on your money to call it quits completely. The swimming fraternity was most worried that option two, serious cuts, was coming. In fact, what UK Sport finally decided upon was option three: keep the investment figure untouched. But it was not as simple as that.

UK Sport was hell-bent on finally making the money work. Above all, they were convinced they had been investing poorly. Over the previous decade, financial support had been given to 282 swimmers and only one of them delivered an Olympic gold. So they wanted answers to questions about how their money was being spent. They wanted to know, for instance: how do we know if we are investing in the right athletes? Do we really know who might win medals? At what point in their development should we know this? What is the peak age for a medal-winner in swimming, and not just in the sport, but for each of the different 34 events? And if we can really identify who we should be backing, how do we know if we have the right people coaching them?

Thus they undertook a full situational analysis of the sport. They seconded two specialists in the science of sports analytics, one from cricket and one from the English Institute of Sport, on a short-term consultancy deal, essentially locked them in a room together and told them not to come out until they had all the answers.

When they finally emerged, this is what they had found. The spread of medal-winners was hugely skewed towards two nations: over the previous ten years, at World Championships and Olympics, the United States and Australia had claimed 41 per cent of the medals. In other words, two nations were doing something very right and everyone else was not. GB's own meagre share of the medal spoils over that time was 3.8 per cent. And of the (few) medals that GB had accounted for, women were outscoring the men by three to one.

Just because you are good as a kid doesn't mean you'll be good as an adult. The transfer of junior medallists to senior is extraordinarily slim. Since 2000, the proportion of junior medallists who have won medals at senior level is just 6.9 per cent. Across the world, only 24 per cent of those who have won medals at senior level ever even finished in the top eight at junior world level. In the UK, though, the percentage of senior medallists who had been in junior finals was 63. This meant that either GB was far better than the world norm at transferring junior talent to senior success (an unconvincing argument), or it had simply been backing its top juniors too heavily and ignoring the claims of later developers (very convincing).

Other areas of GB performance were exposed. Only 13 per cent of GB medals in the previous decade came from the sprint events. They already knew that sprinting, especially freestyle, wasn't a strength, but did it have to be such a weakness? Because if you don't produce sprinters, then you don't just miss out on the sprint events, you miss out on the sprint relay events too. And that is a trick missed because in relay events, by definition, you are not competing against two Americans and two Australians as you often are in the individuals, there's just one of each. Further to that, while the world of swimming is getting ever more competitive, why not look at targeting one or two of the events where the depth of field of competition is not at its strongest, such as the men's 200m freestyle?

The trends of the age-spread of medallists produced the most striking evidence. In some events, medallists were getting older; in others, younger. The golden age for male medallists was 23.7 and women were a good year younger. But a real concern was how many of the GB hopefuls were too far outside the golden age. Of the athletes funded to win medals (called Podium athletes), 61 per cent were not within the desired medal-winning age-spread for 2016. Of 22 Podium athletes, only 12 fitted the competitive profile of previous Olympic medallists; and the stats showed a 68 per cent likelihood that at least six of those 22 would not win a medal in Rio and 95 per cent certainty that at least two would not.

And if the GB wannabe medallists were the wrong age, they certainly were not helped by the fact that they were maybe being coached by the wrong coaches. Of the 24 coaches that put swimmers on the London 2012 Olympic team, only three had ever produced an Olympic medallist. And of those three, only one was still coaching. The question then arose: was GB actually outcoached before it even got to the pooldeck?

Now, you can get lost in a blizzard of stats like this, or you can demand absolute clarity, as UK Sport did from their two researchers. Clarity was what they asked for and this is what they got. When they funnelled all these numbers and all this info into one single filter, it became distilled into one very significant statistic. The number nine. There were nine athletes who fitted the profile of a medal winner at Rio. To a small group managing the funding of the sport, these now became known as The Nine Golden Children.

The Nine Golden Children confirmed UK Sport's position that swimming was not a cadaver on life support that should be just switched off. The question was, how do you breathe new life into it? They applied the question to business: what achieves turnaround in a business? The answer is that you identify your main asset and plan from there. Swimming now knew its main asset – the Golden Nine – so everything then had to start with them. Focus resources, do more with fewer athletes.

So while the total investment into swimming was untouched, UK Sport insisted that the whole funding plan be reconfigured around the Nine and build from there. That was the easy decision. The harder one was from where to take the money away.

The biggest cut was Podium Potential athletes. These are the group below Podium, the group who you hope will make the step up. Once the situational analysis had been conducted, it was suddenly far clearer who really had potential and who did not. Overnight, their number was cut from 65 to 45. Again, do more with less.

The biggest statement, though, was the single cut to the 22 Podium athletes. Just one swimmer lost top-level funding. He had been Britain's best male swimmer over the previous decade with two world titles to his name and four Commonwealth golds. He was still in the world's top eight, but he would be 31 by the time he got to Rio, if he got there at all. All projections suggested that he was just too far away from a medal in Rio, so the brave call was made. Liam Tancock's funding was downgraded; he appealed to British Swimming and lost.

The message was clear: British Swimming was to be more slimline and stronger for it, but turnaround was never going to be as simple as that. UK Sport wanted to manage their investment more proactively; they wrote 11 investment conditions into the new agreement and installed Phil Gallagher, formerly head of education at the Charlton Athletic academy, as UK Sport's equivalent of a management consultant, to sit inside the sport and ensure they stuck to them. One of the key conditions was the streamlining of training centres – to have the best athletes and the best coaches working side by side rather than in different pools around the country. 'Initially,' Gallagher recalls, 'there was a vision of UK Sport parking their tanks on their lawn – with me sitting in them.' He started doing two or three days a week inside the programme. After a while, he was able to describe himself as swimming's 'critical friend' rather than the man pointing his guns at them. Trust was established.

The biggest area of attention, however, was in delivering big performances on the big day. That embarrassing figure from London 2012 – just 20 per cent of swimmers producing their best times of the year – had to be transformed. One of the few genuinely encouraging stats from the situational analysis was that, at London 2012, after the US and Australia, the nation with the most swimmers to qualify for a final was GB. All those finalists for just three medals? Surely that could be improved. Surely some of those finalists could be nudged up onto the podium. If Halsall was becoming a specialist at fourth, fifth, sixth and even disappointing thirds, then there must be a way of transforming fourth, fifth and sixth into bronze, silver and gold. Something had to be done to prevent the Golden Nine and other future stars becoming yet another nearly-but-not-quite generation.

This is how Spice saw it. 'It's nothing to do with the *training*,' he said, 'it's their *coaching*. Where does training stop and coaching start? There's the technical and tactical side and there's what we call "arena skills".' This is a term for psychological weaponry – being able to arrive at poolside on an occasion like an Olympic final and give your best. 'Our coaches didn't deal with arena skills at all before,' Spice said. 'There was just an expectation that you could cope.'

Cope? How would the athletes cope if they were being coached by coaches who hadn't produced champions before and therefore, by definition, did not know what 'arena skills' looked like? British swimmers were doing the opposite, arriving and choking.

Spice therefore had some tough talking to do with his coaches. 'It was about getting them to understand this and embrace it, understand for some of them: "I am not good in that environment, I stress my athletes out." That was the difficult discussion. I was saying to them: "You need to change these behaviours and we'll help you. But if not, you're on the scrap heap."'

To help them, he made one very interesting hire. He employed a man who had never coached swimming before, never swum at the Olympics or World Championships, never swum competitively, never even tried. This was Nigel Redman, a former England rugby player.

Nigel Redman played 20 times for England between 1984 and 1997 in the second row, where the tallest, biggest players tend to play. Maybe more significant was the club he played for: Bath. He was there in the golden period spanning the late eighties and early nineties when Bath were the dominant team in the country. And they were not just notable for their success, but for creating a high-performance environment that they largely policed themselves – if you didn't meet required standards, then the rest of the team would let you know about it quick.

Yet Redman happily tells you that he wasn't very good. Despite all those England caps and those years with the super successful Bath, he is extraordinarily disparaging about his own natural gifts. Growing up, he says, he wasn't much of a sportsman. He was the big guy who they stuck in goal in the football team. Only in his teens, when he discovered rugby union, did he make the following decision: I am a player of limited ability, therefore I will do everything I can think of that will make me better.

So he joined a basketball club to help his movement and ball skills. He started playing water polo because (a) that would force him to get used to handling a wet ball, and (b) in water polo, you need strength in the air when you are rising above the water for the ball and that would be a skill he could apply directly to jumping for a ball in the line-out. He also joined a boxing gym in order to work on his footwork, and he joined a wrestling gym to help with the parts of rugby where wrestling is, effectively, exactly what you are doing. In the wrestling gym, his work regime included sessions with Amir Eslami, an Iranian wrestler and former bodyguard to the Shah of Iran. At their most extreme, their work-outs involved Redman doing weights while Eslami was hitting him with cricket bats and medicine balls. This was intended to improve Redman's resilience.

Eslami's theory on developing athletes was simple: champions are not born, they are carved from stone. This is what Redman did; he chipped away at every possible facet of performance. In other words, he became an expert at personal development. So after he retired as a player, he was an obvious fit for coaching; and when British Swimming advertised for an Elite Coach Development Manager, it was Redman who got the job.

He was initially given a group of 24 coaches to work with, and he met them in groups of 12. He knew, of course, that they would be thinking: this is The Bloke Who Doesn't Know Anything About Swimming. So he told them: it's not about swimming, it's about coaching, it's about people. 'I explained that I'm very open-minded about sport,' he says. 'I think, at the start, as much as anything, they were just curious.'

Most striking for Redman was how individualistic some of them were; there was no sense of them all driving towards the same goal. This is what he recalls from his first group session: 'There was one coach who said, "I'm not sharing any information with any other coach in this room." I said, "Wow! Does it ever occur to you that sharing and developing will enhance everybody?"'

As he did the rounds, he spoke to more coaches, then more swimmers and then more retired swimmers. This is what two retired swimmers said to him, on separate occasions, that really shocked him: 'They said that, before going to a race at an Olympic Games, a coach on the team, who wasn't their own coach, had said something to them that, on reflection, could only have been intended to derail them. I asked, "Why would they do that?" And the reply was, "The only thing I can think of is because my possible success would have reflected badly on them because they didn't coach me."'

Mel Marshall, who was by then a coach herself, was particularly candid. 'She thought about it for an awful long time and then she said, "Nige, I am an open, honest person and I've thought about this and I honestly think my coach stopped me winning."'

Redman's first real task was to work out the answer to the question: what does a good swimming coach actually look like? He knew he couldn't try to make good swimming coaches until he knew what a good swimming coach actually is. So he spent six months going to all the high-performance programmes and watching; then, at the British championships in Glasgow in April 2014, he took the opportunity to interview as many swimmers and coaches as possible with this question in mind. At the same time, he found a document written by a group of people who were most likely to know the answer. A group of American and Australian swim coaches had collaborated in a study: what does high-performance swimming coaching look like?

This was like gold dust. The Aussie/American document was more about the coaching environment; his own findings were more about personal and emotional interaction. He filtered the two into one and established 20 competencies that he felt a top swimming coach required. Then he approached Ashridge Business School, in Hertfordshire, and asked for help. How can I best assess each of my coaches for these 20 competencies? Ashridge had done this kind of thing in business: how do you assess business managers, business leaders? There was not a vast amount of difference. Both swim coaches and business leaders are trying to employ best practice in order to foster high performance. Ashridge came up with five questions for each of the 20 competencies; some of the questions were so directly transferred from business appraisals that the wording merely shifted from 'operative' to 'swimmer'.

Thus armed, Redman got to work with his 24 coaches. They had not done 360-degree appraisals before and they were encouraged to actively engage. They had to find swimmers, managers, support staff who would answer questions about them and thus complete the picture. Even this process, Redman says, started to raise self-awareness. By the time it was done, between the 24 coaches, over 330 respondents had given their views.

'The idea,' Redman explains, 'was not to jump to conclusions but to start a conversation. One of the things that came out was that bottom of the list of 20 competencies were emotional control, emotional awareness, emotional intelligence.'

Redman, then, started a cultural shake-up: the process of re-educating the coaches. Initially it was a lot about holding up a mirror so they could recognise what he was telling them. He needed them to understand, for instance, how their stress levels worked so, during one competition, he hooked them all up to heart rate variance monitors. On another occasion, he wanted them to understand how performance levels and stress levels were related to tiredness, so he hooked them up again at the end of a heavy travel day. He told them that he wanted them to focus less on medals and more on the process by which they can influence medals. 'The question,' he explains, 'which I think is really apt for coaches is: "Who do I choose to be today?" If you're in your hotel room and you're frustrated by something, when you step over the threshold, that door, you need to be somebody for your athlete, so you've got to leave all of your own shit behind and make sure you are the person your athlete needs. It's the understanding of "I need to choose my own behaviour" rather than to start reacting to things which are around me.'

So he started running workshops for the coaches – on managing resilience, on managing stress, on managing themselves – and he brought in outside speakers to talk. He also made it his job to obliterate the culture of each coach out for themselves and replace it with one of sharing information, integrating, working as a team, becoming collectively stronger than the sum of their parts. And he tried to sharpen their technical knowledge too. He really wanted to work on starts, so he brought in coaches from cycling, athletics and sprint canoeing where, clearly, a fast start is a non-negotiable essential.

Redman was so intent that his coaches would be able to perform in Rio that on 10 December 2015, he decided to test them out. Only eight of the 24 coaches would go to Rio; those eight had been selected at the end of 2015 and, on 10 December, were to report to Loughborough for a day entitled a 'performance learning experience'. They were going to simulate a day of the Rio Games, Redman told them on their arrival, and their behaviours were going to be assessed throughout. There were even actors on hand to play certain roles.

The scenario he created was this: It is Day Five in Rio. GB has had success on Day One but none since, so the pressure is growing. You are at the pool. Chris Spice and Bill Furniss, the PD and head coach, have been to a meeting and are stuck in traffic, so you are in charge. One issue of the day to be managed is dealing with an athlete who has not been selected for one of the relay teams. Then there is a breaking Sky News report: there's been an issue with contaminated protein shakes. How do you deal with that?

The entire day was intended to create pressure and stress and to evaluate the coaches and how they responded as a group to crisis management. At the end of the day, there was in-depth feedback and individual assessment of their performance.

One of Redman's best coaches was Mel Marshall. She had quit swimming in 2008 and gone straight into coaching. She was coaching in Derby the following year and remembers the day when a 14-year-old boy called Adam Peaty turned up at the pool for the first time. She knew instantly he was special.

'Straight away,' she says. 'You just saw he had something. As you spent more time, you really knew. I have had that experience with others, but then you see more of them and you'd see capabilities and limitations; with Adam, there just didn't ever seem to be any limitations. Instead there was fight, drive, competitiveness, attitude, skill, feel for the water, focus, technique, agility, speed, potential. He was a born racer. In any race, if anyone was alongside him, he couldn't help himself. He has a killer instinct.'

The story of Adam Peaty, though, is not only about his development. It is also about the development of Marshall. She was put on successive intensive education programmes for high-flying coaches and she had Redman overseeing her progress. The first Redman saw of her, she was still the in-your-face firefighter personality of old. As he recalls, 'I'm on it like a car bonnet' was the phrase she first used to introduce herself. 'Mel was larger than life but you could tell just by the way that she answered that it was a front. There was this veneer.'

She acknowledges how much she changed. In the past, it was always the swimmers whose results were being benchmarked, now it was the coaches too and she found she became more self-reflective and less the old force of nature. Increasingly, she says, 'we were getting a generic measure of what good coaching looks like. What's my listening been like today, what's my interaction been like, what's my set content been like? It is a constant evolution of knowing more. We are wanting to know more and we are accountable for how much we improve our skillset.'

Her learning, she said, 'helped to cement my philosophy'. And what was her philosophy? 'To me, it's about cracking formulas. People are formulas. Everyone who walks through your door has a different formula. Your key thing as a coach is to work out their formula. If you crack it, then you are away.'

Peaty, as a formula, she says, was easy to crack. 'The lucky thing was I was able to mentor him at a key age. He is like a sponge. He is able to cope now because of the conversations we had when he was younger.'

You wonder, does she not wish that she'd had a coach like this herself? 'No' is her firm answer. 'I'm over that. I am a much better coach than I was an athlete. But I wouldn't be as good a coach if I haven't gone through that as an athlete. Now I am just proud of him.'

In April 2015, part of the Peaty formula went up on a blackboard back in Derby. Peaty smashed the world 100m breaststroke record, becoming the first man to go below 58 seconds. However, he and Marshall were not satisfied; they knew he had more and better in him. So up on the board Marshall wrote: 'Project 56'. From then on, everything in Peaty's training would be focused on further obliterating the record, taking it down not to 57 seconds but to 56.

What did it mean to be one of the Golden Nine? It meant that every option, where possible, was considered to aid performance: physio, coaching support, psychology, strength and conditioning. Jazz Carlin, the middle-distance freestyle specialist who was one of the Nine, for instance, needed to improve her starts and her turns. So in the Bath pool, where she trained, an underwater camera system was installed to assist her.

Peaty was not actually one of the original Nine. But the number-crunchers who had carried out the situational analysis had proven that good juniors didn't necessarily make good seniors, so Furniss and Spice were therefore eyes-open to the possibility of late developers and when Peaty started swimming good times, the Golden Nine became Ten.

One of the first changes for Peaty was to take him out of Derby. He started travelling every week to the British Swimming base at Loughborough, to work more closely with the strength and conditioning experts. As Peaty developed, he and Marshall came to agree that their relationship was too pool-based, that they would benefit from a deeper bond that wasn't obsessed solely with Project 56. So he and Marshall were given time away to go walking in the Malvern Hills together.

Meanwhile, Furniss drove the whole squad hard. 'Don't come to me if you want to be normal,' was the way he put it. 'What we do is abnormal.' He demanded world-class behaviours. In the two years leading up to Rio, he made them compete more, so they would get more accustomed to delivering in competition and so that their coaches would sharpen further their arena skills. When the 2016 British Championships approached, which would double up as the qualifying competition for Rio, he set unprecedentedly fast qualifying times for anyone who wanted to make the team for the Games. He wanted to put his athletes under unprecedented pressure, so he could be sure who could handle the Olympic pressure when it really came on.

Can you turn around a failing sport? Was it right to continue funding swimming, or should the investment simply have been withdrawn? The answers would be delivered resoundingly over the first week in Rio.

On Day Two, Peaty smashed the world record that he had already obliterated once. He didn't quite go under 57 seconds, but 57.13sec wasn't far off, and his success seemed to have a kick-on effect. His was the swimmers' first medal in Rio, their first Olympic gold for eight years and, in victory, he seemed to give his teammates the belief that they were no longer black sheep in water-wings. Everyone knew the basic demand: here at the Olympics, deliver your season's best. From the 20 per cent who managed that in London four years previously, the figure rose to 69 per cent here. More medals duly followed. Just minutes after Peaty's gold, Carlin took silver in the 400m freestyle, and on Day Seven she won a second silver in the 800m.

On the last day of competition, it was finally Halsall's turn to compete, in the 50m freestyle. Just like in Barcelona, three years earlier, she held a lead at halfway. Again, as in Barcelona, she got overhauled in the last few metres. And this time she finished empty-handed – fourth. It was one of the most desperately sad, so-near-yet-so-far stories of the Games; but it was no failure, because in the final she had delivered what was demanded of her, her season's best. And on the medal podium in front of her was a former drugs cheat who, in the opinion of many, should never have been allowed to compete. Halsall's fourth was the medal that never was but should have been.

The final race that night was equally unforgettable. Partly because it was the last ever Olympic swim by Michael Phelps (as least so he said), his final final, his final gold medal. He now has 23 of them. Phelps had to swim well, though, because when he started his butterfly leg, the third leg, the US team was in second place behind GB, who had surged ahead because of an extraordinary swim in the breaststroke leg by Peaty.

The silver they won that night was GB's sixth swimming medal. Overall, it was a case of mission accomplished; turnaround had been achieved. Even six medals understates the scale of the turnaround, because they had seven fourth-placed finishers too. Of the original Golden Nine, three didn't make the team, six did and five of them won medals. Mission accomplished there too. As for Peaty's breaststroke leg – split times showed he had gone 56.59sec. He had smashed through the 57-second barrier. Project 56 was successful too.

Chapter learnings by Simon Timson

We were only going to nail 66 medals in Rio if swimming really came to the table. The really important thing about the Nine Golden Children was the principle rather than the practice: you've got a small cohort of athletes that are really precious, you need to focus your effort and resources around them. The fewer athletes you put your effort into, the more chance they'll have of making it. This is not just a message for sport, it's for any walk of life; it's about a hard assessment of where you will get your wins and then streamlining the message and the goal.

Transformative change starts with excellent leadership. British swimming recruited a new senior leadership team that established high-performance expectations whilst providing even higher levels of individual support and encouraging innovative problem solving.

Transformative change takes hold when excellent leaders gather the facts and develop evidence-based strategies. Too often you'll have either the really good evidence-based strategy or a charismatic transformational leader. You absolutely require both.

Success requires an aligned organisation. Think about the chair, chief executive, performance director, head coach – that's the spine of the organisation and individually they are the vertebrae. If any one of them is out of line you've got massive pressure on the nerve and then pain all the way up and down that spinal column. You've got to align the organisational backbone. Chris Spice aligned the organisational backbone and everything flowed from that.

Talent

2

What does talent look like?

Tom Daley, Lizzy Yarnold, Australian aerial skiers

On 22 June 2015, 14 months before Rio, I go to watch Tom Daley training in the London Olympic diving pool. This is indeed a treat, though after admiring his full range of brilliantly executed spins and twists, I am also witness to a rare Daley disaster.

He is going off the 10-metre platform, practising a four-and-a-half-somersault dive, but he spins out. Even my untrained eye can see something has gone badly wrong and that is not just because, by the time he has surfaced, Jane Figueiredo, his coach, has bustled hastily to the pool side, trying hard to under-react but failing to mask her concern. Afterwards, Daley tells me, smiling, 'Jane never understands why, when I spin out, I don't kill myself.'

The four-and-a-half forward tuck is one of the highest-tariff dives and if you want to be Olympic champion, you pretty much have to have it. If you don't do the hardest dives, you cannot compete. Executing four-and-a-half revolutions in the 10 metres between the platform and the water requires extreme power to spin the body, and then grace and timing to unfold and stretch before you hit the water. When you do make contact, you are moving at 30mph. The smaller and tighter the body shape of the athlete, the better the chances of completing the rotations before hitting the water. 'Spinning out' is the term for losing control of the spin. And once you lose control of the spin, in theory you have lost control of how your body is going to hit the water.

Spinning out can therefore cause massive injury. If you haven't injured yourself physically, the chances are reasonably high you may have damaged yourself mentally. When he was 11 years old, Daley was practising off the 10m platform, spun out of a dive, hit the water with his body flat and was so shaken by the experience that it took nearly a year before he was going off the 10m platform regularly again.

On this day, when I go to see him, it is a normal morning's practice; well, it is almost entirely normal apart from the fact that it is a Monday. Daley tends to take Sundays off, so on Mondays his legs are marginally different. What does that mean?

When you spend as much time in the water as Daley, the chlorine dries out your skin. The obvious answer would be to use moisturiser, but divers won't moisturise their legs because that makes them more oily and harder to grip. When you are spinning fast and descending at 30mph, the G-force is extreme and having a firm grip with your hands around your shins is essential to hold the body shape tight; that is why divers rub wax onto their shins – to help the grip. On Mondays, however, Daley's legs have had a day off, out of the chlorine, so they have not had their natural oils and moisture dried out of them as much as every other day he trains. In other words, they are marginally harder to grip.

When Daley attempts this four-and-a-half, he executes the first and the second somersault, but as he rotates into the third, his hands slip and slide up his shins towards his knees. Immediately, he loses his body shape, he is not a tight ball any more, and so the speed of rotation slows and he starts to spin out. The very moment he loses that grip on his shins, it becomes impossible to execute all four-and-a-half spins. This is the danger moment.

However, he is good enough to retain control. Somehow he manages to rescue a dangerous, out-of-control four-and-a-half and turn it into a slightly splashy, get-out-of-jail-free three-and-a-half. It is this that so impresses Figueiredo. She says he is like a cat: you throw a cat in the air, it has an innate sense of how to land on its feet. 'I am not quite a cat,' Daley suggests afterwards. His point is that you throw him off a diving board and he doesn't land on his feet, but what he does have is an innate ability to land head first.

This is how he explains it: 'When I stand on the board I notice everything that's going on; literally everything. When I'm spinning I see everything, which is a good thing and a bad thing. The bad thing is that I get distracted easily because I see everything so well. But also it's a good thing. Today, for example, most people would have just completely wiped out after that dive, but because everything kind of goes in slow motion, I was able to rescue myself.'

This is important – a key talent characteristic. In the search for a diving champion, it is essential.

Figueiredo started working with Daley when he moved to live in London after the 2012 Olympics. For his entire career until then, Daley was coached in Plymouth by Andy Banks, a former diver turned policeman turned coach. Banks runs a big programme in Plymouth and has done since 1992, so when it comes to spotting talent, he knows what he is looking for. Fast twitch muscle, the kind generally associated with sprinters, is essential, he says; unless you are born with it, the four-and-a-half is beyond you. And this other talent, this quality of Daley's – the awareness of where is his body in the air – is special, says Banks, and is something else that you either have or you don't. You can work on what you have, but you can only maximise the talent you have been blessed with. Banks has seen plenty of kids with the athletic ability but not the aerial awareness. He calls them 'twiglets' – 'knobbly knees and legs that don't quite match'.

'Unless there's a high level of talent,' he says, 'then I can't do anything else with them, I can't see someone becoming a Tom Daley. It is impossible.'

If you want to compete as an Olympic nation, then, you can choose to wait for that kind of talent to turn up at the pool. Or, far better, you can go out looking for it.

Chelsea Warr had first started looking for athletes in Brisbane 10 years earlier. That was when Australia had begun to ask the question: given a population size of just 18 million, how can we create successful Olympians rather than hoping they just appear? This is not unlike any business asking: how can we find decent employees and manage success? Olympic sport in Great Britain in the nineties was a long way from asking any such basic questions. The GB system had always lived in the hope that if there were decent Olympic athletes out there, they'd come to us. It was a very long time before anyone properly clicked on to another thought process: let's not make do with those that happen to beat a path to our door, let's take chance and hope out of the equation and get out there and find them. More of them and the best of them.

Back then, Warr was a Talent Search Manager with the Queensland Institute of Sport, which had a good record for producing Olympians. Queensland was regarded as a hotbed of talent and Warr's job was to find new and more systematic ways to unearth more of it and develop it better. Her first attempt was to unearth women weightlifters and she describes it as 'the biggest flop of a Talent ID programme I've ever done'.

She explains: 'Weightlifting is a highly measurable sport. We can benchmark athlete performances and predict what you need to be able to do. We knew the progression rates to become a medalist; it was perfect for talent identification. So we started this initiative, selected a load of girls who had never done weightlifting before, identified the best 15 of them, and within three months every single one of them had dropped out of the programme. I didn't really know what I was doing. I just hadn't thought through the massive psychology around image and going to weightlifting clubs. The attractiveness of the sport – I just totally missed the whole psychosocial aspect.'

She went from that project quickly to the next. She had written a paper on the South Korean women's hockey team and how they had gone from nothing – no hockey culture, barely any hockey players – to winning a hockey bronze medal in the Seoul Olympics *in just six years*. That was her inspiration.

She says, 'I remember thinking: that's really interesting, how on earth did they do that? Because usually, particularly with team sport, they talk about long pathways.'

So she wondered: can we copy the Koreans and challenge standard practice? Women's football was her sport of choice. Instead of finding local players and trying to help them incrementally improve, could she find good local athletes who had never played football before and mould them into something even better?

'So,' she says, 'I'm talking to the leader of Women's Soccer Queensland, and saying: I've got this idea and what we're going to do is we're going to go out and we're going to recruit across Queensland the fittest, fastest, most incredibly athletic women and they're going to be very bespoke for the different positions. Strikers are going to be sprinters and the defenders are going to be from touch rugby and I'm going to create this formidable team, but they're not allowed to have played soccer. We're going to run this experiment to see if we can fast-track them, to understand whether accelerated environments of skill development can work. But the women's soccer fraternity were clearly challenged by this and how it would reflect on existing players and coaching standards. I remember one of them calling it the "Aryan Race Project". Initially, they did not want to do it.'

Eventually they were persuaded.

In late 1997 she recruited, literally, with an advertising campaign. There were 106 responses and, in December, 71 of the women came for a testing weekend in Brisbane. Warr was looking for tall, fast women to be her defenders, high aerobic endurance athletes to be the midfield and agile, long-limbed athletes as potential goalkeepers. None of them were footballers; that was the point of the experiment.

From that weekend, a squad of 24 was selected which, after six weeks, was cut to 17. They trained five days a week, twice per day, but were still so new to the sport that, after two months, when they played a couple of trial games against a Brisbane fourth division side, there was so much concern about their lack of knowledge of the laws that an arrangement was made with the referee that he would stop the game and teach the laws as the match progressed.

The following month, their season started. They were entered into the Queensland reserve team league, they would win 20 of their 23 games and only lose the play-off final on a penalty shoot-out. At the end of the season, ten players were selected for Queensland zone teams. Two of them, Pam Grant and Jess Mitchell, would go on to play for the Matildas, the Australian national team.

Warr had proved a point. For a high skill-based sport, Talent ID and fast-track skill development could work.

Australia in the nineties was an ideal place for Warr to learn this new trade. Just look at the aerial skiers. Australia was not an Olympic skiing nation; it had only ever delivered one Olympic medal on skis. Yet suddenly it was producing aerial skiers. Where from? From gymnastics; it was turning gymnasts into aerial skiers. Talk about challenging standard practice.

The blueprint for this was Kirstie Marshall. She was a gymnast converted to a snowsport aerials specialist and, in the mid-nineties, won 17 World Cup events. She never directly delivered at the Olympics, yet she was the inspiration for Olympic success because, in 1994, Alisa Camplin, a 20-year-old gymnast, decided she wanted to do the same and asked the Olympic Winter Institute of Australia what she needed to do to follow suit. She had never even skied before.

Given some encouragement, Camplin found her new metier had its challenges. She suffered nine concussions, a broken hand, a broken collarbone, a separated shoulder, a torn Achilles and a torn ACL ligament in the knee. When Camplin arrived at the Salt Lake City Olympics in 2002, she was in such physical discomfort from a previous fall that she was examined by doctors – to be told she had two fractured ankles. Contrary to medical advice, she insisted on competing, performed two triple-twisting double back-flips and won gold.

From here a pattern was set. Camplin won bronze at the Turin Games four years later. Four years after that, in Vancouver, Lydia Lassila, another converted Aussie gymnast, took over. In 2000, when Lassila had been first persuaded to join a programme converting gymnasts to aerial skiers, she had never previously clicked on a pair of skis. Within two years, she was competing against Camplin at her first Olympics and within three years she was number two in the world. Injury ruined her chances in Turin, but in Vancouver she finally took gold too. Another four years on and the pattern continued: another Aussie, David Morris, was on the podium for aerials. He had been a gymnast until Marshall, who had by then become an MP, was attending an event at his gym, saw him execute some tumbling lines and told him he should take his talent to the snow.

The line of succession does not stop there. The pathway is now so well established that the gymnastics, skiing and diving bodies in Australia have collaborated with a project called 'Spin to Win'. The next most promising product is Danielle Scott, who has already won World Cup events. And, yes, she too is a former gymnast.

There are crucial lessons in all this for Warr: not just that if you go looking for talent, then you can find it, and not just that skills are transferable, but that the more precise you can be about exactly what skills you require, and what will be required in the future, the more likely you are to be successful. In Australia, it wasn't simply gymnasts who were capable of switching sports; more specifically, it was gymnasts whose specialism was tumbling.

You tumblers out there – get out onto the snow.

In 2001, in the UK, a very different talent search began: Great Britain started looking for skeleton athletes for the winter Olympics. No one in their right minds in Great Britain had heard of skeleton; why should they? Skeleton – that's the one when you go downhill on a tea tray, right? And you go down an ice track, correct? Yes, and Britain doesn't have any ice tracks. And, to be precise, it wasn't 'Great Britain' looking for skeleton athletes, it was just one man in Great Britain. This was Simon Timson; he had been appointed head of skeleton for GB – well, someone had to do it. And, to pursue this curious aspiration to take on the world at a sport his own nation hadn't heard of, he was given an annual £10,000 war-chest to fund it.

Where do you look for a skeleton champion in a country where skeleton doesn't exist? You could go to the British skeleton championships in Austria, where a few British military types competed every year, but Timson decided against that. Timson didn't go anywhere near the mountains. He went instead to the British Universities athletics championships at the Alexander Stadium in Birmingham, where there were no downhill events and none involving tea trays. On a couple of grey, blustery summer days in 2001, Timson hung around the finish line at the end of the 100m straight, handing out his card to breathless athletes who had just finished competing and asked them if they fancied trying another sport.

'What sport?' would be the next question, slightly bemused.

'Skeleton,' would be his answer – and the bemusement remained.

'What's skeleton?'

Of the athletes Timson approached, few took his card and very few then got back to him. Of those who did get back to him, though, one was the jackpot. This was Greg Kirk, a powerful sprinter with the imagination to embrace a new competitive challenge.

Timson had one absolutely unswerving opinion that would govern all his decisions: that the £10,000 that had been spent annually on skeleton in previous years had been wasted. The old military types that used to compete for GB would simply travel the circuit and enjoy the racing. Timson's opinion was as follows: if all you are doing is what British skeleton athletes used to do – race and prepare to race – then when are you going to get better? When does skill development come into it? When are you going to learn by trial and error?

So Timson spent almost all his £10,000 on training. Racing was allowed to grind pretty much to a standstill. Pretty much all Kirk did was train. The target in the first year was to do 80 training runs. Towards the end of the season, when the money ran out, Kirk was in Igls, Austria, and refused to go home. The first night, he went up the mountain to the ice track, broke into the starter's hut and slept there. His sleeping bag wasn't up to much, though, so the second night he tried the local church, the third night a barn, and then finally he found an underground car-park with a tap and running water. That way, that season, he got nearer 180 training runs.

By not even halfway through the following season, Timson had spent all his £10,000, pretty much all on training. So he went back to UK Sport and asked for more. He was given a proper telling off. 'If you give me another £10,000,' he said in reply, 'we'll get you a world junior champion.'

Timson did get his money. The following season, Greg Kirk became world junior champion.

In 2001, Warr was recruited by British Diving to work on Talent ID and put in place a development pipeline to sustain success. In order to spot world-class potential, the first step is to build a profile of exactly what world-class actually looks like. In diving, world-class looks Chinese; China is, by some distance, the best diving nation in the world. In the last four Olympic Games, of the 32 gold medals on offer, China has won 26. And so Warr went to the Chinese elite and literally measured them up. How so?

Almost every year, some of the Chinese national team would come to the UK for a World Cup event or a training camp. Often they would base themselves at the pool at Crystal Palace. They were told that part of the deal for using British facilities would be that they would make themselves available for a 'research experiment'. OK, deal done. In goes Warr; she measures, she photographs, and she goes away with a very exact codification of what makes the world's-best diver.

Here, again, she was using 'skills' she learned in Australia. Before the swimming World Championships in Perth in 1998, by way of another research experiment, the Australians had also codified the Chinese swimmers.

She first went to Plymouth in 2002 with Chen Wen, the British head coach. She knew what she was looking for – not the Chinese finished product, obviously, but children whose physiology could one day become that. The format had been established: they would only go to towns or cities with diving pools and, within a ten-mile radius of that pool, they would visit as many schools as possible. They brought with them a trampoline because a number of the children they were testing couldn't swim. If it wasn't a problem that the Aussie aerial stars couldn't ski, Warr concluded, why should it matter if Britain's next generation of young divers couldn't swim?

The tests they put the children through were fourfold, looking at flexibility, speed and jumping ability. Chen, meanwhile, concentrated on the crucial body parts. 'No, no!' he would say, very matter-of-fact. 'This shoulder will dislocate. Next!'

This bit, finding genetically physically gifted people, Warr says, is the easy bit. In her own words: 'It's not hard to do the first shake of the tree and scoop up that top small per cent of the population.' The harder bit is refining the group, and she has an analogy for that too: 'A bunch of people will have enough points to get you into the Frequent Flyers Club, but actually what we're trying to find out is who can fly first class. How do we go from frequent flier to getting enough points to get into first class? That's the bit we need to focus in on.'

Daley was at St Edward's School in Plymouth at the time, but he missed the testing day at school. He had, though, already found his way to the Central Park Pool in Plymouth, and Warr and Chen tested him there. This is Daley's recollection: 'The first thing that I remember is that you had to do jump tests, stretching tests, somersault tests and you would go in a line one after another and you could see what the person in front did. And of course I just wanted to beat the person in front. I wasn't thinking about going as high as I could, I wanted just to beat that person. The competitiveness just came out in me.'

It clearly did the job. His records show good power ratios, that he was pingy, with good fast-twitch muscle fibre and listened to instructions. He was in. He would work with the coach who was running a Plymouth diving programme, Andy Banks. This is Banks's first impression of Daley: 'He was zippy, he was fast, he was aware of where he was and he had an ability to get through the water really quite well. The other thing that impressed me is when you said to him, "You're doing *this* but what I want is *that*," his ability to make changes was significant.'

Here were two genuine signs that Daley could be more than a Frequent Flyer. One: he had that sense of where he was in the air. Two: he had the capacity to learn. So it wasn't long before Daley was on an advanced junior programme and invited to national junior training camps. This was not a happy experience.

Warr recalls: 'Our ages were eight to thirteen years old and he was eight, he wasn't used to being away from home and was desperately clingy with Mum and Dad. They drove him from Plymouth to his first camp in Southampton and he was the youngest. The first day, in the pool he does OK, and then as soon as night time came and dinner and everything with everybody, he just went into meltdown, completely lost it to the point where I remember the team manager says to me, "Come into Thomas's room," and I'm like, "What's the problem?" "You need to come in."

'I walk into his room and you see these windows – the kind of hotel windows that only open so far – and he's standing, balling his eyes out, trying to push the window going, "If you don't call my parents now, I'm going to jump, I want to get out of here, I'm not doing this."

'I was there a long time, listening, reassuring him, reminding him we were there to help him achieve his big-dream goals, and we finally got him downstairs to dinner and he sat right in the corner and all he ate was Jaffa Cakes. It was a two-day camp and he got through a day and a half and in the end we had to call his parents to say, "He can't do this just yet." What was really interesting was when we put him in the pool he was so excited and just got on with it and did all the work and was brilliant, but when it came to the night-time, he went to pieces. I remember he would just refuse to eat. He would sit at the end of the table, with just tears and Jaffa Cakes.

'His parents were desperately passionate not to come; they wanted him to do it. So we didn't take him off the programme, but we said: "For the next six months, you need to go and do five sleepovers, and once you've done that and done it really well and liked it, then you can come back and stay for the camps. But you need to go and practise sleepovers." So he did.'

And that is where Daley's lucky monkey comes from. He recalls: 'The diving part made me so happy and I was fine all the way through the day until it got to bedtime. I'd dread the evenings. After dinner, it was, "Oh no, now I've got to go to my room, I've got to go to sleep," and I'd start getting upset. I used to cry because I never used to want to sleep in a hotel room. I used to not be able to sleep, to threaten to jump out of windows. It used to terrify me, even if my mum and dad were staying in the hotel next door. They were trying anything to get me to stay with the other divers, they were like, "What do you want?" And I said, "I want a trampoline and a monkey. A real monkey." They were like, "OK, we'll get you a monkey if you stay in that hotel room." So I stayed that one time and the next day I come down and, in the back of the car, there's a monkey with velcro hands and one of those mini-exercise trampolines. That's where that lucky monkey comes from; it travels with me everywhere still. It's crazy really; it sits on poolside, even during the Olympics.'

The making of Tom Daley, though, was more than just genetics and a few sleepovers. Of course it was. The question Warr is asked more than any other is: 'What is talent?' Her short answer: 'Potential.' A longer answer: 'It's a question of who's got the headroom? What I mean by that is: who has the room to grow? It's like investment bets in potential. The trick is to try and find out who's got the most headroom because they're the ones you want to invest your time, money and emotional effort into.'

So it is all very well Daley being genetically blessed with the required physiology and that innate aerial awareness, but it was never going to grow on its own. Arguably, if Daley had been born anywhere other than Plymouth, it would never have grown at all.

This is Andy Banks, The Life Story, in short. Brought up in London, moved to Yorkshire in his teens, had no interest in school, was a kind of lightweight, middle-class punk, won district titles for diving, dropped out before A-levels, joined the police, did a bit of diving coaching. Decided, then, that diving was what really interested him, so, with that in mind, left the police and went to Carnegie University in Leeds for a degree in Human Movement.

'In my school career,' he says, 'I couldn't see the point in anything. Why the hell do I need to learn the area of a circle? I'd had no interest in that whatsoever, but when it came to diving, all of a sudden biomechanics and how it worked and why it worked was really interesting.' Thus he graduated and pursued a career as a diving coach.

In the UK of the eighties and nineties, though, there was little education system for any sports coaches, least of all diving coaches, and certainly not to elite level. How on earth do you become an Olympic coach, then? 'Head-sitting,' as he puts it, was the solution. This is what he means: 'You have to go and sit next to someone who knows more than you and bleed them dry, and then the next one and the next one and the next one. I was an absolute pain in the arse. I sat on everyone and anyone I possibly could. I'd go away to competitions and sleep on someone's floor, film everything that was going on, talk to coaches, ask them what they were doing, why they were doing it, how they progressed it. I was trying to build up a knowledge base. If someone like Tom came along, I wanted to be ready for them.'

Banks's most valuable head-sit? John Wingfield. Wingfield is an American coach who was responsible for the career of Thomas Finchum.

Like Daley, Finchum was a prodigy who developed early and fast. He pursued his talent so hard that he was home-schooled through most of his high school years in Indiana so that he could spend more time at the pool. When Daley, aged 14, went to the Beijing Olympics as the great young future hope of British diving, Finchum, four years older, was at the stage when people were expecting him to deliver. Long before they got to Beijing, Banks head-sat Wingfield and asked: 'How have you done with this Thomas?' He wanted to suck up everything he could about developing exceptional young talent.

While Wingfield passed on his learning about exceptional youth, he also reinforced a coaching philosophy that Banks was working on which he calls 'Everything Everywhere'. This involves using all the different heights of the boards and building up a skill chain from the lower levels, adding more complications to a dive the higher you go. By switching between heights, Banks reinforces the learning of the skill chain, and this enforces consistency of control and thus confidence. In effect, he is allowing them to learn what they are doing and where they are in the air. In other words, that innate skill that Banks looks for and that he says Daley was so blessed with – his aerial awareness – has been nurtured and improved.

There were some huge crises along the way. 'I used to be a little brat,' is how Daley recalls the early years. He could also suddenly develop a deep fear of heights and would spiral so far downwards that, when he was 11, he genuinely thought his career was over. At the 2005 junior international event in Aachen, Germany, as a ten-year-old competing in the category for 14- and 15-year-olds, he won silver on the platform. The following year, expectation preceded him to the same event in Aachen, but so did a comparatively minor incident in training when he had tipped his feet on the edge of the board when he was spinning. That seriously freaked him out.

In Aachen, he had no Andy Banks to calm him. 'I was just so terrified and nervous of the whole thing,' Daley recalls, 'and my dives weren't going so great and I was just really scared. So I said, "I can't dive, I don't want to do it." It was so embarrassing and horrible. But I was told

"We're going to do the competition," so we started the competition and when it got to the dives that I didn't want to do, I was told, "If you don't want to do it, pull yourself out." The recorders at the competition were sat in a stand up a three-metre ladder, so when my name, Thomas Daley, came up on the board, I had to go and climb up this ladder in front of everyone, crying, and tell them I wasn't going to do it. It was brutal. That was the competition where my dad had flown over, so I went over to him; he was crying and I was crying.'

When he returned home, his confidence was shot. He wouldn't even climb the ladder to the 10m platform. The boy with all that aerial awareness had been stripped of his powers. 'He wasn't in control,' Banks says, 'his body was doing stuff that he wasn't in control of.' That was when Daley himself was convinced that his diving career was over.

Banks, however, knew what to do. He took it back to basics and started to rebuild the skill chains. No rush. Indeed it took nine months before Daley was doing his full repertoire off the 10m platform again. The result, though, was an improved model with stronger foundations and, crucially, greater aerial awareness. Banks had taken his potential and found a way to allow it to grow.

On 13 February 2014, Lizzy Yarnold stood at the top of the Sochi Olympics ice track, preparing for her last run in the Games. What she was about to prove was that Olympic success can be engineered. There are a million and one factors that go into Olympic success, and no two Olympic champions are the same. But the chances of a non-ice nation winning the Olympics with a non-ice woman are simply laughable. Unless you get your engineering spot on.

If you are brought up as a kid in a German town with an ice track, you will very likely spend Wednesday afternoons after school doing PE on it. The women that Yarnold was competing against had therefore had around 15 years' experience in the sport; Yarnold had had five. Her story told a simple truth: find the right talent and give it outstanding training and you can beat the traditional accepted systems of sporting success. There were no 10,000 hours here, nothing close.

Greg Kirk had been the prototype for British skeleton. Seven years after finding Kirk, Timson et al had refined the profile of what a skeleton Olympic champion might look like, so that when they first clapped eyes on Yarnold at the Manchester velodrome on a warm weekend in June 2008, they knew she might be a decent fit. This was the key to their success: the more precisely you can establish what success might look like, the higher your chances of finding it. She had been a regional level heptathlete and had answered the call of a Talent ID campaign called Girls4Gold which was intended to find future Olympic champions in a variety of different sports. All she had to do was fill in a short questionnaire, get weighed and measured, and then complete a vertical standing jump and a 30m sprint. After the Manchester try-out, the letter she received said that she had made it through the first filtering stage as a potential athlete for skeleton. She did not know what skeleton was.

Fast-forward five and a half years, and she was in Sochi. At the Sochi Olympics, the kind of danger that skeleton presents was experienced by Noelle Pikus-Pace, the American regarded as Yarnold's greatest rival. On one of the final training runs before competition, Pikus-Pace had had a serious crash when the G-forces created on the ice had caused her to black out mid-run and bang her head. Pikus-Pace had dusted herself down sufficiently to make it to the start line. Yarnold, conversely, was so relaxed that she had prepared in the Olympic Village by knitting and watching episodes of *Downton Abbey*.

After the first two runs on Day One, Yarnold had built a lead over Pikus-Pace of 0.44 seconds. In skeleton, that is considerable. On the first run of Day Two, when all her rivals needed to start reeling her in, Yarnold broke the course record. For her fourth and final run, she was a dead cert. She would win gold by 0.97 seconds.

The London Olympic final would put Daley's skill chains to the ultimate test. Daley's first dive was greeted by a blaze of flash photography and he lost the dive in mid-air. This was a moment of high drama, because he scored so badly that he was as good as out of the competition, and high tension because Daley and Banks immediately launched an appeal against the illegal and off-putting use of flash photography. For Daley, it was also a moment of sheer terror; however well drilled you are, losing a dive from 10m is terrifying. As Daley would later admit in an interview in *The Times*: 'My instant reaction was that I just didn't want to go back up there. I wanted the referee to say no, but he ordered a re-dive. I was the most terrified I've ever been in my life, thinking I could lose it again in front of 18,000 people.' Under that pressure, nevertheless, Daley nailed the dive. After the re-dive, he was in second place. By the time they got to the podium, he was in third.

Whatever happened to Finchum? He had won two US national titles by the age of 16, a bronze at the World Championships when he was 17 and a silver at the Worlds when he was 19. The Beijing Games, however, didn't quite work for him; he finished fifth in the synchro event and twelfth in the individual. Four years later, he failed to make selection for the London Games and the day after that team was announced, without his name on it, he retired from the sport to pursue a career as a country music singer. He had reached the heights, but never soared quite as high as hoped; that happens sometime with prodigies.

Daley is still trying to prove that is not the case with him – which is strange to say, given that he now has a second bronze, from Rio, to add to his first from London. Yet he wasn't happy with Rio. After bronze in the synchro event, with partner Dan Goodfellow, he seemed in prime form to fulfil his pledge to win gold in the individual which followed. The individual event was a disaster, though, and he failed to make the final. 'At the Olympics,' he said afterwards, 'you can get your dreams crushed.' He also said that he intends to pursue his dreams another four years to the next Games in Tokyo.

Daley remains the only Briton ever to win diving medals at successive Games so 'crushed dreams' is a tough assessment. He doesn't want it to be the conclusion.

Chapter learnings by Chelsea Warr

The common denominator of any high-performing organisation is having hugely talented people. When people discuss talented people, they often say: 'They've just got "IT".' But what exactly is 'IT'? How can we confidently know they really have 'IT', and how can we separate performance from potential?

You can't teach a brick to float. Sorry, strivers, talent really matters. Whether it's physical, physiological, psychological or technical, proper talent has proper super strengths. You require several in order to achieve at the highest level. In the examples in this chapter, the super strengths were clearly defined and measured.

Zig-zagging. As Daley teaches us, the route to excellence is rarely linear. The pathway to the top is often referred to like a game of snakes and ladders. Mistake-making and risk-taking are a large part of the journey.

Put square pegs in square holes. We would never have heard of Lizzy Yarnold if she had stayed in heptathlon. How many of your employees are working in the wrong roles? How often do you encourage job swaps to optimise a better matching of talent to task? What might Talent Transfer look like in your business?

Diversify your talent recruitment methods. Throw your net wide to capture talent, challenge the status quo on your traditional recruitment methods, fish in alternative talent ponds. That enhances your chances of unearthing your future performance genius.

Experiment. The hallmarks of any successful great high-performance environment are two words – curiosity and experimenting. Leaders, coaches, athletes and parents in this chapter were prepared to try both.

3

Where to find talented people

If Australian women had been better at rowing, then maybe we would never have discovered Tom Daley or Lizzy Yarnold at all. Only because the Australian women were so hopeless did the seeds of modern Talent ID in British Olympic sport take root. In 1988, the Australians could not find one single female rower to take to the Seoul Olympics and, even worse, Peter Shakespear, the women's head coach, could not see where the next one was going to come from for the following Olympics. As he puts it, in his own laconic way, 'I was in deep shit.'

Any industry in any country around the world that employs people is, in its own way, involved in identifying talent. For many of the most advanced, Talent ID – the business of selecting employees – is an exceedingly sophisticated business. The first step to successful talent-spotting is knowing what a talented person looks like. The problem for Shakespear was that in 1988, when there was a general acknowledgement in Aussie sport that the absence of female rowers was an indignity that should never be repeated, he did not really know what he was looking for.

What does talent look like? How should you know? How do you know what is potential, or which young athletes have what Chelsea

Warr describes as 'headroom'? Shakespear asked himself those questions many times. He had been a rower himself and had competed in two Olympics, in 1972 and 1976, so he thought he had a reasonable idea. But more specifically? The exact profile of a future Olympic star? No. He accepted that his knowledge was too limited. So he elected to learn from the real masters. While there was not one single Australian female rower at the Seoul Olympics, at the opposite end of the scale were the East Germans. They won four of the six Seoul gold medals. Shakespear, therefore, decided to look there.

East Germany, the communist state whose sporting system is ethically denounced and at which the western world turns up its nose, was there first with Talent ID. Peter Shakespear may be the godfather of Talent ID in the western world, and his methods would soon start to work when he brought them to the UK, but it was from East Germany that he learned his early lessons. The UK today is simply attempting to perfect the systems that East Germany was toying with 40 years ago.

It was not just the East Germans that Shakespear looked to. The second most successful nation in the women's rowing at Seoul was Romania, so he decided to look there too. He made one trip to the old East Germany and his timing could not have been better: when communism began to crumble in the old Eastern Bloc and the Iron Curtain fell, the state secrets and inside knowledge of their sporting system that had previously been so militarily locked away suddenly started to seep out through the cracks. Shakepear was ready and willing, hands cupped, to collect any scrap of information he could catch. While the western world viewed eastern European methods with disapproval, Shakespear realised that he was collecting invaluable intellectual property. And some eastern European coaches, waking up to the fact that they might need to make friends fast in foreign countries, were only too happy to share it.

'When the Wall started to come down,' Shakespear recalls, 'we started to look at other countries. We had this incredible window when they would tell us almost anything.'

He invited two high-performance directors to present at a conference in Australia. One was from East Germany, the other from
Romania, and immediately two different approaches to Talent ID became apparent. 'It was interesting to look at the process of how they
tested their kids,' he says. 'Not how they developed them – that was
pretty horrendous – but how they tested them.'

The East Germans tested children aged 12–14 and recruited in large
numbers. The Romanians did not have such a comprehensive infrastructure; they tested 16- to 18-year-olds and recruited in smaller numbers. The East Germans had a far higher attrition rate; their kids were
fodder and they would lose around a third of every intake every year.
The Romanians had a higher success rate and, for two reasons, Shakespear concluded that their version was the superior model for his purposes. One: testing children before puberty, the way the East Germans
did, was not a good indicator of talent. Two: a programme on the massive scale of the East Germans was not remotely one he could copy; he
needed a better production line, something far closer to the Romanians.

In fact, a 'production line' was, at that time, far from the realms of
possibility. But what he did get off the ground was a pilot study. Long
before Chelsea Warr was looking for weightlifters and footballers in
Queensland, Shakespear started searching for rowing talent in Canberra.

He recruited a local young Canberran coach, Paul Thompson, to
help him and they went to a number of schools that didn't do rowing
and recruited their maiden group. As Shakespear acknowledges, they
still didn't really know what they were looking for. Some coaches insisted that they should be identifying girls who showed a natural ap-
titude for picking up technique. When they first put their new cohort
onto the water, they wanted to keep 12 of them. The twelfth-ranked
girl was called Megan Still, who was a good athlete, with impressive
upper-body strength from doing the throwing events in athletics, but as
an oarswoman, the least impressive. 'We put her in the boat and she was
terrible,' Shakespear says. Indeed, she was so terrible as an oarswoman
that every time she took a full stroke, she would unbalance the boat.

However, Shakespear noted this with interest; it was only her extreme power that caused this to happen. This he saw as a flash of talent so he decided to keep her.

Within two years, Still was competing at the World Junior Championships and two years later she was in a coxless four that came sixth at the Barcelona Olympics. A year later, Still was put in a coxless pair with another girl, Kate Slatter, and, with Thompson as their coach, they became world champions. In 1996, at the Atlanta Olympics, Still and Slatter then became Australia's first ever female rowing Olympic champions.

Shakespear had proved that what worked in East Germany and Romania could work in the western world too. He had also taken significant steps in discovering what talent looks like. The rower with the real headroom is not the one with the natural gift to be an oarswoman, it is the woman gifted with the natural horsepower. Rowing can be learned; natural power cannot.

What is the best model for talent identification? Who does it the best? And not just in sport but in any walk of life? This is what Chelsea Warr wanted to know, and so she didn't just look at sport, she looked to music, medicine and the military.

By 2008, she had moved on from working for British Diving to a position overseeing talent identification, confirmation and development programmes across all Olympic and Paralympic sports within UK Sport. So she needed to know how best, with limited resources, to find talent pools that would supply the whole of the British Olympic system. The biggest talent scouting system in the country is in football, where boys are recruited from the age of eight. At any time, some 10,000 boys will be with football club academies or centres of excellence and thousands more will be with other development squads. From these vast numbers, less than one per cent will make a living as professional footballers. As a model, it may work yet it is exceedingly ineffective, the numbers and costs are vast and the wastage is huge. In football, if you are recruited, you are very unlikely to succeed; Warr needed completely the opposite. Where football is very high numbers, very low success rate, Warr needed to be delivering to the Olympic and Paralympic sports low numbers of athletes who were highly likely to succeed. Every pound had to work.

How you hire and who you hire is clearly an art, as Sydney Finkelstein studies in his book, *Superbosses: How Exceptional Leaders Manage the Flow of Talent*. When Ralph Lauren, the fashion giant, meets with prospective job candidates, he asks them to talk him through what they are wearing and why. The policy of Bill Sanders, the real estate guru, was that if you couldn't hire someone great, then you shouldn't hire at all. Those who successfully made it through the job application process to join his companies would have been invited to his ranch in New Mexico to complete a hike up the 7,000-foot peak on his doorstep with him and some of his managers. Only when new candidates had been up and down the mountain did Sanders feel he knew enough about them to know who to hire and who not to.

Warr busily cross-referenced with other worlds to learn how to build a system that could compete with the best in the world. She looked at the European Space Agency and invited Tim Peake, the first British ESA astronaut into the International Space Station, to make a presentation to British coaches and talent managers. How do you talent-spot an astronaut? That is one piece of recruitment you really cannot get wrong.

Three key influences were elsewhere. One of the highest-achieving models she could find was the Yehudi Menuhin School for Musical Excellence in Surrey: 95 per cent of its pupils become musicians. In the world of performing arts, the Royal Ballet School does do better – 100 per cent of their graduates go straight into performing contracts, but they weed out a considerable number of their recruits en route through the school.

Another was the SAS: when you have got through stage one of recruitment for the SAS, you are dropped into the Brunei jungle for seven weeks to see how you survive. What, she wondered, does the SAS expect to learn there?

One day she found herself watching on television a programme called *Surgery School*, about how surgeons in the UK make it through the selection process, and she saw a model that tested heavily the ability to make good, clear decisions under extreme pressure. The cross-over to sport was clear.

Yehudi Menuhin School

The school receives 300–500 applications a year for children aged eight and above. Applicants are asked to send a 15-minute clip, audio or video, of them playing. Between 50 and 60 are then invited for a day at the school to audition, with their parents, and the best of those are then invited back for a three-day residential stay without them. Between 10 and 15 a year are then selected.

What are they looking for? This is Nicolas Chisholm, who was headmaster for 22 years up to 2010: 'The number of music lessons or how far they'd got before we saw them was irrelevant really, because actually what was much more exciting was what we felt was their potential, and in the three-day stay we could see how receptive they were to ideas, how quickly they pick things up. To us this was much more important than seeing somebody whose parents had tied them to the piano. I can think of those who appeared to be fairly flashy playing the piano, for example, but if you really drilled down to what they were actually doing, they probably weren't as exciting as somebody who had only been playing the piano for six months but just had something else, some sort of quality of communication.'

What qualities are they assessed on? Assessment is based on the four Cs: co-ordination, concentration, commitment and communication. Of these communication is the most subjective. Chisholm: 'It's the communication – that sort of hairs-on-the-back-of-your-neck quality – which after all is the most important thing because that's what an audience wants.

'A lot of people ask me whether I can spot the stars from the word go. You can't necessarily, but Nigel Kennedy was very a talented individual and an amazing violinist and was obviously, from the age of seven or eight, going to go right to the top and become an international soloist. In my very early days, we had an eight-year-old come in who'd only been playing the cello for about three months. That was Cheryl Frances-Hoad, who is now the most wonderful composer. We gave her a place and it was one of the easy decisions.'

What are the crucial parts of the talent ID process? 'The three-day stay was our real clincher because we realised that actually you really need to see somebody when they've relaxed and they're not hyped up by their parents being there. Motivation is crucial; is it internal or, deep down, is the child only doing the music because of being pressurised by the parents? We brought in the three-day stay five years after I'd started. We'd give them a lesson, possibly two, on their instrument and see how much they could assimilate in those three days. And we'd watch the way they fitted in – they'd kick a football around, we'd get feedback from the other pupils, who'd say "Oh, we like that person."'

What did Warr learn?

1. Understand exactly what it is you are looking for. She says: 'I remember, they were really clear on their talent profile of what made expert string musicians and concert pianists. I thought: "Right, they really understand, with absolute clarity, what they're looking for." What was stunning was: why is it that kids 11 years of age will voluntarily go into a cubicle in the school and will practise completely on their own without any tuition or encouragement or coaching – they just do it? And they will do it for hours. They are looking for kids with intrinsic motivation and commitment and

they absolutely find them and then provide an environment that optimises their development.'

2. It is not about how excellent you are when you are tested, it's all about how far you can improve. She says: 'It was the notion of trainability that was essential to selection. The initial talent characteristics are not always the best predictor of what someone's going to be able to do in the future. It's more how you respond when you start to give them a training regimen – or that first lesson or two on the residential stay. The ones that rapidly improve over a set period of time are the ones that are more likely to keep adapting. So we have to test adaptability, trainability, plasticity in responding to training loads and pressure. It's one of the key differences between performance and potential.'

The Special Air Service

The numbers. Each SAS selection group starts with about 100 wannabe recruits. The first selection phase is four weeks of physical training; from this phase 40 per cent make it through. The second phase is seven weeks of jungle warfare training in Brunei; after this, there are 13 per cent still standing. The third phase is two weeks of combat survival; if you have made it through Brunei, you will probably survive this too. Between 10 and 11 per cent of most intakes go the whole way.

The man Warr went to for her learning was Floyd Woodrow, who was 14 years an SAS soldier before taking over as head of recruitment. Fittingly, when he arrived to make a presentation to Warr and a group of coaches, it was in a helicopter. It was the jungle phase that interested Warr most.

This is Woodrow: 'Talent is the most important thing; we can't survive without talented people. I can always spot the top 2 or 3 per cent; there is just something special about them, they stand out, there is a presence about them. They are easy to spot. However, sometimes they are not the ones who give you the full fulfilment of their potential – because they haven't experienced failure. They arrive so very confident. I am more interested in the larger proportion of people who do have potential and who, with careful management and skills training, I get a better chance with.

'I am looking for all-round skills: your physicality, your intellect, your ability to be coached, your ability to work under pressure, to adapt, how you work with a group of people, whether your ego comes to the fore, whether you're going to be disruptive. You won't see these skills in a short space of time, so you need to put them under pressure and that is what happens in the jungle.

'In Brunei, you will lose a stone in weight, it is very arduous, physically and mentally tough. If you don't look after yourself as an individual, you suffer. You have to stay focused all the time. In the SAS, the expectation is: you do not fail anything, you go on. So it's about looking after yourself as an individual and as a team, because you are split up into groups so we see how you operate in a unit. No mavericks; it just doesn't happen. The biggest driving factor in an SAS team? Forget doing it for your country, your nation. You do it for your mates, it's a massive drive.

'As much as anything in the jungle, we are testing their attitude, but we don't motivate them, we want people with natural drive and ambition. The big test, though, is their mental toughness, resilience. What they actually do in Brunei is not out of the ordinary: simple infantry tactics, patrols, ambushes, a man-down, how they respond. But it is relentless. There is one big, tough day in the jungle, in particular, when you are on patrol the whole day, there are loads of different incidents, it is physically debilitating, you are absolutely shattered and you still have to think, still have to perform. That is the one day people remember as the tough day when you could easily jack.'

What did Warr learn?

'In the jungle, you have basically just got to survive, and if you make it through, which most don't, then you start to get to the really serious end of the selection process. I asked Floyd, what are you trying to get out of those seven weeks there? What questions are you really trying to answer? What do you need to know and why? And he described this talent confirmation process: how they respond to pressure, their ability to work as a team, to organise themselves. He explained that these qualities are fundamental to being able to succeed and you can't know if they have them until they have been tested in an environment like this. No pen or paper or one-off selection testing will tell you this – but you need to know.

'So it is one thing finding your talent pool, but then we need to confirm that each candidate is really going to fit into the environment, and not only survive, but thrive. I thought, we need to be doing this, not just spotting talent, but confirming it more carefully. If we confirm, we'll have a much higher hit rate. So we took the concept of seven weeks of jungle survival and we thought: that's "talent confirmation" and that's what we'll do with our sports, we'll create a set of experiences and tasks and apprenticeship phases to better test all aspects of their future potential to fit into the high-performance environment. And we have to do that as part of our process before final selection and really making the investment.

'It's like when a business hires people what do you do? You give them a six-month probationary period. What are you doing during that time? You're assessing them objectively, you give them targets, you're giving them feedback, you're watching. You are making sure that when you hire someone, you know that there's a very high chance of it being right – for them and for you.'

British Surgeons

Once a year, application is opened. Between 1,000 and 12,000 qualified doctors apply to join the ranks as trainee surgeons. Over a two-week period, they are interviewed, three ten-minute interviews each, which takes the number down to 600. Karen Daly, who used to run the London training programme and is now a consultant orthopaedic surgeon at St George's, London, acknowledges that this half-hour interview is a 'blunt tool'. The 600 selected will then be on a two-year programme, during which 10 per cent of those will leave because they decide it is not right for them (as Daly says: 'There is a lot of self-filtering'), and 1–2 per cent drop out for other reasons. Some 500 will qualify.

This is Daly: 'We are trying to identify people who have potential, because effectively they haven't done any surgery, even though they are qualified doctors. We are trying to assess commitment and potential, and increasingly that revolves around their personal skills and attributes rather than whether they can tie knots and do that technical side of things. You have to have a basic technical ability, but it is more about commitment, attitude, ability to learn, team-working, taking in information, decision-making, situation awareness. It is really hard to assess those soft skills.

'There is a small, hard-core group who possibly have the ability, but don't have the mindset and definitely don't have any insight. They are the really challenging ones. We spend 90 per cent of our time looking after this 10 per cent of our trainees. They think they are God's gift to surgery, they think they know it all and want to pursue their own pathway rather than work within the framework. They are the mavericks. The politically correct term for these is: trainees in difficulty.

'Decision-making is so important and it's one of those things that is really hard to capture. There are people who can talk the talk, but you put them in the hot seat during an operation and they can't do it. It's about decision-making and judgement under pressure. How do we assess this? Two ways, really. It's being in the operating theatre that makes the big difference, so you have an expert assessor. My senior trainees will be doing the operation and I'll be right there, standing behind them, watching. That in itself creates a certain amount of pressure. But then I challenge them: "Tell me why you are doing it that way." You start, then, to get a feel of how people perform and their thought process. The reality is we don't let our trainees get into difficult situations. Historically we used to. In one of my very first operations, for instance,

I started operating on the wrong leg. It was a young boy, I had only made the incision, but it was one of the worst and most informative experiences of my life.

'To test and train decision-making, you can simulate too and we do that throughout the training programme. There are sophisticated hi-tech simulators where you can do key-hole operations. We do quite a lot of scenario mock-ups. We do work-place scenarios as well; the idea is rehearse for the rare things. You can make it as tough as you like. The really advanced simulations use mannequins who talk, whose pulse goes up, who can die as well. If you have a really good facilitator who says, "These are the decisions you have to make, come on, come on, we've got to move fast, you've got to tell me what to do," you can really ramp up the pressure. People get hung up on the fact that it's not real life, which of course it isn't. Real life is not a different thing, but it is a level beyond that and if someone can't do it in simulation, they won't be able to do it in real life.'

What did Warr learn?

'How they deal with mavericks was interesting. There was a bit of cross-over there. And Karen also described to me specifically what surgeons will need to be like in the future, and how the profile of the surgeon has changed; it used to be very clinical and now it is more than that, it is about teamwork and communication and complex problem-solving using an array of experts. I thought, that's the same for us. We need to think: if Jessica Ennis-Hill came along in two or three Olympics time, would she win? She probably wouldn't, because the profile of the Olympic heptathlon champion will have changed. So we shouldn't be looking for Jessica Ennis-Hill clones; we should be asking what the Olympic 2024 champion might look like and trying to match that kind of profile.

'However, the big learning for me here was about making decisions under pressure and making accurate decisions quickly. Olympic and Paralympic sport is all about performing under pressure. In many sports, decision-making is a key skill too. You wonder: can you really test those for those kinds of attributes? My answer is of course you can.'

In February 2007, Helen Glover, a 20-year-old studying for her PGCE in Plymouth, responded to an advertisement that was considered extraordinary at the time: Great Britain was looking for big people to compete in the Olympics. Can you make the grade? More specifically, women had to be over 5ft 11in, men had to be over 6ft 3in, the required age range was 16 to 25, and if you met those criteria, the message was: your country needs you, you could go to the Olympics. Never before, in Britain, had there been a nationwide recruitment drive of this nature. It certainly didn't feel very British. It was a programme called 'Sporting Giants' and the cynicism that greeted it was such that Steve Redgrave, who was the front man for the campaign, was interviewed by Matthew Pinsent on the BBC, with Pinsent in effect saying: c'mon, Steve, this is never going to work, you really think you can find champions this way?

A similar opinion was voiced in the *Daily Mirror* by Oliver Holt, one of the best and most respected sportswriters in the country. He wrote: 'Much of the preparation for the 2012 Olympics has already gone beyond plain embarrassing and past hysterically funny to the point where now it just seems like utter farce. Yesterday we witnessed the launch of a campaign to attract – wait for it – "tall athletes" to compete in the London Games. Tall athletes? Next, it'll be small athletes. Or squat ones. Or big ones. Or maybe bald ones. Or long-legged ones with stubby fingers. Please tell me we've got better brains than this in charge of 2012. Please.'

Around 4,800 potential Olympians thought otherwise and applied. Glover soon found herself among the hordes at a testing day at Bath, the nearest of the offered venues, where she discovered that, contrary to her belief, she wasn't actually 5ft 11in at all. She had to go on tip-toes to survive the very first test but she was allowed through. An initial briefing was given to each cohort by Chelsea Warr and Peter Shakespear. Warr, by then, was in her broader role with the Olympic and Paralympic sports; Shakespear had been recruited from Australia in December 2001 and was Performance Development Manager of British Rowing.

There was a lot of whooping and shouting and motivating in the sports halls where phase one of Sporting Giants was taking place. They had two priorities: one, they wanted everyone to feel welcome and that they had had a good experience; two, they didn't want anyone to leave with the impression that the pathway to the Olympics was going to be anything other than phenomenally tough.

Glover made it through phase one and was invited back for a second weekend where girls and boys were tested on consecutive days. It was there that she really raised eyebrows. 'I remember when she came in,' Natalie Dunman, the number two in Warr's team, says. 'She was physically impressive, confident, you could see she was serious but easy to talk to. She wasn't the best physically, so she almost wasn't noticed by some of the coaches. But there is one test that is very important in rowing, on the Schwinn arm-leg bike which is a test where the intensity of effort increases and increases. It is basically the go-until-you-die test. It's the test where you see if people are really up for it or not, the one where you either back off or are on the floor being sick into a bucket. The score itself is very important, but so is your attitude. One of the things we are looking at is whether you pass what we call the "mongrel" test. Do you back off or do have that real gritty fight inside you? If you pass the mongrel test, you'd get an M by your name. Helen certainly got an M.'

If you made it through phase two, you were then invited to a 'Confirmation Weekend'. It was there that you would be interviewed one-to-one with a coach who, if you made it through to the end of the process, might be your coach when you got there. Glover was interviewed by Paul Stannard. 'The small conversations you have with athletes around the testing and around an event show a hell of a lot about their character and what they are thinking,' Stannard says. 'I interviewed a girl who burst into tears and told me that she was doing it for her parents and she wanted to make them proud. Helen, though – she was leaning forward in her chair, eyes laser-beaming into your own eyes saying: "This is what I've done so far in hockey and cross-country, but I know I can do better. I want to go to the Olympics."'

Sporting Giants, which had seemed to some like a bit of a desperate, unspecific and very un-British attempt to find champions, was actually a very sophisticated big-numbers recruitment programme. Long before its inception, Warr had collaborated with the individual sports to refine the picture of exactly what each of them were looking for. And Shakespear had certainly perfected the profile of a future international rower. In the Australian team he had left behind, the number of women who had only made it there through Talent ID was 60 per cent. He had toyed with various different types of testing. At one early stage he was giving his triallists bleep tests, a running exercise that examines endurance, but he found that the coxes were doing better than the actual oarswomen. The bleep tests didn't last long.

For rowing, three attributes became the key indicators of talent: levers (height, arm span), strength and endurance. Potential recruits would be assessed against all three. A light green value indicated that you were at the lower end of acceptable; dark green across the board was ideal. 'While these scores are relatively accurate,' Shakepear says, 'it did not guarantee success if the psychological area was not strong. Conversely a few athletes could be world champions if they were extremely strong in other areas, especially the psychological attributes.' Glover fitted the latter profile; light green on the levers, very strong psychologically.

For Shakespear, part of the skill in assessing physical potential was in finding a test that that ironed out skill or prior training and best revealed innate horsepower. He found a bike that worked arms and legs simultaneously was the best predictor; when he arrived in England, he discovered that Schwinn were already making a commercial version of it. But he knew, too, how to identify other characteristics of potential. When he wanted a look at their competitiveness and ability to perform under pressure, he would position his triallists on a number of ergos (rowing machines) in a semi-circle so everyone could see each other. To crank up the pressure a little more, he would often do this with the parents' gallery in view.

For Warr, the key learnings were all in place too. From the SAS, she knew a process of confirmation was required. That was why Glover and others spent months back in Bath. And when they were back on these confirmation weekends, they would be analysed particularly to see how fast they learned technique and how much they improved athletically; this was the Yehudi Menuhin influence: what is your trainability, how far can you be stretched? The influence from Karen Daly and the Talent ID of surgeons came in decision-making; this did not affect rowers so much, but when Warr was trying to find potential Olympians for tae-kwondo and handball, it was fundamental.

In Paul Stannard, Shakespear had found an able and willing assistant. Stannard is not shy. If Stannard is in a supermarket and sees someone who fits the physical profile of a rower, he won't ignore them, he will invite them to come and be tested. Once, in a pub, where a hen party was taking place, he made the same approach to a girl dressed as Superwoman.

Shakespear liked Stannard's mind too. Stannard was as driven as most of the champions he would coach. When he was at university, Stannard wasn't a rower, he was a rowing coach; he had been coaching in some shape or form since he was 15. Shakespear first came across him at a regatta in Belgium. Stannard was coaching a girls' four and they won the junior event on the Saturday; the next day he entered them for the senior event but he had a hunch that they could go even quicker so he changed the order in which they were sitting in the boat and they finished third. Shakespear liked that and offered him a job.

Stannard was given a role in finding new talent; success for him therefore equated to finding as good, or better, new athletes than other people finding new talent. So when he was given the basic minimum height that was the requirement for recruitment of potential new rowers, he added a few centimetres. That way, he reasoned, his talent pool would be even more elite.

Based at Bath University, Stannard knew that his big opportunity would be in September when the new student intake arrived. He asked around a bit and worked out a plan. More than 90 per cent of fresher students, in their first week, go and pick up their student union card. In that same week, a large number of second and third year students, who have lost their cards or need re-registering, go to the same place: a room at the university with 20 to 30 computer terminals where they can register online. This, he reasoned, was probably the highest concentration of the student population he would find. So Stannard measured up the door frame into the room and stuck up two pieces of red tape, one at 1.80m, for the girls, the other at 1.90m for the boys. In four days, around two thousand people went past his strips of red tape. As the students stood in line, Stannard could see down the corridor, where there would be around forty in sight at any one time, and work out who merited a conversation. On average, he reckoned, he had around five minutes to talk to one tall person before the next tall person came along.

The conversations were easy. In their first week at university, students are so used to giving out details that they spilled out to Stannard everything he needed: age, course, halls of residence, phone number, email address, previous sporting history, personal highlights, the lot. As Stannard recalls: 'If I'd asked for their bank details, they probably would have given me them as well.' Anyone in whom he was interested would be invited to testing the following Tuesday or Thursday evening. He was specific about the date – this testing was in the *second* week of term, not the first. You try doing Talent ID in Fresher's Week, when there are other priorities more nocturnal and interesting than becoming an Olympic rower, and your talent pool might just dry up.

So, in week two, Stannard took his search further with standard testing: height, weight and armspan measurements, and then physical efforts on a Concept II Dynamometer, a type of rowing machine, and the Schwinn arm-leg bike. He was also observing the psychology of his possible recruits. On the first day he ever did this, he recalls, two stood out: the one that went first – because his hand went up first and he was therefore courageous and gung-ho. And the other – because he sat in the corner and took it all in, watched everyone else do it, listened to Stannard coaching them all through it and last up, went himself. His was the calculated approach. Stannard wasn't far wrong with his assessment; these were the outstanding pair and, though one was forced to drop out of the training programme due to glandular fever, the other would be the first Bath recruit to ever get selected for GB rowing.

Stannard's best find at the university would be in the May of his third year when he got the whole of the university rowing club to come for a 2km ergo test. The university club was a very different, totally amateur entity and entirely separate from his search for elite, possible future Olympic rowers. One of those uni club rowers was a girl on a British Army scholarship who spent a number of her weekends away on her military duties and had therefore only rowed occasionally. Somehow she had she slipped past the Freshers' Week red-tape test, but no matter, Stannard got her in the end. She smashed out a time of 7min21sec, which was the best of all the girls, though what particularly impressed Stannard was that she did it at such a low stroke rate.

He remembers the moment well: 'She did it, stood up, and walked away from it barely having broken a sweat and said, "What do you think of that?" She had absolutely no idea what a good ergo score was or what she was doing or how she was doing it. Awesome and very exciting. You've got someone who is physically very capable and just has no idea about how good they could be; that is the bit that makes the hairs on the back of my neck stand up. It's what excites me about coaching Talent ID athletes; they will do stuff that surprises you and them on a regular basis.'

So he invited her to join the GB Rowing 'Start' programme. She then won the student event at the national indoor rowing championships in Birmingham and within 18 months had won a world under-23s gold medal. This was Heather Stanning.

By the summer of 2007, Sporting Giants had filtered the numbers so finely that five women received invitations to go to train at Bath University. They were to be trained by Stannard, whose welcome message was: 'Only 1,763 days to go to the Olympics.' In itself, this was fascinating. Trendy thinking at the time had it that it took ten years or 10,000 training hours to reach world-class standard; here was the 1,763-day counter-argument.

The women started by proving Shakepear's theory that it was innate power that was important, not innate technique. On their first day on the river in Bath, a former horse-rider called Vicky Thornley fell in three times. On day two, she fell in twice, the same again on day three, and that was the pattern for quite some time. It was some months before it really clicked for her.

Stannard was dry of humour and liked to come over as grumpy and unsociable. His rowers saw through that, warmed to him and wanted to succeed for him. They hated his regime, though. He made sure that nothing came easy, he made them graft; it was his belief that only the grittiest among them had a chance and so he would let them rise to the top. They didn't get paid for being on the programme; all they got was an elite coach and elite facilities. Glover could not afford a car, so her best mode of transport from home to work to training to home was running.

'Whenever I think how hard I am training now,' she says, 'I think about how horrible that was. I was trying to fit in teaching and training; I was making myself ill, I was totally broke.'

Stannard also managed to instil a furiously competitive environment. 'That's why I think it worked,' he says. 'They'd bash themselves to bits trying to beat each other.'

But he was an inspiration too. 'At one point,' Glover says, 'I started lifting well in the weights room and it got to the point where lifting shoes became really important for me. They prevent injury and help you lift more. But I was never going to be able to afford any, no way. They were £80. And one day he turned up at my door with a pair of lifting shoes and would never talk about it.

'I remember we went to race at Dorney Lake, which could be the venue for the rowing at the London Olympics. I had been rowing only for a few months. I raced my first race; I wasn't pleased. I was not very good at all. And afterwards, he said to me: "You are going to be here rowing at the Olympics." He had that much conviction that he started referring to 2012. He just had utter belief.'

The concept of accelerated learning started to work. When Glover won her first race, nine months after she had started, people really started to notice her. Eighteen months after they had started, Thornley got a seat in the women's eight at the Under-23 World Championships in the Czech Republic and she came home with a gold medal.

In May 2010, Glover won a place on the national team and, for the first time, qualified for lottery funding. Then, the following summer, one single and extremely significant decision was taken: to pair up Glover with another of Stannard's recruits: Heather Stanning. Glover and Stanning would become one of the great British double acts. They won silver in their first World Championships. A year later, back at Dorney Lake for the Olympics, they were favourites to win.

What happened next is, really, a story of what happened over the next five years. In London, Glover and Stanning made history when they became the first ever GB women's boat to win gold. The following month, Stanning reported back for duty at Larkhill garrison to recommence her other life as a captain in the Royal Artillery. A year later, and after a six-month tour of Afghanistan, the Glover–Stanning team were reunited and their winning streak continued. It continued all the way through to Rio; by the time there were done there, they had five years and 39 races unbeaten and a second gold medal round their necks. Without Talent ID, British Rowing would not have had either of them, let alone both.

Chapter learnings by Chelsea Warr

Whatever business or walk of life you are recruiting in, the key message in this chapter is to understand what 'really good' will look like, and not now, but in the future. Once you have established that talent profile, you can find people that measure up to it.

Know the difference between performance and potential. Performance and potential are words that often go together in the talent arena, but are fundamentally different when forecasting success. Just because someone is performing now doesn't mean they will be successful in the future. This is the difference between 'shouting talent' and 'whispering talent' – the shouters are the obvious ones, the whisperers are not so obvious but may have greater long-term potential.

Talent confirmation. The trainability of potential recruits is a stronger marker of their future potential than their starting talent characteristics. Character assessments, mindset and attitude are instrumental in your assessment of trainability.

What can we NOT live without knowing? Often when we've done Talent ID testing, I would start with this question. In skeleton, for instance, we had to know: can they live abroad, in unpredictable weather/ environment conditions, deal with foreign languages, confined room-sharing for months? We therefore created opportunities to discover if they were responders or non-responders in this environment.

It's like watching a racehorse run within a pack of donkeys. Great coaches know talent when they see it. Experienced coaches have a large catalogue of reference points which means they know talent when they see it. The combination of art (their eye) and the science (the harder metrics) can maximise your chances of making a star pick.

4

Challenging conventional thinking

Lutalo Muhammad

According to Paul Stannard, 'The Talent ID is the easy bit. You could probably teach anyone to do Talent ID.' Indeed you could if it was just coloured sticky tape, measuring heights and ergo tests. That's the bit that Chelsea Warr describes as 'the first shake of the tree'. But what if it is fighters you are looking for? Here is the question: can you properly spot talent when you are looking for information that is far more complex than basic statistics? What tree do you shake? In the curious case of looking for people who could become Olympic fighters, the following became the solution: make them fight each other.

That, at least, was the answer that taekwondo came up with. Literally. *Mano a mano*. You want to be an Olympian? You fight for your future.

Paul Buxton, who was helping run taekwondo's first Talent ID programme, remembers arriving at one session, in Roehampton, south-west London, just in time to see an ambulance taking away one wannabe Olympian who'd had his nose broken. More memorable was the occasion when one 'player' had some teeth knocked out – and when the call immediately went out for a dentist, the guy who had knocked them out said, 'I'm a dentist' and put them back in himself.

Taekwondo had been asking, with good reason: how are we to compete on the Olympic stage when our numbers are so small? The UK population of participants under the World Taekwondo Federation rules is around 16,000; of those, from the most junior 'piwis' through the age groups to the seniors, only around 500 a year compete in the annual national championships. In other words, the talent pool was minuscule. However, there was a solution: double the talent pool overnight.

Here is a brief, relevant history of the sport. Taekwondo is a Korean martial art. It is the national sport of South Korea. Long after Korea split in two, taekwondo split too. South Korea is the heartland of the World Taekwondo Federation (WTF); the International Taekwondo Federation (ITF) is the same sport but with slightly different techniques and scoring systems and was favoured by North Korea. However, taekwondo's Cold War politics which started in Korea went global. In the UK, for instance, there is WTF and ITF and the numbers in each are not far different. According to Buxton, there is little love lost between the two – 'it is like mods and rockers'. The significant point here is that the body that is ratified by the Olympics happens to be the WTF. But if you were a parent taking your kid to his or her first taekwondo experience, what are the chances of you knowing that? Would you even be interested? You would most likely go to the nearest taekwondo club, and if that club was an ITF club, you probably wouldn't have a clue that you were putting your child into the non-Olympic version of the sport.

What, then, if the GB taekwondo team could select those other kids, the ITF ones? What if it could be picked from both the mods *and* the rockers? Even better, what if it could be picked from kickboxing too, or karate or kung fu, ju jitsu, soo bahk do or any of the other numerous (applicable) martial arts in the country. Then, all of a sudden, you don't just double the size of your catchment area, your talent pool goes from the 16,000 to roughly ten times that number. And then you win more medals, right?

In theory, this was an excellent idea. In practice, there was still this Cold War. Purists from the WTF argued that ITF players could only come over from the dark side if they did the WTF training and got their WTF belts – in other words, if they started pretty much from scratch. And purists from the ITF wanted to protect their patch and keep their best athletes. And, in martial arts, instructors can be more like spiritual guides than sports coaches, and you don't leave your spiritual guide, do you? It's like changing religion. Thus did tension, snobbery, protectionism and division rule the day. While amalgamation would seem common sense, in martial arts such common sense does not apply; it certainly doesn't in the United States, Canada and most of Europe.

That is why, when GB Taekwondo finally broke down the barricades, in 2009, it secured itself a major advantage. It didn't exactly smash those barricades down; it was more a case of carving out a small hole and allowing an escape route. It required months of gentle politics, softly softly persuading each side that the other wasn't so bad and that the ITF fiefdom was not being taken over. This was a minor invasion that made taekwondo generally look better, whatever the acronym you go by – that was the message that was eventually accepted – and so finally, GB Taekwondo started advertising around the other martial arts. The invitation went like this: come and try your hand, you could become an Olympic champion. They called it the 'Fighting Chance' campaign.

At the same time, Ian Yates, a Talent ID specialist, started researching the rival codes, scouring the results and the websites to identify which fighters might genuinely straddle the divide. While this was an open invitation to different fighting codes, Yates wanted to find not just those who *might* make it, but those who probably *would*. And he ensured that invitations to Fighting Chance went directly to them.

Soon, over 1,000 applications had been received. This became taekwondo's version of *The X Factor*: a panel of expert judges attended a select number of venues around the country and watched as athletes

were put into pairs, given a quick résumé of the new rules, and then sent
out to fight for their future.

This wasn't Talent ID by numbers; a few body measurements were
taken, but it was almost pure subjectivity. The judges – coaches and current athletes – had to assess which of the 1,000 were worth an invitation
to the second stage of the process, a boot camp at the GB headquarters
in Manchester. They weren't spotting winners and losers on the mat in
front of them; they were trying to assess which of these athletes, who
were playing a sport to rules that were new to them, had the attributes
to become Olympians.

One of those caught in the political crossfire in Fighting Chance
was Wayne Muhammad. He was an instructor in ITF, ran his own taekwondo school and one of his star pupils was his son. But ITF was the
wrong code, the non-Olympic code, and though he wanted a bright
future for his boy – of course he did – he was uneasy about him cross-
ing codes. A sequence of written correspondence then passed back and
forth between himself, GB Taekwondo and UK Sport. GB Taekwondo
gently tried to persuade Wayne at least to let his boy try out, and eventually the father relented. It was a decision that paid off. Three years
later, at London 2012, his son had an Olympic bronze medal around his
neck. This was Lutalo Muhammad.

Can Talent ID work in fighting sports? Muhammad was the living
proof and four years later, in Rio, he sought to settle the argument for
good. In Rio, it seemed that Muhammad had made the leap to the
top of the podium. On Day 14, he was in the gold-medal fight against
Cheick Sallah Cissé, of the Ivory Coast, and he appeared in control.
At least that was how it looked all the way until the final second of
the fight. He was 6–4 up, he was a second away from gold. He just
needed to stay out of range. Yet, in that last second Cissé turned and
flicked out a high reverse kick with his right foot and though it was
barely a brush with Muhammad's face, the contact was enough. The
head shot was worth four points. Muhammad won silver and broke
down in tears.

So that was two medals to Fighting Chance.

There were no surprises then when, after London, Fighting Chance II was launched. That was followed, in 2015, by a third campaign, searching specifically for heavyweights. By this stage, GB Taekwondo knew better how to find what they were looking for. They found that kickboxers, in particular, could make the transfer. They identified, too, a method to better filter the talent: can you fire off 35 high kicks in a minute? Below 35 and you surrendered the right to a fight. And they set more store by the talent confirmation process; Boot Camp became two weeks long.

'At the end of Boot Camp, some people would be really physically and mentally pushed,' Buxton recalled. 'Very quickly into sessions, there would be two or three athletes in tears. That flushed out many of those who couldn't handle it.'

On one fight day at Fighting Chance II, in October 2013, Gary Hall, the performance director of GB Taekwondo, sat next to Yates behind the judges' table waiting for the trials to begin. The triallists were being shown a brief video that explained the rules of WTF; they weren't expected to be able to conform to them completely, but it was, at least, a guide before the action could commence. The very first fight of the day was a women's contest. Personal details on each competitor are given to the judges, and the notes they had for this fight showed that one had been an ITF world champion, while the other, a Welsh girl, was a good junior athlete who said she'd done a bit of kickboxing. In no time at all, the junior kickboxer had annihilated the world champion. Hall recalls this vividly: 'We were sat there with our mouths open. I said to Ian, "How old is this girl? Get her in now." And he said to me, "We might have a problem." I asked why and he said, "She's only 15 years old."'

This was their first glimpse of Lauren Williams. Within six months she was world junior champion. Two ankle injuries followed. Then, in May 2016, aged 17, fighting in the seniors, she became European champion. Too young, too late to make it to Rio. Muhammad may be the present; here is the future.

Chapter learnings by Chelsea Warr

Lutalo and his two Olympic medals were the direct product of courage and curiosity: the courage to expand into new markets and the curiosity to question the accepted norms and traditions and to embrace what 'even better' might look like.

Take risks, challenge convention. Always be prepared to look beyond the accepted norm. There were senior people in taekwondo who said, 'This won't work'. Nevertheless, there was enough belief elsewhere to challenge convention. And look how it worked.

Persist. Taekwondo spent many long months making this happen, against the odds.

Understand what you are looking for. Only after the first Fighting Chance did they really establish that kickboxers were such a good fit and that helped in talent-spotting thereafter. Whatever field you are working in, knowing the profile of what you are recruiting is crucial.

5

What the super-elite look like

SIXTEEN OF THE GREATEST GB OLYMPIANS EVER

Talent-spotting a future winner is one thing, finding a serial winner is another job altogether. What do they look like? Do they look the same? What is the difference between athletes like Chris Hoy, who won six gold medals, or Michael Phelps, who won 23, or Carl Lewis, who won nine, and all those thousands of other Olympians in history whose greatest single, most joyful moment in their sporting lives was that single day when they got on the podium once? There is some real value in finding the answer. Between the Atlanta Games and Rio, Great Britain won 96 gold medals, but just 12 people won or contributed to 49 of them. What made them different? Is there a difference between the elite, which is pretty much anyone who ever got to an Olympics, and the super-elite, which is that tiny, narrow band of over-achievers who came to dominate them? Do super-elites in sport share the same formulae as super-elites in other walks of life? If we could understand better the miracle formula of the super-elite, could we nurture it?

These were questions pondered by Chelsea Warr. Do we actually know the difference? And, if not, is there any chance that we can find out?

Because here in Rio, the super-elites were really doing the business for GB. The rowers, Andrew Triggs Hodge and Pete Rudd each won their Olympic gold; Charlotte Dujardin, the equestrian, won her third. Mo Farah, who won double gold in the 5,000m and 10,000m in London, pulled off the astonishing achievement of successfully defending both of them. He tripped and fell in the 10,000m final but even that didn't stop him. The most super-elite household in the country must have been the home that the soon-to-be-married Jason Kenny and Laura Trott returned to; Kenny brought home three gold medals and Trott two.

These were all extreme over-achievers. Warr had watched Hoy and the Olympic knights do the same in previous Olympics: Steve Redgrave (five golds), Ben Ainslie (four). What is it that sets these people apart? Can we learn from them and can we therefore develop multimedallists more successfully in the future?

As good a place as any to find the answers might have been the Maria Lenke diving pool on Day Five of the Rio Olympics. By the time the Games were over, Rio would become the most successful Olympics for Great Britain for over a century, but on the morning of Day Five, it looked very different. British competitors had been posting a flurry of fourth-place finishes. A gloom appeared to have set in. It was three days since Adam Peaty's victory in the pool and GB was still search of a second gold medal, now in twelfth place in the medal table, lagging behind the likes of South Korea and Hungary.

It was under the grey clouds of an overcast Rio that afternoon, in the open air of the Maria Lenke diving pool, that the picture started to change. The diving pool has long been the stronghold of the Chinese, but now Jack Laugher, from Harrogate, and Chris Mears, from Reading, broke their grip. Laugher and Mears were best friends and housemates and here, in the springboard synchro event, they were on the verge of gold. They had a new dive, never seen before in Olympic competition, known to them as The Washing Machine dive, known to the judges as a forward two-and-a-half somersault with three twists, and known to all as a make-or-break, all-or-nothing gamble. The gamble worked.

For Laugher, it was not just a gold, not just a one-off jackpot. That year, he had already won gold in the European championships; the year before, he had won two bronzes in the world championships, and come first in the World Series; and the year before that, he had won two golds in the Commonwealth Games. So by winning gold in Rio, he had established himself as a super-elite. What was it that made him that way? What had set him apart?

Arguably the most exhaustive research into these questions had just been completed. Warr had never been content just wondering. She commissioned the pursuit of the answer. Over a period of three-and-a-half years, over 1,400 hours of interviews were conducted with a group of athletes who collectively had won over 100 medals at Olympic and World Championship level. The purpose was to get to some kind of truth: if we want to find more multi-medallists, what do they actually look like?

This would become the Great British Medallists (GBM) study, a collaborative venture between UK Sport, Bangor, Exeter and Cardiff Metropolitan universities and a number of sports in the high-performance system. To compare elite with super-elite performers, they traced backwards the competitive history of a number of British multi-medallists and, for each of them, found a twin, an elite athlete of the same sport, same discipline, same sex, same age with whom they would have competed in the bright days of their competitive youth. To qualify as the twin, the elite had to have competed at a standard which would be the stuff of most people's dreams: they had to have represented their country at senior level and won a medal at a minor international competition. The performance graphs of almost all the super-elites and their twins show them rumbling along in pretty much the same direction in their formative years until, at the point they reach world-class level, the elites flatten out or dip and the super-elites suddenly shoot upwards. Why did one go up and the other not?

What, for instance, was the difference between Jonny Wilkinson, who is the most garlanded England fly-half of all time, and James Lofthouse, who is not? Wilkinson and Lofthouse were the leading English young fly-halves of their age group; at junior level Lofthouse would get picked ahead of him. So why was it that Wilkinson (super-elite) accelerated to superstardom and kicked a World Cup-winning drop goal and Lofthouse (elite) chased his career around a number of clubs and then retired at the age of 20?

The first recruits to GBM were four 'ambassadors' – all of them multi-medallists who were themselves going to commit to the study. These four then put their names to a letter to other super-elites, inviting them to come on board. Then, when the super-elites were on board, the process commenced to find their elite twin.

Academic work on the subject of talent is hardly thin on the ground. Qualitative studies tend to probe a set of psychological skills and characteristics in search of the ultimate answer: what is the secret? Where does your talent come from? Is it nature? Nurture? Practice? Personality? These are all a part of the story, but not the secret. GBM attempted to go deeper and asked for the entire life story, a developmental biography interwoven with certain themes related to their career, their inter-personal relationships with coaches, family, critical life events. In such a study, it is hard to say 'You're fantastic, why?' and expect a proper answer, even if the athlete had one. This study was an attempt to go the long way round. Two two-hour interviews each, one on the athletes' history of practice, training and competition, the other on the whole psychosocial gamut. And it was not just the athlete who had to commit; to qualify for GBM, both twins had to have a coach and at least one parent commit to the interview process too.

The recruitment was complete with 16 pairs of twins on board; 32 athletes in total. Absolute confidentiality was therefore part of the deal. Nobody knew who was their twin. Nobody knew who else was in GBM. In the report, no parent's occupation is referred to. All are referred to as male for anonymity purposes. The athletes are referred to by a set of codes. Locked away somewhere is a document with another set of codes which explains who is who.

Qualitative studies can be emotional for the interviewees, and this was designed to be a psychologically arduous journey. Leading the study with Warr were researcher Stewart Laing and Lew Hardy, Professor of Health and Human Performance at Bangor University and former head psychologist at the British Olympic Association. 'We drilled in very hard,' Hardy said. 'Super-elite athletes are amazing. But they aren't necessarily the most well-adjusted, happy people. If they were, they wouldn't do what they do. Often with the parents, there was a moment of realisation that something they had done somewhere in their child's upbringing had had a major impact. Some athletes cried in the interview, but a larger number of the parents did – a moment of realisation, not necessarily good or bad, about what their son or daughter had become.'

For a taster of what GBM tells us about super-elites, this is a quote straight from the study: '"Normal" people do not win one gold medal, let alone a gold medal plus at least one more. Thus, it seems unlikely that super-elite athletes would have "normal" personalities, "normal" interpersonal relationships, or fit comfortably into a "normal" sporting system. Rather, one would expect them to have some idiosyncrasies that make them exceptional.'

That is a kind way of putting it. Super-elites hardly come out of the study looking like well-adjusted people. Maybe that is no surprise, but what is surprising is the vast gulf between super-elites and elites. It is not in the amount of hours of practice, it is far more the extreme differences in personality. And remember, the elites are not 'normal' either in their levels of achievement, for they are high performers. They spent most of their lives winning; it was only when they got to the very top of the world that the vertigo hit them.

Need to succeed

An innate, absolute non-negotiable requirement to be successful lies deep in the super-elites but is not universal in the elites at all. Thirteen out of the 16 super-elites reported an elevated 'need to succeed'; only six of the 16 elites did.

Here are some of the reflections of the super-elites:

'Every sports person will have something in their past that gives them the need to win. Those things are absolutely fundamental in becoming good in sports, because I needed it more than other people did.'

'When I lose, I will go over and over it, I will torture myself over it … I see it in a different colour almost.'

This is one super-elite talking about another: 'He just desperately needed to win. It is pretty nasty. Sport can do that. It is such an unreasonable thing to do that it is weird to witness people who desperately need it more than anyone else.'

These are the coaches of two paired twins. The coach of the elite athlete: 'It's not life or death to him. He loves [his sport] and needs it, but doesn't need to win.' And the coach of the super-elite twin, recalling the day he asked the coach to coach him: 'He arrives at my door and he stood there; he was anxious, and he was nervous, and I looked at this kid and his eyes were burning. I have never seen such desire, nothing has ever mattered to anybody that much! He was burning.'

This is another elite: 'You know some kids totally throw their toys out of the pram and absolutely can't accept not winning; I've never been like that. I'm a bit laid back. I like to win – I don't like to lose – but at the same time it's not the be-all and end-all for me, which is probably why I never reached the very top in sport, because I don't have a big enough drive for it.'

Ruthless and selfish

Personality traits that 'normally' would be judged undesirable work away deep inside the super-elites but, again, not the elites. Super-elites would rather be successful in their sport than be liked or deemed considerate by others. They can switch the ruthlessness and selfishness on and off, but the moment it is required, it is flicked on again. Acknowledging that you are ruthless or selfish may not be the most comfortable of confessions, but 14 of the 16 super-elites admitted that they were; only two of the 16 elites said the same.

While the super-elites' honesty about their take-no-prisoners approach is striking, so too is how far on the opposite extreme the elites sit. The elites rated being 'nice' and pleasing other people higher than being ruthless and selfish in order to achieve. The elites even seemed to recognise that ruthlessness and selfishness were advantageous for high achieving, yet they couldn't bring themselves to behave that way.

Among the super-elites, one said that he had 'dumped' two girlfriends, not because he didn't like them, but because he thought he would be more successful single. Another acknowledged that he had been a poor carer for his sick parent because his sport had 'given me a great excuse to be very selfish'. Another, when asked where he differed from slightly lower achievers, replied: 'Being quite mentally tough, and being comfortable with being terribly single-minded and pretty ruthless. They're not necessarily nice things to be and lots of people aren't comfortable being those things, but that is what I have been.'

This is a coach of one of the super-elites: 'He doesn't really [care] about what anybody else thinks or does particularly. This is a big generalisation, but most very successful people are incredibly selfish. You have to be selfish, because you're so far off the scale in terms of normal human behaviour, that if you're not being selfish, then you are not doing your programme justice.'

In comparison, here are some comments from the elites: 'I always tried to help people. I'm definitely a helper.' 'I would be bit too nice.' 'I don't think I could have been an Olympic champion. As much as I am really competitive, I'm just not ruthless. I'm a bit too nice probably.'

The elites' parents seem to recognise this too: 'Perhaps it would have been better if he was selfish ... but I think I would prefer him the way he was and what he achieved ... not selfish to the point of "at all costs".' 'I often say: "You're too nice." But I'd rather that than a killer instinct and walking over someone.' 'An athlete has to have that killer instinct and he hasn't got it. It's almost like he's the goodie instead of the baddie.'

Obsessiveness and perfectionism

Here was another gulf between super-elites and their lower-achieving twins. Fourteen of the 16 super-elites reported either consistent obsessive or perfectionist tendencies, but only five of the 16 elites did.

Here are two typical comments. The super-elite: 'I don't think there's any point in doing anything unless you're going to do it really well. I've tried to kill that a little bit in me [since retiring] because it gets a little bit boring for people around me.'

The elite: 'I was conscientious. Not as obsessive as some of the people. [Another squad member] wasn't the most naturally gifted but is a true example of the awesome graft that they put in. They just go at it again and again and again and again and keep pushing. I have utter respect for [that] because I know that I don't have that.'

The relative importance of sport

Being a professional athlete, it is generally acknowledged, requires sacrifice. You cannot party when you might want, you certainly cannot booze, socialise, earn well or start a 'normal' career when you might want. For super-elites, though, this is not a problem. Super-elites do not wish they were doing these other things, they do not see their life-style as a sacrifice at all. The elites, again, are different; they see the grass as greener on the other side. The GBM results show that for 15 of 16 super-elites but only three of the elites, sport held a greater relative attraction than the benefits of 'normal' life. Elites shelve normal life out of a sense of sacrifice and often resent or begrudge it; super-elites just shelve it and aren't bothered. Some elites referred to 'they' – as in another class of athletes who they competed with, who were different, who were able to make sacrifices willingly. They, the super-elites, like the structure and simplicity of their black-and-white existence; they have a narrowness of vision that the elites do not.

This is a typical super-elite comment: 'As an athlete you are so one-dimensional, so focused on your performance, and all the other stuff almost gets left behind, it's almost like being frozen in time.' And this is an elite: 'The monotony of being a professional sports person is just mind-blowing; how they do it is beyond me.'

This deeply ingrained supremacy personality in super-elites translates clearly into the way and the success with which they perform. The distance between super-elites and elites is marked here too. For instance, there are two types of mindset attributed to those setting out to succeed in a sporting arena: 'outcome focus', which is winning pure and simple, the very process of beating the opponent, and 'mastery focus', which is an assessment of the quality of the performance, or mastering the discipline. When athletes use the expression 'I want to be the best I can be' – that is mastery focus. In the study, it was the super-elites who would be parroting that very line as if it was in their DNA.

The study results showed that super-elites had a dual focus: both outcome and mastery. For them, simply winning was not enough. Of the elites, though, only three of the 16 were focused on both. Most of the elites were just focused on outcome.

Here, for instance, is the testimony of one pair of twins. This is the super-elite: 'It is all about beating other people and being first. But to cope with that I would force my attention to being the best that I can be. There is a subtle difference. I had to keep forcing my attention there.' And this is the coach of his elite twin: 'I think he was [motivated] to win. What I mean by that is, if he didn't think he stood much of a chance of winning, I don't think he would work hard, he'd just work enough to [complete the race].'

Just to make the point here, GBM carries this quote from Ian Thorpe, the Australian swimmer (five Olympic golds), clearly super-elite and clearly mastery-focused: 'For myself, losing is not coming second. It's getting out of the water knowing you could have done better. For myself, I have won every race I've been in.'

No doubt this obsession with performance as much as outcome helps sway results in the super-elites' favour too. Significantly, the extent to which super-elites smashed the elites in 'performing under pressure' was striking. Remember, again, these elites have spent most of their lives as high achievers, it was only when they reached the very highest levels that that ceased to be the case, yet only two of 16 said they could maintain a high level of performance under the pressure of high-level competition. Only two of the 16 super-elites said they could not. Super-elites and elites have so much in common, yet when they get to the ultimate judgement day of winning on the world stage, they are miles apart.

Very early on in researching this book, I conducted a long and unflaggingly interesting interview with Peter Keen, a former director of performance at UK Sport, at the end of which we were talking about Bradley Wiggins. I asked him about athlete management and how you deal with superstars, like Wiggins, who we know can be difficult. Keen's reaction was beautiful. He looked at me curiously. 'You think he is the outlier in terms of being complex?' he asked, and then answered his own question. 'Bradley is not an outlier among gold-medallists. Bradley is the norm.'

'What about Chris Hoy?' I asked. Hoy is as balanced and decent an Olympian as you will find; he is a head boy on wheels. 'It's Chris who is the outlier,' Keen replied. And then he explained further: 'On the question of "What is extreme talent?" – it's a very unusual mixture of personality traits and drives which, by any definition, is not normal. Deeper needs, deeper drives, more extreme behaviours are not normal. Bradley might be a bit more visible in how that plays out but I don't think he's unusual in terms of being complex. You'd find very similar insights in the majority. There's a need in them to succeed and to dominate others which in its worst case is psychopathy; it's essentially a trait of a psychopath taken to its absolute extreme. If you look at the most extreme it's a desire to dominate others, immunity to anxiety, a separateness of mind which is unhealthy actually.'

Keen is not the first to suggest that outstanding high achievers are also psychopaths. In 2012, a group of American academics published a paper in *The Journal of Personality and Social Psychology* entitled 'Fearless Dominance and the US Presidency: Implications of Psychopathic Personality Traits for Successful and Unsuccessful Political Leadership'. The paper referred to research that 'showed psychopaths and heroes as twigs from the same branch and conjectured that the fearlessness associated with psychopathy can predispose to heroic behaviours'. It explained: 'Psychopathic personality (psychopathy) is a constellation of personality traits encompassing superficial charm, egocentricity, dishonesty, guiltlessness, callousness, risk taking, poor impulse control, and, according to many authors, fearlessness, social dominance, and immunity to anxiety.'

The paper went so far as to give all the US presidents, up to George W. Bush, a rating for Fearless Dominance, which 'reflects the boldness associated with psychopathy'. The top three were Theodore Roosevelt, John F. Kennedy and Franklin D. Roosevelt; it seems appropriate, then, that Theodore Roosevelt was variously nicknamed 'The Lion', 'The Driving Force' and 'The Dynamo of Power'. The study concluded that 'the boldness often associated with psychopathy may confer advantages across a host of occupations, vocations, and social roles, such as positions of power and prestige in politics, business, law enforcement, athletics, and the military'.

Psychopathic behaviour can, therefore, reveal itself in extreme success as well as extreme criminality. What links the two is the fact that they are extreme. Katherine Grainger knows this pretty much as well as anyone; besides the five Olympic rowing medals she has earned – one gold and four silvers – she has a PhD in Criminal Law with a focus on serial killers. This is her take: 'Yes, there is this branch of successful psychopaths. Because of the culture we're in, people see psychopaths as murderers or nutcases. All psychopathy is a social or personality disorder. It doesn't mean you will become a criminal. The traits that might drive someone to some awful criminal act are the same that could drive others to be phenomenally successful in other fields. There is drive and fascination in one particular area, there is less empathy generally, less guilt or concern for others. There are people with psychopathic traits who will be at the top in corporations, in the army, in sport because it takes a certain mindset. There is a certain mindset that leads to success.'

Does this mean that she and all her teammates are psychopaths? She does not quite go that far. 'I think a lot of athletes are empathetic, especially in team sports,' she says. And empathy is very much not a characteristic of a psychopath.

Yet in the GB Rowing squad, she says, there is a shared personality trait which she would describe as 'extreme': 'It's not a normal choice in life. There are no guarantees of success, a happy ending or the right medals; selection is never guaranteed. It isn't a comfortable existence to choose – and yet everyone on some level really wants to do it, and that's what makes us all a bit crazy. There are some strands that run through everyone. There has to be a real resilience, a toughness. You cannot do this every day. You get battered physically and mentally in all sorts of ways. So the ability to focus and narrow the mindset on one or two things at the expense of everything else – that is quite strong. There is a lot of ego. Athletes can go after something, go after it with a hunger, knowing that it will have an impact on their own lives and other people's – and still go after it.'

What is it that drives the hunger, the narrowness of the mind? Where does all that ruthlessness, selfishness and obsessiveness, that are so distinct to the super-elites, actually come from? The GBM was not just content to identify what makes super-elites different, it wanted to know why. That was the purpose of all those hours of interviews which tracked every athlete's journey from childhood through to the world stage.

Of all the striking evidence that GBM revealed, here was the single most striking fact, the one that hits you right between the eyes. Every single one of the 16 super-elites reported experiencing a significant negative critical event during their primary developmental years. Only four of the elites experienced the same. These negative life experiences included the death of a parent, a parent attempting suicide, parents at war with each other, being bullied by a teacher or another pupil, being dominated by a sibling – and, interestingly, a number of super-elite athletes and coaches acknowledged that there is a connection between this booming driving force within them and their past.

This, for instance, is one of the super-elites: 'I think every sports person will have something in their past that gives them the *need* to win and *need* to stand out from the crowd.' This is another: 'I think it is very clear that I am driven by a sense of inadequacy, and needing to prove something, and I do think that this goes back to very early when my brother was always older, stronger, cleverer, better, and not ever being able to keep up with him at anything.' The parent of that super-elite is in agreement: 'Sibling rivalry gave him a thick skin to strive for achievement.' Has it shaped the person he became? 'I think it possibly has.'

This from another super-elite: 'The biggest [early critical event] was my dad being diagnosed with [a life-threatening illness] just before my last year at school started. That was the moment that I decided I wanted to be an [athlete in my sport]. I wanted to be really good at [my sport], and prove to him before he dies that I would actually have something in my life that I could be really good at.'

These are the reflections of the coaches of a set of twins. The coach of the super-elite: 'He had a bloody difficult childhood, his parents had all sorts of troubles. One of the big things was that his mum [had] a secret [mental health problem]. He came home from school one day to find out that his mum had re-mortgaged the home and spent all the money and his dad had just found out. So his understanding of stability and control and all the rest of it was warped by that experience. I definitely think that his early childhood years were absolutely fundamental in forming him as an athlete.'

And the coach of the elite twin: 'He is in that position where "Life's ace: I've got a lovely great big room, a lovely house, loads of money and what do you say I have to do? Go [and do my sport]? Of course I want to. Why wouldn't I?" You could stand back and feel really envious because everything is laid on a plate, [but] I think he had been delivered the worst of all worlds really. I mean, it's absolutely the classic story of a kid having no fire because everything is laid on for him. I think happy, comfortable kids who get too much support don't ultimately make great athletes.'

This particular coach is questioned further, more generically, on the subject. He is asked: 'Is it the uncomfortable truth that maybe a bit of unhappiness is not such a bad thing?' To which he answers: 'That is 100 per cent right … I say it to my friend all the time … who is this wealthy guy with three kids … and he's got this son who is just a brilliant athlete. [My friend asks]: "What do you think I should do?" I said: "Kick him out. If you want him to win, kick him out on the streets [because] you'll make him a nutter but … he'll just throw himself into his sport." Happy kids don't make great sportspeople in my opinion.'

Anecdotally, in her autobiography, Kelly Holmes discusses her unsettled childhood and her later struggles with self-harm. Likewise, Steve Redgrave has discussed his dyslexia and how that was a traumatic developmental event in his life. And here is one very famous coach, on very similar lines: in his book *Leading*, Alex Ferguson says, 'I have an abiding belief about the virtues of tapping the hunger and drive that can be found in people who have had tough upbringings.' Ferguson says that he would use team talks to remind his players of the hardships in their past. 'We all felt ourselves to be outsiders in some ways, and people who feel like outsiders do one of two things: they either feel rejected, carry a chip on their shoulder and complain that life is unfair, or they use that sense of isolation to push themselves and work like Trojans.'

Here is another major difference between the elites and super-elites. Of the 16 super-elites, 15 experienced a significant turning point which increased their focus. Only one of 16 elites could say the same; indeed they were often turned off their sport by the same kind of experience.

Here, for instance, are the coaches of three of the super-elites. One: 'I think he's still got scars over [finishing outside the medals at the Olympics] ... but it made him more determined to prove everybody wrong.' And another: 'I'm absolutely certain that his whole mentality is driven by the fact that he finished fourth in [the Olympics] and finishing fourth – as you know – is the cruellest place to finish. That flicked a switch with him.' And the third: 'My view is that he went through a complete transformational phase in his life. The death of his father was an extraordinary event in his life. It was an absolute trigger point to him committing to excellence.'

Compare those comments to these from the elites. One elite said: 'I realised that I was never going to make the Olympics. I was good but I wasn't that good. I'd enjoyed my time on the programme, I'd achieved probably all I was going to achieve and it was time to move on.' And this is the parent of another elite: 'He just sort of lost the will to do it after [the Olympics].'

The traits in psychology run strong in both groups here. The elites, who have had the greater comfort in their upbringing, are simply not triggered the way the super-elites are. The GMB quotes Greg LeMond, the three-time Tour de France winner, who seems to put this into words. LeMond was sexually abused as a child, and he says: 'Cycling saved my life. I know it did ... It allowed me to reinvent myself.'

Similar sentiments were expressed recently by John Eales, one of the greatest rugby players of all time. When he was the Australia captain, in 1999, Eales led Australia to become world champions; 17 years later, in a column in the Australian business magazine, *The Deal*, he talked of his older sister Carmel, who died of cancer when he was 18, and how that motivated his playing career. 'I remember her final moments as if they were yesterday and I always will. With her last breath a tear rolled down her cheek. For many years I thought about it before every major challenge I faced or big match I played. My sister had a love of life and rich potential which was never realised. Here was I with an opportunity to live and to achieve. I owed it to her. I owed it to myself.'

A similar inspiration lies behind another of the all-time great Australian athletes, Cathy Freeman. Ten years before Freeman's moment of fulfilment, winning gold in the 400 metres in the Sydney Olympics, her sister Anne-Marie died of an asthma attack, and it was at her funeral that Cathy made a vow that henceforth she would run every race for her. Some years later, Freeman put it into words: 'You know how people say someone is like the wind beneath their wings? Well, she's like a tornado.'

There is an over-simplistic way to interpret the GBM study. We could conclude that, if we are to find super-elites, we should just go round recruiting from single-parent families or find those who had a sibling die early or were bullied at school. This is Lew Hardy's response to that: 'I'm not saying: we need to go out and find out if people have had early life negative events and if they haven't just dump them because they're never going to be a super-elite. I'm really not. For me the more important thing to understand is: are these going to be easy people to work with or difficult people to work with? When I look at the people in this study, I think: they are not going to be easy. And then: how do we prepare our coaches and performance directors to work with people that are like that? Do our coaches know what they are working with? What can we do to help coaches to understand how to work with people who are ruthless and selfish, because it's not easy, yet it is an essential part of the journey to success? I do think that, at the very least, this study could help coaches to understand and be more aware that frequently this is who they are working with; that's a start. Then when people behave a little oddly instead of the coach just getting upset and having a rant, they've got some material to go: "Ah yeah, that's one of those, isn't it, and if I don't want him to be selfish and obsessive then I should go and work with the guys who are in the third team."'

Two other highly significant conclusions from Hardy and Warr. One: this study isn't really about sportspeople. It is a model for high achievers generally: musicians, artists, businesspeople, academics or US presidents.

Two: who wins? Do the super-elites find reward and happiness in their achievements? This is Hardy's hunch: 'I suspect that a higher proportion of super-elite athletes end up having unhappy lives than the elites.'

By the time that Day 11 came round in Rio, GB were flying. The early, first-week gloom had completely lifted. They had even nudged ahead of China on the medal table. And Jack Laugher was back for his second campaign. This was the individual 3m springboard event and the Washing Machine was, again, his signature dive.

His psychology in the final was interesting: in qualifying, he hadn't dived well and sneaked into the final with the lowest score of all the finalists. In the final, though, this worked in his favour. The order of divers was in reverse order of their qualification scores which meant that he would dive first. In all six rounds, then, he could put pressure on those who would follow him. He relished the opportunity.

Laugher's dives carried the highest collective degree of difficulty; he was all high risk, high reward and, as he nailed them, one by one, the challengers fell away. Only Cao Yuan, the Chinese diver, stayed with him. Theirs became a duel, Yuan so technically excellent versus Laugher's showman brilliance. It came to be settled by the Washing Machine: Laugher landed it with slightly too much splash, and with that, Yuan opened a lead and would not be caught.

What the silver medal confirmed, though, was Laugher's position among the super-elite.

What is it that drives him, you wonder. What is it that spurs him to such high achievement? Laugher believes he knows the answer, and much of it is rooted in the bullying he was the victim of when he was a child, most of it in his early diving club years.

This is his take on what he says 'felt like hell': 'The other kids would call me names, make me feel very lonely. If a lot of kids are doing it, a lot of people jump on the band wagon and so I didn't have one friend. Rumours would be spread about me for no apparent reason. Just silly things. And there were rumours spread around my club by other parents. They would constantly called me gay as a kid and tell me to shut up. My coach was actually a brilliant coach but it was done without the coach knowing really. I don't think I'm the only one to experience that, but it is horrible.'

Laugher says he hated the training camps. He recalls the drive home after one of them, feeling on the point of quitting. 'I just didn't want to spend another week with these people that called me names constantly.' His mother talked him out of it. 'She said, "Don't quit, show them." And that's exactly what I do with everything that happens to me now.'

His motivation, then, was to prove himself better than his detractors. And where are those kids now? 'Some of them have quit, some of them have become low lifes as it were. But some are my friends. It's what kids do. It does feel good to have been in that position and to be where I am now.'

Proving people wrong has fuelled him ever since. 'A lot of people along the line have told me, "You're not going to be successful." So it's almost out of spite that I want to be successful.' This carried on all the way to the top. When he and Mears wanted to team up as a synchro pair, the national performance director told him: no, you're not good enough. 'He told me, "Your front and inward rotations aren't good enough." So I said, "Right I'll work on it" and got it really good, did them really well and very consistently and now they're some of the best dives on my list. And when I came back to him he still said no.'

Why still no? 'I don't know. But in a way, that has made me better as a diver.'

He certainly shows the traits of a super-elite. A need to succeed? 'I always want to win. If I finish second I'll be annoyed. In my junior career, I won four world gold medals and one silver and I was more upset for the one silver than I was happy for the golds. I want to be the best.'

Ruthless? He tells the story of when he left school against his parents' wishes. He went to the Barcelona world championships in 2013, performed poorly, didn't even make the final. 'That was the kick in the nuts. I said to myself there and then: "That's it, I'm moving out of home, quitting school, I'm going to do this full-time." I told my parents and they said, "You're stupid to do that." My mum was almost heartbroken. I said, "No, I'm going to do it."'

And how did he respond? 'I tried a lot harder than I've ever tried before – to prove them wrong.'

And is he obsessive and perfectionist? 'If I'm passionate about something I will never take no for an answer.'

Chapter learnings by Chelsea Warr

Do not make the mistake of thinking that we have to go round recruiting athletes – or employees – who are from broken homes or who were bullied or who lost a parent when they were young. That would be the wrong interpretation.

Organisational Fit. Understanding the life journeys, including early childhood experiences and family backgrounds, of your top performers is one way to better understand your people's values, opinions and organisational fit.

Rocky roads. Elite performers need resilience and determination to thrive in high-pressured environments. For some, this is developed in their upbringing (negative experiences, broken homes, etc). For others, these characteristics can be learned by exposure on the development pathway to a number of stressors. In other words, make the road rocky, don't make it smooth.

Super-elite people expect the abnormal to be normal. There's a paradox here: you've got these extraordinary and somewhat maverick people who may find it hard to operate in a structured, supportive organisation. It is important that coaches/staff/employers are equipped with the skills and education to deal with super-talents – people who are ruthless and selfish.

Mastery goals. Athletes – employees – should be encouraged to focus on mastery goals and not be purely outcome focused.

Transformational Leadership

6

The power of learning from foreign models

MAX WHITLOCK, LOUIS SMITH

In sport, as in business, the world is eternally searching for the next big thing. How can we get ahead? What can we do that no one else is doing? How can we innovate? We race away with the obsession of getting a lead on the opposition by conquering new ground. Park that thought for a minute, though, because innovation may sometimes be overrated; the elixir of life may sometimes be found not in breaking new ground at all, but in being the best copycat. This was an observation made by Ndubuisi Ekekwe, founder and president of the African Institution of Technology. In an article for the *Harvard Business Review* he recalls attending a tech conference in Nigeria and being approached by a venture capitalist looking for investment ideas. Ekekwe made some recommendations but they were all rejected. Why? The investor explained that he was not interested in taking a chance with new ideas; he wanted to copy ideas that already had been successful. As Ekekwe writes: 'He explained that Nigeria should not be pushing for innovative start-ups, but should instead be looking for ways to incubate copycat companies.'

Ekekwe's article was headlined 'When you can't innovate, copy'. It was partly with that in mind that in 1989 Paul Hall, a wannabe young

British gymnastics coach, boarded an Aeroflot flight to Moscow. He had been invited over by Sergey Simakov, a Russian coach, and he jumped at the chance. In return, all Simakov asked for was for Hall to bring a starter motor for a Peugeot 305 – which he did. So Simakov drove for three hours in an old minibus from Novgorod, where he lived and ran a gymnastics programme, to pick Hall up from the airport in Moscow. Their journey back was even longer, because at one point there was a road block and Simakov had to take a detour through a ploughed field.

In those days, British gymnastics was, like Nigeria, a third world country. Britain were nowhere; girls fell off beams, the men were such notorious flops in one particular discipline, the pommel, that, at junior or senior level, no Briton had won a medal ever. So, innovation was not an issue, hardly even a thought; the only issue to those who cared was catching up.

Hall really cared. He was inspired in the seventies by Olga Korbut and Nadia Comaneci but, by the eighties, he had come to terms with the idea that he wasn't going to be an Olympic gymnast himself, so he decided the next best thing was to teach someone else to be one. He was obsessed by Eastern Bloc gymnasts; the Soviets in particular. The problem, then, was information. Most of the world's best gymnasts were from behind the Iron Curtain, and that is where the intellectual property that created them remained; even if they hadn't guarded it so closely, you couldn't Google their training methods or YouTube their performances. Hall had attended coaching weekends at British Gymnastics HQ in Lilleshall, Shropshire, but these were deeply theory-based programmes and Hall wanted more. He had already had a tiny glimpse. The very first time he had been to Russia was five years earlier, on a structured tourist holiday to St Petersburg, when he had managed to break away from the heavily managed trip schedule in order to find a shop where he could buy some technical manuals on men's and women's gymnastics. He pored over them with relish.

Hall already had a bit of Russia in him. His grandmother, Sonia Galperina, was Russian; she had fled a smallpox epidemic after the Revolution and come to Scotland. When Hall was a boy growing up in Canvey Island, Essex, his grandmother lived in the family home and he would listen at her knee as she told him proudly about his ancestry, the Motherland, recounting stories and reciting Russian poems. He picked up some scraps of the language and he would later top that up with a Russian O-level. So when he returned home with those manuals from the trip to St Petersburg, he was able to have a reasonable go at translating them and, in the process, it dawned on him how much more there was to know.

Four years later, an opportunity arose that was better than a Russian manual – a Russian coach. Hall received a call from a friend: there was a Russian coach here in the UK, on a visit at a gymnastics club in Sutton in Surrey. Would he like to come and meet him? It was not a difficult decision. These were his thoughts at the time: 'The Soviet system was an established system with thousands of coaches going through a university degree. I knew their country was doing incredible things that I couldn't imagine myself doing and I wanted to know more.'

So he went to Sutton and that was when he first met Simakov. Being able to manage a conversation gave him a natural advantage, the two men got on well, and by the end, Simakov issued him the invitation to come to Novgorod.

This is how Hall recalls that first trip to Novgorod: 'Very interesting, amazing to see how their system worked. I stayed with some families who were extremely hospitable. At the time, there were a lot of shortages so I remember having a lot of soup or food that wasn't perhaps the best standard but I remember also so much friendship. And lots of vodka. I felt very welcome. The gym itself was a real eye-opener. We still complain about gyms in Great Britain, but going to Russia and seeing these amazing gymnasts training in gyms where they made kit from bits of old trampolines had a big impact on me. It really was cobbled together with what little money they had, yet they were producing the highest level of gymnasts. And they had really innovative ideas on conditioning and the many ways of learning a skill. They had a tried and tested regime of how to train twice a day, sometimes six days a week; the kids were tough. The fact is: the communist regime was harsh and there wasn't really a way out, so for them to work really hard and deliver in their sport for their country probably was it. It was an opportunity to break out of their system. I think that had an effect on making the kids tougher.'

Hall returned with his head full of thoughts, one of which was how much harder young athletes could work than he had ever imagined; another was that a capitalist country wasn't very conducive to high-level sport. Just as importantly, he had made a proper friend. Simakov passed on to him some more manuals from his university coaching education; Hall insisted he return again to England but, next time, to his own gym. Thus began a real exchange; Hall has now made ten trips to Russia; Simakov has been back twice as often. They both could offer each other something valuable beyond their friendship: Hall was a sponge to Soviet coaching methods; Simakov was a sponge to the new western world. With the Iron Curtain coming down, the funding programmes that had underpinned his living started to change; in the commercial west, he realised, his knowledge would have a price.

Simakov was not the only Eastern Bloc coach thinking this way and Hall was not alone either in seeking Eastern Bloc expertise. John Atkinson, a PE teacher who became national gymnastics coach in 1973, made his first fact-finding trip to the Soviet Union in 1967 and, like Hall, saw exactly how far advanced their infrastructure was. Where possible, Atkinson would entice an eastern European coach back to England; once the walls of communism came down in 1990, the occasional drip-drip of this expert foreign intellectual property started to become more of a trickle. The key question quickly changed. Previously it had been: how do you get your hands on the information? Now it was: how do you use it?

There is an art and a science to borrowing intellectual property. The Japanese car industry used to blatantly copy American design and really started dominating the market in the seventies and eighties. Then the

Americans tried to work out what they could copy in return; they seized upon Japanese efficiency and lean production methods, tried to implement change and saw their own efficiency worsen.

Conversely, maybe the most infamous and successful copycats in business are the three German Samwer brothers. Living in San Francisco in 1998, they noticed the fast-rising success of eBay and hurtled back to Germany to start up a version of their own, Alando. Alando quickly hit the market and, within a half a year, it had done enough for the Samwers to sell to eBay for US$43million. This became their modus operandi: executing other people's ideas can be just as successful as coming up with your own. Once they had hit the jackpot once, the Samwers started taking aim again. They backed StudiVZ, a German clone of Facebook; they went to Indonesia and started Lazada, an Asian clone of Amazon; they took note of the success of Zappos, the American online footwear retailer, and set up Zalando in response. Often they would sell their own product back to the company they had mimicked it from. By 2012, they were rated among the top ten wealthiest tech entrepreneurs in Europe. They didn't top any charts for universal admiration; many have criticised their controversial tactics. On the rare occasions that they can be persuaded to comment, they explain they wanted to build companies, not ideas. And they are pretty effective at it.

The skill in learning from successful models is identifying exactly what can be transferred. The idea of sports coaches going abroad on fact-finding trips has long been accepted wisdom. Dave Brailsford is relentless in his pursuit of knowledge from other success stories, be they from sport or, more recently, Silicon Valley; he would consider it a dereliction of duty if he wasn't. We have already seen in this book how the seeds of knowledge in Talent ID were taken from East Germany, planted in Australian rowing and then replanted into the UK high-performance system.

Paul Hall knew exactly what he wanted to take from Russia and sow into his gym in Huntingdon. He learned technique, he learned the acquisition of skillsets, but one of his clearest conclusions was that one reason why Britons fell off the pommel was because they did not work hard enough. Thus, Hall came to regard the pommel differently to other GB coaches, viewing it as an endurance discipline.

By the mid-Nineties, another foreign influence had come heavily into this sphere: Gheorghe Predescu, a top Romanian coach, who had also relocated to the UK. The contrast between Romania and Russia was numbers; in Romania they had fewer world-class gymnasts, so, when the good ones came along, they had to treasure them. The same would be said for Huntingdon. Hall's thinking, encouraged by what he saw in Russia, was that because 8- to 11-year-olds have a low body mass, they could cope with greater loading. So he asked Predescu: can we double the workload without breaking them? Can we do pommel every day? The answer: yes.

On a daily basis, Hall thus had squads of kids spinning large numbers of circles on handles on varying sizes of pommel horses. The 8- to 11-year-olds, for instance, would do four 30-minute sessions a week. Hall kept charts and statistics. The best children aged 10 could spin 140 to 150 circles without stopping. He remembers very well the day when one kid brought the gym to such a standstill that soon everyone was standing around, cheering and counting. The kid got to 336. This was Louis Smith.

Hall's success with foreign learning, however, was not mirrored by British Gymnastics. The late nineties brought double opportunity: the influx of eastern European coaches and the influx of lottery money. This allowed Atkinson to implement what he had witnessed and admired in the old Soviet Union: centralised training. Let's bring everyone together under one roof, at the National Sports Centre in Lilleshall, one high-performance sweat-house where we can all train full-time, compete with each other, learn from each other, where the improvement curve goes only upwards. Atkinson was right in theory, but not quite right in implementation. As he would prove, one culture does not transfer directly into another.

One obvious problem was a language barrier with some of his imported coaches. The problems went deeper than that, though. For

Soviet kids, being selected to go to a centralised training site was the golden ticket, it brought clear rewards: on-site schooling for the children and financial support back home for their families. At Lilleshall, though, these rewards did not exist. An invitation to Lilleshall did not equate to a financial windfall. The athletes themselves did not qualify for enough lottery support, so they would end up having to go on the dole. Craig Heap, who won two Commonwealth golds, had to double up by working on his parents' farm; a number of his peers were recruited by Cirque du Soleil and headed for the door. For the girls, who tended to be younger, it was even harder. They would be centralised in Lilleshall and bussed into nearby Newport to go to school; it was either that or tutors being brought into Lilleshall itself.

The effect of permanent centralisation lost its competitive *raison d'etre* too. The theory that the nation's top athletes would spar with each other daily and collectively improve through collective practice did not hold. Instead what formed was a pecking order; soon everyone found their place in it and the pecking order barely changed.

Indeed, despite all the great intentions, the changes saw British Gymnastics hurtling downhill. At the World Championships in Anaheim in 2003, the nadir was reached. The men finished twenty-third. As a final confirmation of their place in the greater order of things, lottery funding was thereafter withdrawn. The plan had failed.

The story of modern British gymnastics is not the descent to Anaheim, but the comeback after it. Here then, is an example of good use of foreign input from the year that followed it. Hall was preparing his young prodigy, Louis Smith, for the European Junior Championships in Ljubljana, Slovenia, and he wanted Predescu's advice. Smith was 14 then, the youngest in the GB team; it was his first pommel competition at that level. Romanian gymnasts weren't the most aesthetically beautiful but they were renowned for being well prepared for competition and Hall wanted to know how. Predescu gave him specific advice on the heavy number of repetitions required to have his routine ready for competition and, with that, Hall agreed with Smith that, in the month before the Championships, he would have to do 50 clean routines. For a British gymnast, that was considered a crazy workload, but Hall and Smith stuck with it. Sometimes Smith would do four or five routines in a session. The day they were to leave for Ljubljana, he was on 49 and they went down to the gym just to get in a fiftieth. They had no real hopes for Ljubljana apart from getting into the final; Smith, however, would win gold.

The victory was a huge landmark. No Briton had ever before won a pommel medal. More significantly was the message it sent to fellow British gymnasts and coaches: success was not beyond reach, Britain needn't be a third world gymnastics nation.

One man who got the message loud and clear was Scott Hann. In the late nineties, Hann had been a decent junior himself; he had been a reserve member of a junior national team, but he realised he wasn't going to make it himself and, just like Hall, resolved to help someone else to make it instead. He was not short on self-belief either.

This is Hann looking back on the confident young man he was as a young coach in the early noughties: 'I don't know why or where it came from but I was obsessed with coaching. I believed that I could take on anybody or any team and turn them into some sort of champion – which is ridiculous. I was just determined to create a world champion; that's all I felt I wanted to do. I had a huge ego. I thought I was better than everybody else.' Even when he started moving up the echelons and started coaching in respected company, he had an offensively high self-regard. 'If I didn't believe that another coach had something to offer, I wouldn't entertain them coming over and offering me advice – which is just stupid. It would offend me back then. There were only a few people that I listened to and Paul Hall was one of them.'

What he shared with Hall was the philosophy that Hall had learned in Novgorod. Hann's own view was very specific: Britain didn't produce champions because they didn't give athletes the opportunity. He explains: 'I wanted to give people the opportunities that I never had. As a gymnast, I had had the time to train but I didn't have the coaching. And while there was full-time training going on, it was only as you reached your older teenage years. So what I wanted to do was bring youngsters in regularly from school. They soon started coming in, two or three times a week, from the age of about seven. It was far from the norm then, but now everybody does it.'

When Hann started coaching, at Harlow in Essex, he was 19 years old. He wanted to devote all he could to coaching, so he did most of the coaching for free and earned a living in part as the gym's cleaner, in part in a local nightclub and in part by driving for his father's minibus company at the weekend. He then got a job as head coach in Basildon and started driving forward a high-workload training programme for his youngsters. When the parents of a 12-year-old called Max Whitlock rang him one day, asking if Max could switch from Hemel Hempstead to join his programme, he said: 'Fine, as long as he is here three times a week.' No problem.

Among his other juniors reared on this heavy training regime was Brinn Bevan. In 2014, Bevan went to the European Junior Championships in Sofia in Bulgaria and returned with multiple medals. But Hann was reassured long before then that his philosophies were paying off. Even before Bevan or Whitlock got to junior level, Hann had been experimenting by taking his juniors abroad to events in Russia, Bulgaria and Slovenia, and he liked what he saw.

'I just thought I had some really good kids,' he recalls, 'and I wanted to go and show them off and see how good they were compared to the best. And it was a real confidence booster. People would come up to me saying, "Wow these kids are fantastic." I can remember my guys on the floor doing some basic tumbles and the Russian coach coming up to me to ask questions about them. I remember looking at these great seniors in Russia in particular and thinking "How do we get to be like that?" and then looking at their juniors and thinking "I'm actually doing better than them." I felt like my eight-year-olds would have beaten their 15-year-olds. It gave me an experience and an insight into what other people were doing outside of the country, but it also made me realise that what I was doing was right. It drove me on even more.'

The rise of Louis Smith was the start and the inspiration. A cavalry charge of other young Britons followed. After his initial breakthrough in Ljubljana, Smith successfully defended his European junior pommel title in 2006 and thereafter, the gold medal has remained in British hands for a decade, handed down between four other young British gymnasts. In 2010, Whitlock won it. In 2012, it was won by Jay Thompson, another who joined Hann's Basildon cohort.

This new generation represented an almighty opportunity. Funding was switched back on in 2006, but the focus was all on the future, not the present. Smith and the new cohort were initially not even allowed to train with the senior gymnasts for fear that the seniors would ruin them. The juniors were more professional than the seniors; they had a better idea of how full-time athletes should conduct themselves than the seniors; they trained harder – they didn't need to pick up bad habits.

The new British Gymnastics hierarchy now redesigned its structure, this time using foreign influence for all it was worth but not following it unquestioningly. On the men's side, now, there is an executive director who is British and, beneath him, Eddie van Hoof, a head coach who is British too; there are two Russians on the staff, Andrei Popov and Sergei Sizhanov, who are technical coaches, but the language is not a problem because Popov has been in the UK since 1990, when Liverpool Gymnastics Club brought him over, and Sergei Sizhanov followed in 2001 when he was employed by Notts Gymnastics Club.

The centralised programme that had once proved so unwieldy was redesigned too. Instead of complete Soviet-style centralisation, Lilleshall became a semi-centralised hub hosting regular team camps every year. There the team enjoyed the bonding and sparring, growing as a team, establishing their personality as a unit, in which Smith was the loudest and Whitlock the quieter perfectionist. But why would you take Whitlock permanently away from Basildon, or Smith from Huntingdon, if that is where their coaches are?

And the new system worked. Smith led the way. If ever there was an oh-my-God moment, it was in 2008 at the Beijing Olympics. He won bronze and, as Hann recalls, 'That was it. That was what told us: we can do this, this is actually happening. And: OK, great, now we want *that* too, let's go and do it.' Four years later, in London, they did. Whitlock got bronze on the pommel behind Smith in silver, though the greater statement about how far the young generation had come was the team event result: the team that were a laughing-stock twenty-third in 2003 were on the podium in third.

So what British Gymnastics has now is not a copycat from Russia, but a very British system with strong Russian influence. It has a star team who were given the foundations of intensive early training, as learned from the Soviets, but with a battalion of British coaches who learned much of their art abroad. Speak to people around the sport and they will tell you that Van Hoof has been a master at blending the two.

If you watch Whitlock closely, you can see the two at work. His tumbling and his twisting are heavily influenced by Alex Shiryaev, a Ukrainian coach. His parallel bars routine has strong shades of Shiryaev too. But his signature move on the floor is very much home-made. Back at the Basildon gym, when training sessions were officially completed, Whitlock always wanted to stay around, essentially to play around. He would bug Hann to stay, too, and, for a while, he became obsessed with seeing if they could teach themselves a breakdance move he wanted to copy. The move starts in a handstand, with legs split, and goes into a spin, pushing off from one hand and then effectively catching the move on the other. Whitlock cracked it to the point that he wanted to see how many spins he could do in a row. When he had got into double figures, Hann eventually came up with a better suggestion: let's tidy it up and apply the move to a routine. Watch the BBC footage of his floor routine in Rio, and it is this breakdance move that the commentators rave about – until they are eventually able to declare him the Olympic champion.

In one glorious afternoon, on the middle Sunday in Rio, learning, experience and expertise all came to fruition. Whitlock barely had the time to take in the fact that he was Olympic champion on the floor before he was competing with Smith on the pommel. This was the master versus the apprentice. It was also the climax to the rise of British gymnastics. This was no longer Britons trying to get to the top; it was two of them right up there as high as you could get, peerless, fighting their own private battle for gold.

Smith went first, looking to set the bar as high as he could go. However, he nearly made an error at the start of his routine and immediately he decided to switch from his original plan. He had set out to do the hardest routine in his repertoire; hardly had he got going than he opted for something marginally safer: execute it cleanly, he thought, give myself a chance. He did pull it off brilliantly, but he had already given Whitlock a chance too. If Whitlock could execute a clean routine, with a harder tariff, then he would edge ahead.

This was the moment when the generations passed. Whitlock was inspired and too good. When he had flipped off the pommel, his landing perfect and clean, he had edged past his teammate. So it was Smith silver, Whitlock a double gold. And Britain's gymnasts were on top of a world in which they recently didn't belong.

Chapter learnings from Simon Timson

As St Francis of Assisi preached, 'Start by doing what's necessary; then do what's possible; and suddenly you are doing the impossible.' The transformation of British Gymnastics from a team that was a laughing-stock was founded on willingness to learn and to look beyond their own boundaries. Hall, Hann and van Hoof were never so bold as to think they had all the answers, and continually searched to find them. The story of this transformation highlights three principles of successful change:

Contextual application of best practice enables successful change. The skill of learning from successful models is identifying exactly what can be transferred. Ask yourself and your peers, 'Precisely what elements of best practice can be transferred to our environment and used in our culture?'

Develop a clear and simple formula that's easy to understand and can be applied by people at all levels on a daily basis.

Start with the changes people are ready to make, and capable of making to maximise the likelihood of transformative change.

7

Empowering female talent

WOMEN'S HOCKEY, REBECCA ROMERO

It was after the Beijing Olympics that Danny Kerry realised what an appalling job he had been doing. Kerry was coach of the GB women's hockey team, and they had finished sixth: not great, no medal, but it was better than their world ranking before those Games (eleventh), so not bad either. Respectable, you might say, and Kerry felt he had worked damned hard to get them that far. But then, after the Games, came the body blow. A post-Games review of their campaign was conducted, as it always is. The review took in the players' feedback and, to Kerry's astonishment, his players ripped him apart. He was hugely hurt and very pissed off; he could not believe that his group of athletes would turn on him. They said he was grumpy, miserable, unapproachable. He wondered: I worked every hour God sent me. What more could I have done?

He discussed it at home with his wife, Liz. He told her he was considering walking away. Maybe he was just not cut out for this. She wasn't so sure. She asked him: 'Do you think the person that your players have described is really you?' No, clearly not, he said. 'Well,' she surmised, 'you must have worked in a way that makes them think that's who you are.'

The moment when Kerry really saw the light was not far off. He had once heard a talk by Steve Peters, the psychiatrist who had been doing such good work with British Cycling, but at the time he had dismissed as nonsense Peter's interpretation of the difference between male and female behaviour. He regarded it as gender stereotyping. After Beijing, though, Kerry was sent on a coaching course and it so happened that Peters was speaking again. Again, he talked about women – how they are hardwired through evolution to be anxious and how they worked in groups because it served the purpose of keeping them alive. And he talked about men – how they are hardwired to be competitive/aggressive and they don't necessarily have the need to work in groups. And he talked about the neuroscience, about how the male and female brains are wired up slightly differently, about brain function and hormone systems.

This second exposure to Peters held a mirror up to Kerry's soul. He started retracing his steps and, in his mind, re-reviewing the Beijing campaign that he thought he had conducted with such diligence. He rewound to 10 August, their first game in the Olympics, a late evening match against Germany ending in a 5–1 defeat, a spirit-sapping start to their Games. He thought back to that night post-game: the players did ice-baths, did anti-doping, food, travel and then when they finally got back to the Olympic Village, he convened a team meeting. The 16 women in the team looked at him with faces that said 'What the hell are we doing here?' And then he rewound to 11 August, when he was preparing for the Argentina game the following day glued to his laptop, reviewing selection, performance and the tactics against Germany and looking for answers for what he should do for Argentina. But did I go to the rooms and talk to the players, he now asked himself. Did I have conversations with the athletes? Did I ask them: how do you feel about last night? Do we want to discuss the plan for Argentina tomorrow?

Kerry had been a successful coach of a men's university team, and then the successful coach of the England boys under-18s. He was used to coaching in a male environment where his job, as he saw it, was to provide answers around tactics and technique. To give instructions. Here's the schedule, let's get on with it. The mistake he made was to transfer the same thinking from a men's team to a women's team.

In summary, he says: 'I got it horribly wrong.' A second exposure to Steve Peters had shone a light on the errors of his ways. 'I realised I needed to lead and work with a group of high-performing female athletes in a very different way to the way that I had worked before,' he says. 'Actually I needed to leverage on the strengths of what a lot of high-performance female athletes can bring around nurturing and a want for social cohesion and use those hierarchies for good, not for bad.'

Yes, this chapter is straying into dangerous territory and doesn't Kerry just know it. It is the very fact that it is such precarious ground that prevented him from working it out for himself earlier. 'In western society,' he says, 'it is taboo to talk about men and women as if they are different, and that actually creates as many problems in the performance world as anything. But if you aren't aware that the types of hardwiring that exist are different between men and women and then how the hormones impact on that hardwiring, and the fact that the performance world is an anxious world – then that's a pretty deadly cocktail. My experience in the many years I've been working in this area is that you ignore this stuff at your peril.'

Dan Hunt would have appreciated Kerry's advice, had he not already learned the hard way too. Hunt started as a coach in British Cycling in September 2005 when he was put in charge of the women's endurance programme. There are four parts to the track cycling team, and the women's endurance was the one department which showed not the remotest sign of future success. So when the team went to the Melbourne Commonwealth Games, six months after he had started, the expectations were not great; the pressure to deliver, at that stage, was still low.

One day at the Games, he found himself having lunch with Victoria Pendleton. Not planned, they just happened to be in the food hall at the same time. Pendleton was in the sprint team, so she wasn't coached by him, but she was close enough to the endurance women to know what she was talking about and senior enough to feel able to do so. She said to Hunt: 'How do you think you're getting on?' He replied equivocally: 'Oh, not too bad.' At which point she appraised him of the cold reality: 'Well actually you're not doing well at all.'

Bluntly but not too brutally, Pendleton handed down the information: he needed to change in the way that he was interacting, coaching, communicating and managing the women's team. 'I was doing it almost like a bull in a china shop,' is how Hunt recalls his management technique pre-Pendleton lunch. 'I just assumed that I knew what I was doing and that I was going to give them what I thought they needed. The problem that I had that I didn't really recognise for the first six months was that all the advice I had been given about coaching was being given by men who coach men about coaching men. So a lot of the advice I was happily receiving as a rookie coach was wrong, and I'd have done a lot better to have sourced a coach of high-performance female athletes because that is what was standing in front of me.'

After Pendleton's firm nudge, Hunt went on a brief journey of enlightenment. It took him via two other male coaches who were coaching female athletes, who could both relate to his story, and to the man who had given Kerry the tablets of stone: Steve Peters. A series of conversations with Peters thus commenced. As Hunt explains: 'He really helped me to understand what their demands were, how female athletes are different and how they look at the world. I think that the whole piece around communication is very different from coaching a group of female athletes rather than male. They are far more tuned in than the boys; they're much more receptive to changes in body language, tone, inclination. They connect on a much more personal/emotional level; the boys are much blunter tools. Boys worry more about what's being said rather than how it's being said. There was a lot of emotional management to be done with the girls, and yes, a lot of it was quite common sense and yes, sometimes I think I was just being a dick. Once I'd got that awareness that I needed to change, Steve was the person who really helped me understand what was standing in front of me.'

It may be tempting, here, to conclude that Kerry and Hunt were being male and emotionally unintelligent, but (a) you won't find many more emotionally intelligent coaches in the Olympic arena, and (b) that misses the point. Their point is that you manage males and females differently – and they are not alone in making it.

One more point from Hunt: 'Certainly when I was coaching the lads they never had one of their girlfriends or wives on the phone to me asking questions or challenging things. And that is absolutely fine but boys don't tend to have such a commanding influence in their life as many of the girls. If I went back into coaching girls again I would invest a lot more in those people. Your decisions go home with the athlete and get talked about. You could really manage things very well by engaging those people – the husband, the boyfriend – so they understand what you are doing.'

In skeleton, in the early noughties, the GB team stumbled into another key difference between the male and female athlete. Why was it that some of the most promising women dropped out of the programme, yet most of the men stayed? The women would all drop out at roughly the same stage; and what was more perplexing was that the point at which they elected to drop out was just when the whole thing was getting interesting.

If you have received an invitation to go to the mountains on mainland Europe to start training as a potential Olympian in skeleton, you will already have gone through two very strict recruitment filters. Lizzy Yarnold, who won gold in Sochi, for instance, first showed up in Manchester during the Girls4Gold recruitment programme. She and hundreds of other women went through a series of physiological tests; from that group, 28 were then invited for Phase Two at Bath University. Yarnold was a heptathlete and was hoping she might get to transfer into modern pentathlon; when she received her 'congratulations, you've made it through' letter, which informed her that her Bath group was the skeleton group, she didn't even know what bob skeleton was. Nevertheless, she and 27 others showed up for Phase Two, after which nine were selected to progress to their first real experience of the sport they were being considered for: a three-week induction programme in Lillehammer, in Norway. It was once they got to Phase Three – in Lillehammer, Altenberg in Germany, or wherever each group happened to be located – that some of the women would drop out. On one of the first runs in Lillehammer, one of the women broke her leg. But that wasn't the reason anyone dropped out at all.

Some of the men dropped out too, but their reasoning was straightforward. They were solely interested in their training times and 'Am I faster than you?' – and if they weren't fastest, they'd consider quitting. They weren't winning so they wanted to find something else in which they could.

The women were different. Sometimes it was the best who would leave. Why? Simon Timson, who was skeleton performance director for a time, explains: 'Our answer was the social factor: maybe they weren't getting on with the coach, for instance, or they weren't having a good time with the other girls. For the women, the social environment in the early weeks was more important than the sport itself. You take 17- to 20-year-olds who have never seen an ice track, and some who have never been out of the UK, and you are shoving them into Norway or eastern Germany for three weeks – they need to have fun and enjoy the environment. No one in Great Britain wakes up, even now, thinking "I want to be the next skeleton champion". So, the first thing you have to do is romance the athlete with the sport and have them fall in love with it. How? The boys are inherently competitive and just want to compete and race. For the girls, particularly in a foreign environment, it's a shared experience and they want to be part of it with other people and they need the relationships as much as they do being the fastest.'

To try to stop the men leaving, Timson simply switched off the clocks in training so they couldn't see how fast they had been and couldn't know if they were the best or not. For the women, the answers were different: they introduced girls' nights out, pizza evenings, games nights. That way they wanted to stay.

There is nothing clear and definitive in this apart from the science. We do know for sure that there are anatomical differences in different parts of the male and female brain, we do know for sure also that there are differences in the way certain transmitter systems work, and we do know that the brain is connected slightly differently according to gender. Scientific studies have tried to prove, for instance, that the difference in size and functioning of the male and female amygdalae, two almond-shaped groups of nuclei which help process decision-making and emotional reaction, can explain why, under stress, men might be more likely to respond with a physical reaction and women with an emotional one. We know, too, that the ventromedial prefrontal cortex (VMPC), located in the pre-frontal lobe, has a greater dominance in the right-hand side of the male brain and the left-hand side for the female brain. As the VMPC also plays a part in decision-making and emotional response, there is further evidence therefore to support the idea that, neurologically, there would be gender-based behavioural differences.

In 2013, a study by the University of Pennsylvania employed diffusion tensor imaging, a technique which could map neural connections in the brain to observe the different ways that men's and women's brains were, effectively, wired. They mapped the neural traffic of 428 males and 521 females and found the distinct difference – women's neural activity was far more across the left and right hemispheres of the brain and men's was more front to back. The left of the brain dominates logical thinking and the right intuitive thinking and here were the women's minds flicking from one to the other in a perfect display of multi-tasking. As Ragini Verma, the researcher on the project, observed of the findings: 'I was surprised that it matched a lot of the stereotypes that we think we have in our heads.'

This is the science, though it is limited. By no means do scientists understand everything about the brain and gender difference. And

every brain is different anyway. Just as you cannot make blanket statements about cholesterol because different bodies process food in different ways, we cannot come close to predicting how different brains react.
Humans are not robotic. And thank goodness for that.

This is how Peters sees it: 'I could never say "All men do this, all
women do that", because it is not true. If you go down the route of saying to coaching staff, "If you have a men's group, you act tough, you rally
the troops" and "If you have a women's group, you act very gentle", then
you end up not functioning optimally at all. My message would never
be "If you have a male athlete, these are ten things you can do" and "If
you have a female athlete, here are ten different things you can do". I
would never advocate that. Yet typically within a men's group you get
a lot of ego; typically, within a women's group you might find that ego
is not the driving force and it is more to do with the interpersonal play
among the team members. When I am advising people, I do keep saying, "It is helpful sometimes to understand that men and women may
have different approaches." Because we know that there are these anatomical differences, this would imply that we are going to perceive the
world slightly differently and interpret it differently.'

And anecdotally, it is not just Kerry who discovered as much with
his hockey team, or Hunt with his endurance riders, or Timson, in the
mountains with the skeleton women. An interesting take from a different angle comes from female coaches. Giselle Mather, one of the
highest qualified and most successful female rugby coaches in England,
has coached men and women and she, too, acknowledges that there are
clear differences. 'Females ask more questions,' she says; 'they will ask
and ask, whereas guys will just do it, though eventually guys will feel
comfortable enough to ask questions too. But while girls really want to
understand the answer and talk about it, boys just want to do it.'

Another take on the same subject is this from Paula Dunn, the head
coach of UK Athletics' Paralympics team. She says she is only conscious
of gender differences significant enough to require a different approach
to her coaching when the athletes go from individual performers

(which they tend to be) into teams (such as for relays). 'When a group of women come together, it can be different,' she says. 'When I have coached women's relay teams, that was definitely more about emotional intelligence.'

Mather, however, says that yes, there are clear differences, but no, that doesn't mean she will coach differently. 'I have a way of coaching,' she says. 'First and foremost, I coach the person. The best coaches I had when I was playing, did they unlock the female in me? No, they unlocked the athlete in me.'

One of the stalwarts in Kerry's hockey team was Hannah Macleod, and she sees it from two points of view too – from the women's team, that she is part of, and from her professional part-time work as a nutritionist to individuals and teams, male and female. 'You can tell guys to do things,' she says, 'and they'll go and do it. But girls want to know why they should do it; they'll want to discuss it. And if they don't, you don't get their buy-in. I see this with the hockey at Bisham Abbey, where we train: the men, for instance, if they have a bit of conflict, are happier sorting it out there and then, whereas the girls tend to take it off the pitch. The girls know that we have to discuss everything. We generally won't accept being told: "Go and do this." This is what I see in my work as a nutritionist too. It's much easier working with men, they are much more straightforward.'

Kerry, at least, became convinced that he had to start over with a fresh approach. Here, he gives five examples of how.

Collective agreement

Kerry: 'You have to allow the space for a lot of clarification as to why we are doing what we are doing, otherwise you get group discussion and anxiety about what those decisions mean for individuals and for groups. You have to be very explicit about your rationale and, interestingly, if you do that, you then get the very beneficial thing where collectively the women as a group feel part of the process and feel valued. It can then be an incredibly tight unit that wants to go and do things. But you have to manage that constantly.'

After Beijing, Kerry felt that if the group were to make the step up to contend for the podium, they needed proper change. One option was to centralise their programme, to have everyone move to Bisham Abbey, their training base, and to train as full-time professionals. This was a huge call: a lifestyle change, a demand on people to leave jobs and education, to postpone careers. Kerry floated the idea of centralisation, fully aware that forcing it on them was out of the question. Only when the group had discussed it and agreed it did it go through. The team went so far as to decide themselves when centralisation would start. They even designed the schedule of the working week.

Kerry: 'They genuinely felt it was their programme. And when people feel they own it, they are very precious about it, very proud about it.'

Ownership

Kerry: 'There is a lot of business talk about people owning their performance. The key is to find a way to genuinely get people to own it, actually give them the opportunity to input, contribute, shape. I will definitely be a voice, but the athletes will feed in. The strength for the women is, if you can make them accountable and own the performance, they will really do everything in their power to bring everybody with them.'

Captaincy, then, became not his own selection decision but the group's. They selected their captain by democratic vote.

Even more significantly, he introduced 'Thinking Thursdays' where, each week, new challenges would be presented and it would be up to the players to overcome them on their own. On Wednesday nights, the players would be sent an email with the three teams for the next day – Alpha, Bravo and Charlie – along with the crucial news of which team would get the supposedly 'lucky' bibs, plus the special circumstances for the competition between them the next day, be it extra points for goals from the left of the pitch, for instance a game where minutes in possession beats number of goals scored, playing when the opposition have a player sin-binned, whatever. Immediately on receiving the email, the three teams would set up WhatsApp groups and start exchanging ideas and tactical plans. The following days' sessions at their Bisham Abbey HQ were furiously competitive. Sometimes Kerry would change the rules mid-game, he would force one team to play short-handed, for instance, or stage a penalty shoot-out. And he would drive them with the sole message: you have to find a way to win.

Thinking Thursdays worked on two levels. One: they created an intensely pressurised environment: two hours of physically and mentally hard training, being worked to the limit of intensity and having to think their way through games when they were absolutely dead on their feet. There are matches, at the top of the game, where that is what it is all about.

Two: they encouraged independence, the necessity and thus the ability to think on their feet, to remain mentally sharp and to solve their own problems. In other words, he forced them to own their own performance and they loved it.

Selection

Kerry: 'Selection is the biggest single risk in women's team sport.' For the Olympics, a head coach has to cut the squad from the 30-odd players in the squad to the 16 who go to the Games. For Beijing, Kerry's plan was that he would announce the 16 and all athletes would be granted a face-to-face meeting thereafter if they wanted. He concluded after the Games that he could hardly have been more wrong if he had tried. As he discovered, rather than be dictated to as to how this was going to happen, his athletes wanted to own the process; they wanted to input how they would hear and who they would hear it from; they wanted reassurance that the process had been completely thought through.

Kerry: 'If they don't have that reassurance of what the process is, then what you get is the athletes talking about the process, they'll then attack the process, and in doing so it will undermine the outcome.'

For London, then, the players were invited to design the process themselves. They agreed that individually they would be able to decide how they would hear the news (text, email, phone), where they would be when they heard it and even how they would want their housemates/teammates to respond. They agreed they would have a week where they could have their face-to-face with Kerry and that they could bring another person in with them.

Kerry: 'Effectively, for a week, I was sitting in meetings where you've got athletes who, in their world, have had their lives shattered. Some of them had prepared written things because they knew they wouldn't be able to hold it together if they just spoke. It affected me deeply. I couldn't sleep well through that period.'

However, it worked. The team had also agreed that though the Olympic squad was 16, they would need the 30 to stay together for the three months between selection and the Games, because a squad of 16 cannot train half as effectively as one that can train as a full 11 versus 11. The test of the process would be how many of those whose Olympic dreams had just been cut dead would return to train. Within four days, 28 were back out at training.

Encourage female strengths

Kerry: 'They want to nurture. That sounds like a stereotype, but ultimately that is what is occurring. They want to look after the collective of the group. Men are sort of task-orientated whereas women – these women – are cohesion-orientated. If you can get to that point where they want to cohere and look after one another and pull one another along that is an incredibly powerful force.'

Kerry staged a number of surprise sessions that involved intensely hard, physical training where the players knew neither what the physical tasks would be nor how long they would last. This is called 'dislocation of expectation'. Kerry found that when he dislocated expectation, the players would come together, because they wanted to look after one another. This kind of exercise maximises their strengths: nurturers nurturing, the group getting stronger.

Grumpy face

Kerry: 'You have to be conscious of the higher-level anxiety which can exist within the performance environment. A low-level issue can become a group problem very quickly. You have to ensure that the most mundane thing doesn't become a bigger issue than it is. You see that happening constantly.'

It is not as if Kerry has to remember birthdays (though that is appreciated). But he does have to remember the problems with his 'thinking face'. On the side of the pitch, he has his thinking face on a lot and that makes him look grumpy and unapproachable. And then, if someone then talks to him when he looks grumpy, they can get the wrong impression.

Kerry: 'If they're anxious they'll read into your body language that somehow he doesn't like me any more and he's not going to pick me.'

Kerry cannot stop himself thinking at pitchside, but what has started is an awareness. 1) He does remind himself to smile more. 2) He has explained that the grumpy face doesn't mean he is grumpy. 3) As a group, they spend a lot of the time trying to reinforce the need to have their responses governed by logic rather than emotion.

If we could produce a manual saying 'This is how you manage men' and 'This is how you manage women', then life would be indeed simple. And probably dull. The reality is of course complicated and much more interesting. For Dan Hunt, it was hard, too. Lunch and enlightenment at the Melbourne Commonwealths had not suddenly left him with the world at his feet.

After those Games, he made some tough decisions. One of the cyclists he coached had won a bronze, but even that was not enough to persuade him that she, or any of the squad he had inherited, could be good enough for the Beijing Olympics two and a bit years on. So he released all his athletes from the British Cycling funded programme and elected to look for his talent elsewhere. This was the ballsy gamble he took: to jettison the mediocrity of the current squad and opt instead for the complete unknown. That complete unknown was Rebecca Romero, who already had an Olympic silver, but not in cycling – it was in rowing. Romero had never even ridden in a velodrome before.

She was interested in switching sports, though. Yet neither she nor Hunt knew if it could be done; it hadn't been done before. But after bringing her up to the English Institute of Sport in Manchester for a standard testing session on an ergobike, Hunt was convinced it was worth a go.

'What happens on the ergo is you start off at 85 watts, nice and easy, and it gets progressively harder and harder until you stop.' Hunt explains. 'They are pretty demoralising tests because you know you can't win, you're just going to pedal yourself into a sweaty mess. So this is Rebecca: after five minutes, she's still going but she's starting to look a bit hot. Another couple of minutes go by and I'm thinking: this is over in a couple more. But eight or nine minutes later she's still going. She absolutely turns herself inside out. I've run hundreds of bike tests, and I've never seen anybody do that to themselves on a bike. She eventually collapsed over the handlebars and looked up and said: "Do you think I'll be good enough?" I didn't even look at the numbers.'

All that was required, then, was to persuade UK Sport to release funding for an athlete who had never pedalled a bicycle in competition before. Simple.

Both Romero and Hunt needed this to work. Romero needed to prove that moving from rowing, where she had already shown herself to be world class, wasn't an act of complete madness. Hunt was in his first big job as a coach and was staking his reputation on an unprecedented gamble. But Romero liked what she saw in Hunt: 'I thought he was definitely far better than any of the other coaches in rowing I'd had. I don't remember thinking: we're a male coach and a female athlete here. For Dan and me, it just clicked. Within a couple of hours, I didn't see him as anything else but a world-class coach. I didn't even think: is he the right coach or not? I straight away, instinctively trusted him. In weeks it all fell into place. I didn't question it at all. He understood me. He listened to me, interpreted my ideas and it was just so simple or easy. It was everything that I needed in a coach, that I knew I had been missing in the past.'

While Hunt may have been masterly at managing one female athlete, he was not so smart at managing two. His other hope for Beijing was Wendy Houvenaghel, an Ulsterwoman, formerly of the RAF, who was working as a dentist in Cornwall. Houvenaghel wasn't on the world-class programme, she trained and coached herself, and yet she regularly beat the cyclists he had taken to the Melbourne Commonwealth Games, the ones who *were* on the British Cycling programme. Naturally, Hunt wondered what she could she achieve if she was on the programme too.

With Romero and Houvenaghel both on the programme, Hunt's gambles started to look good. At the 2006 National Track Championships, Houvenaghel got gold in the individual pursuit, with Romero in silver. They went to compete in Moscow later that year and Houvenaghel pipped it again. At the World Championships in Palma the following spring, the tables turned. It was there, Hunt recalls, that, for Romero, 'it really clicked'. Houvenaghel came fourth; Romero got the silver.

'Palma was a bit of a turning point,' Hunt acknowledges, 'because the relationship between Rebecca and Wendy at that point started to disintegrate.' It would never mend.

Romero describes her relationship with Houvenaghel as 'the biggest negative I had in cycling'. They would train together and then compete together. 'I know so many other personalities that I would have been able to work with in that environment,' she says. 'I was used to managing that proximity and that intensity from rowing, when you are all competing to be in the top boat. But I think the differences between Wendy and me were just so extreme. There was never really any hope of it mildly working out. It was a real shame because we spent a long time training together, racing together. I always wished that it could have been someone else.'

What did Hunt do? 'Steered clear of conflict,' by his own admission. Thus, the coach with whom she had clicked so quickly now started to irk Romero. 'Dan wasn't very good at dealing with conflict and managing conflict,' she recalls. 'It did frustrate me a lot of the time, always treading on egg shells and not disciplining situations.'

Hunt had an awkward triangular relationship that he needed to keep in place. He knew he was really onto something good with both of them, particularly Romero. At the World Championships the following year, in Manchester, Houvenaghel was again fourth and Romero now in gold.

This is his take on the dynamic: 'I never dealt with the Rebecca and Wendy issue, not ever. I really did think about it a lot but actually, as uncomfortable as it was, I don't believe either of them would have got the performance they got without being chased by the other one. They drove each other on for sure. If that was what it was going to take, I was prepared to plaster over some cracks.

'But if I'm honest, I look back on that time and I was probably weak at times as well. I wanted to be recognised as doing a good job; I wanted people to say: "Wow, Dan's turned that programme around." To me that would have been like winning ten Olympic golds, and to do that

I needed these girls. I think that there were a lot of times when we needed to have a conversation but didn't. At times, maybe I should have said: "Look, you don't like you, and you don't like you. Get on with it, get over it, because we're here to operate in a professional, productive way," but also I didn't want to rock the boat. I thought: if we get this just about right, we're in with a sniff of a chance. This was how I rational-ised it: most of what was coming at me was manifested stress, so don't hit stress with stress, just let it wash over you.'

Hunt's management was skilful, or head-in-the-sand, take your pick. It probably did not help that the two girls shared digs in the Olympic Village. Beijing was harder for Romero because she had family issues at home and then a back injury which was kept completely secret from the media. 'Out in Beijing,' she says, 'I just fell to pieces.' No one knew how her back would hold up; her first practice session in the Olympic velo-drome was appalling. 'Mentally and physically,' she recalls, 'I'd reached my tipping point.'

She and Hunt nevertheless managed to hold it together and a sem-blance of form returned at the last minute. The inevitable conclusion was played out on 17 August when Romero and Houvenaghel went head to head in the Olympic final. Romero won it, though her recollec-tions are painful in the extreme. 'It wasn't winning an Olympic Games. It was just a horrible experience. Everyone on the British team has seen the decider race between us, Rebecca gold, Wendy silver, and all you get is the team with its back turned to you. Afterwards, nobody wants to unsettle Wendy so no one is congratulating me, Dan can't acknowledge it because he doesn't want to be seen to in front of Wendy and it's totally subdued, as if it never happened. It was horrible, not even a clap or a cheer. I didn't have tears because I was happy but because it was a shit feeling; I couldn't believe it happened that way. We got gold and silver and went back to the village as if we've just done a training session. I felt bad for myself but even worse for Dan. He had two athletes win-ning gold and silver and he couldn't celebrate. It was just so wrong that it had to be like that.'

Hunt's own recollection is not vastly different. His achievements were remarkable; he had inherited a going-nowhere squad and, in two-and-a-half years, won gold and silver and turned a rower into a cycling Olympic champion. He was a success, he had delivered, and, yes, he did have people going: 'Wow, Dan's sure turned that programme around.' But this is how he sees it: 'The Olympic Games is meant to be one of the best things you ever do. And I just thought: "Fuck, I want this over."'

At the London Olympics, Kerry's change of direction was vindicated. The women's hockey team won bronze. He had done well; so well, in fact, that he was promoted from women's head coach to performance director of the whole sport. That meant that he wasn't coaching the team any more, and within two years that really showed: in the 2014 World Cup in Holland, the team finished eleventh. That summer, their coach lost his job and Kerry took control again. The following summer, they beat Holland in the final in a penalty shoot-out to become European champions.

Fast forward a year and they were in another final, the Rio Olympic final, and again, it was against the Dutch, the double Olympic champions. Technically, the Dutch were the superior team and both teams knew it; anyone could see it. They utterly dominated the third quarter, after which they held a 3–2 lead and showed no signs of relinquishing it. By that stage, they had forced ten penalty corners and GB none.

Alex Danson, GB's main goalscorer, recalls the tension of the end of that game: 'In the last quarter of the final, one of the girls said: "Right, it's Thinking Thursday. We've been here before, we're back at Bisham, except this time we're all in the same team. Find a way to win."'

The challenge this time was to score a single goal against the run of play, to drag them into a penalty shoot-out. This is Macleod's view of that final quarter: 'We were skilful, but not as skilful as the Dutch. We were never going to be a gold-medal team based on skill. We were only going to do it by being the best *team* in the world.'

Where they struggled was to force the possession from the Dutch. The chink of light came when Laurien Leurink, the Dutch midfielder, was yellow-carded. And now they really were in Thinking Thursday territory: they had a man over, they were fatigued and in the most pressurised situation of their lives, they *had* to make the most of any scrap of possession, they had to find a way.

In the time that Leurink was off, they forced their first penalty corner, and it was saved. A second followed immediately, a shot from Danson rebounded and it was flicked in for the crucial equalising goal.

By this stage, back in the UK, nine million people were on their sofas to watch the penalty shoot-out that followed. Maybe the only person feeling relaxed, at that stage, was Kerry at pitchside. He knew this team had beaten Holland on penalties before. He had every confidence that their minds were straight enough to do it again. They had done this so many times. And they reminded themselves once more: it's just another Thinking Thursday.

As the sky darkened, the intensity gripped tighter as the final drama was played out. In Maddie Hinch, GB had a heroic goalkeeper, not only brave but smart, with a gameplan for every one of her Dutch opponents studied and written down in a notepad. One by one, Hinch repelled the Dutch attacks; meanwhile GB edged ahead. Helen Richardson-Walsh scored with a penalty flick – that was the lead. Then Hollie Webb buried her penalty inside the right post – and that was the gold medal.

A month later, I asked Kerry: do you really believe that a major contribution to this triumph was your attitude to managing them, to managing them as *women*? He was absolutely convinced that it was. 'What I've found with women is your role is to provide constant reassurance. People might say that is applicable to a men's group as well, but I am not so sure.'

Then I asked: would the team themselves recognise this, that his management approach had become so gender-orientated? 'Probably not,' he said. For all the information he shared with the team in his second two Olympic campaigns, he never actually explained that this was why he had so completely changed his approach.

So I asked a couple of the team. Did this approach work, because of your gender? Danson seemed surprised. 'I've never really thought about it,' she said. 'There definitely was a shift in Danny. Previously, he would be pitch- and laptop-orientated; then, after Beijing, he shifted to understand another side that he hadn't tapped into. We became more cohesion-orientated. You could argue that is a more female trait; I don't know.'

Then I asked Macleod the same question and she said: 'Definitely.'

I think that actually there can be no definitive answers. No blanket rules, as Steve Peters said. Humans don't work like that. Yet if Kerry and the hockey did not lay down a blueprint, they surely at least shone a light.

Chapter learnings from Simon Timson

Doing it the right way matters as much doing the right things. American management guru Ken Blanchard stated, 'In the past a leader was a boss. Today's leaders must be partners with their people … they no longer can lead solely based on positional power.' This is what Danny Kerry learned and executed with his hockey team. His leadership became all about fostering engagement in group goals. The hockey gold medal demonstrates that the power of engagement is costly in time but cheap in financial terms and it creates great levels of ownership, commitment and perseverance which you require to succeed.

Listen to your team. Accept feedback as a gift, but types of feedback are important here. You have clean and dirty feedback: clean feedback is given for the benefit of the receiver to help them improve their performance; dirty feedback is given for the benefit of the person giving it in order to get it off their chest.

Always be very explicit about your rationale for decisions, especially with women, in order to make teams feel part of the process and make people feel valued. This takes time and effort but creates buy-in and unity.

Challenge team members to creatively and innovatively solve problems. Rather than presenting solutions to your team, empower them to find them themselves. This will generate a collective responsibility and accountability.

8

How to turn around a failing sport

On Day Three in Rio, British journalists covering the rugby sevens in the Deodoro suburb, an hour and a half out of the city, started receiving phone calls from their sports editors. Question: 'Can you leave the rugby?' Answer: 'Well, if I have to.' 'The shooting venue is nearby, isn't it?' 'Yes.' 'Well get yourself over there quick. We're about to win a medal.'

The medallist was Ed Ling in the men's trap shooting. His Olympic record, until then, was hardly indicative of medal potential. He had finished twenty-fifth in the Athens Olympics, didn't qualify for Beijing and then came a glorious twenty-first in London. So he hadn't exactly been a magnet for media attention. Yet in Rio, those who made it over from the rugby to the Deodoro shooting venue arrived just in time to see him win bronze.

Two days later, shooting was not such a secret. The British media were a bit better prepared, and they needed to be. This time, in the double trap, there wasn't just one GB shooter in contention but two, and they ended up in a head-to-head shoot-off for the bronze: Steve Scott versus Tim Kneale. Scott, who had finished twelfth in Beijing and hadn't even qualified for London, won it.

So, two days after that, a decent crowd of GB media turned up to cover the last of the British medal hopes: Amber Hill, who was 18 years old and had become European champion a year earlier. Hill would reach the final and finish sixth – so she didn't win a medal, but she certainly contributed to the impression that GB shooting knew what it was doing. This is important, because a few years earlier, it didn't.

British Shooting had sent six athletes to the Rio Olympics, of whom four reached the final and two won medals. That is a good return. Yet, three years earlier, shooting was a failing sport that needed rescuing, and this had led to the question: how do we turn around a failing sport? One question was met with another: what if we treat it like a failing business?

On the evening of 8 January 2014, Steve Headington, an operating partner in a leading London private equity firm, received a call out of the blue from Lew Hardy. Hardy, a psychologist and academic who worked as an occasional consultant to UK Sport, was an old contact of Headington's but hadn't spoken to him for around four years. 'I have this interesting project,' Hardy said. 'Can I run something by you?' And then, slightly more unusually: 'Can I interview you?'

Hardy explained that he was ringing on behalf of UK Sport. At UK Sport, where they managed and funded Olympic and Paralympic sports, there were a number of sports that weren't pulling their weight. Some, like basketball and water polo, had already had their funding dropped altogether; they had shown no reasonable sign of delivering Olympic medals in the next four to eight years and there was a firm argument for stopping their funding. And there were others teetering on the brink. These others were in a bracket known as Risk and Opportunity sports. There were a number of them including swimming, judo, weightlifting and shooting. All are sports where there were lots of Olympic medals available but where GB was simply not winning enough of them.

Hardy's point was this: these are failing sports that need turning around. You, Steve, are in private equity where your specialism is in taking over businesses that need turning around. We are wondering: is there much common ground between the two? Can you apply the principles in private equity to winning Olympic medals? Hardy also wanted to know: how did Headington operate in private equity? Was he the kind of operative who liked to take businesses apart or was he more the kind who built them up?

The phone call left Hardy convinced sufficiently that this was, at least, an avenue worth pursuing. Three weeks later, Headington received a call from Chelsea Warr, who wanted to know more. Headington recalls: 'I explained how a private equity firm works, how we make very focused, conviction-based investment bets, how we think very hard about the effectiveness of what we are doing to make a difference. Chelsea was asking me about the core principles to doing successful turnarounds and how we might apply them to better case-managing underperforming sports. I said there are ways to do something like this really well and drive alpha returns – as in beating the market returns. I told her I set out with a mindset that my job is to make heroes out of management teams. That is my starting point. Then I said: "I'm happy to come and have a chat."'

Two months later, Headington arrived at the UK Sport offices for what would be the start of a long association. 'I was intrigued by it as a mission,' Headington recalls. His own sporting background was limited – national age-group swimmer, Loughborough University water polo team – but he liked what they were trying to achieve. 'I liked the inspirational agenda. I remember 2005 when Coe stood up when we won the bid for the 2012 Olympics and made that speech: inspire a generation.'

At UK Sport HQ, Headington explained further how private equity works, by raising funds from sophisticated investors and then selecting companies to invest in – a bit like UK Sport deciding which sports to invest in. 'What is our core business? Investment decision-making. What is the core business of UK Sport? Investment decisions that drive medal winning success. Not much different.'

He then revealed more about his own modus operandi: 'Private equity used to be: raise money easily, buy companies cheap, do a lot of financial engineering and sell at a high price. That world, in the last 10–15 years, has fallen completely by the wayside. Now, the only way you can outperform the market is to work with management teams to help them improve their business. It's a more competitive world. And the misperception about private equity being cost-cutters and vultures is so old, it's 1970s.'

Headington's own role seemed a good fit too. He takes second-quartile firms – good, under-managed companies, just like these Risk and Opportunity sports – and works with management teams to build better businesses of them. 'We are not quick-flip merchants,' he said. The more they all talked, the more it became apparent that the challenges UK Sport faced as investors in athlete medal success had direct parallels with private equity. 'In that sense,' Headington says, 'our day-to-day professional experiences collided.' The chief difference was scale. Headington, at the time, was involved in the acquisition of a large retail business with over 1,000 locations across European markets; this was somewhat bigger than, say, shooting.

Finally, Headington left them with a couple of weighty observations which seemed to resonate. Beware the big noise, he said, the idea that the answer to every business problem is to restructure. No, it is not. And then a classic Headington line: 'Underperforming organisations that re-organise underperform underperforming organisations that don't.'

He also said that he was, 'concerned at the number of funding conditions these sports were required to meet, the number of changes they were attempting and the short time they were given to implement them.' So he told them about peanuts versus coconuts: with a handful of peanuts, you are dealing with lots of small issues; you will achieve so much more if you identify one or two big issues; these are your coconuts. Focus on the coconuts.

When you ask Headington exactly what he does and how he does it, he refers you to a 2002 article in the *Harvard Business Review* entitled

'Value Acceleration: Lessons from Private Equity Masters'. One of the masters within it is Bain Capital and the story in one of the article's case studies is a straightforward account of turnaround in a contact lens business that Bain purchased in 1995, Wesley-Jessen. The business had a very specific point of difference in the contact lens market; it sold specialist lenses: coloured lenses and toric lenses, which are used to correct astigmatism issues. In its desire to expand, though, Wesley-Jessen had moved mainstream and started competing with the two giants of the industry, Johnson & Johnson and Bausch & Lomb. This was a fight it couldn't win; Wesley-Jessen over-expanded and simultaneously lost touch with its key corner of the market. By 1995, it was working at a dangerous operating loss; that is when Bain bought the business. Bain had performed an investment review and its conclusion was that Wesley-Jessen needed to return to its core market. The $100million factory that had been constructed in order to pump out the more standard lenses was thus re-equipped to start making more specialist lenses. There were some spending cuts made, but largely to reinvest in growing the product range in the specialist market. It all worked so sweetly that in two years Bain's equity had earned a 45-fold return.

After Headington's initial meeting with UK Sport, he received an email from Warr asking if he would join their Mission 2016 panel as an independent business expert. Mission 2016 constantly reviewed the health of the Olympic and Paralympic sports; if a sport got a red light, it meant it had triggered extreme concern and it would get a polite demand to see the Mission panel. As Headington observed, a summons by the Mission panel can sometimes feel like being put on the naughty step, 'but what it is really about is helping them improve by challenging and supporting them.' His role on Mission 2016, though, would be primarily to work with the Risk and Opportunity sports. Just as Bain had turned around Wesley-Jessen, Warr was hoping Headington could do a job on some of the underperformers on the Mission.

The first question for a private equity investor is where to make an investment bet. Headington, like Warr, was quickly convinced that an investment in shooting could produce dividends. One of the hack-neyed old sayings around shooting is that 'anyone can win on the day'; the performance of GB shooters in recent years had certainly provided corroborating evidence. They didn't win often, and they hardly ever won in the Olympics, but every now and again, one of the group of leading GB shooters would pop up at a major event and take a medal. The exception, which kind of proved the rule, was Peter Wilson, who had won gold in the double trap at London 2012. Wilson, though, had operated outside the system; he had not been funded by UK Sport for most of his Olympic campaign and he was not coached by a GB coach. Instead, he had been talent-spotted by the 2004 double trap Olympic gold-medallist, Ahmad Mohammad Al Maktoum, who happened to be a member of the Dubai ruling family, who had of-fered to coach him himself. Wilson was proof that there is talent in GB worth backing.

To the private equity mind, an investment in shooters could prove good value because of their longevity. In most Olympic sports, you have a brief window when you are athletically at your peak. In the London 2012 shooting, medallists' ages ranged from 20 to 49. In other words, if you invested in the right stock, it could keep producing medals for three decades.

It just so happened that a 16-year-old shooter had just been voted the BBC's Young Sports Personality of the Year. This was Amber Hill. An ideal investment. One of the first interventions of Mission 2016 fol-lowed a discussion about Hill and the question: how do you make the transformation from a young girl into an adult medal-winner? One of the answers was to introduce Hill to Jessica Ennis-Hill. Jess would give Amber guidance.

At this first meeting with British Shooting, Headington was keen to leave one strong message. He wanted some clarity in the way they were planning the way forward, so he introduced them to what he calls 'the 60-second elevator test'. You are in a lift with someone and you have 60 seconds, before they get out at the next floor, to tell them what you are focused on. That is what British Shooting needed: real clarity of purpose, a 60-second elevator answer to the future.

It was not only Headington who was pushing for a bigger, bolder vision. Warr was too. In 2013, she had recruited into British Shooting a new Talent Pathways Manager, Steven Seligmann. He came from the English Cricket Board and was highly rated. One of the problems immediately identified with British Shooting was that there was no pathway, no formal method of recognising future talent, nurturing them, coaching them and developing them into the stars of tomorrow. In other words, shooting was still stuck in a world where it would keep its fingers crossed that enough young good 'uns would float occasionally to the surface. This was Seligmann's problem to solve.

He was appointed in July 2013. A month later, his solution was presented to Warr in the form of a 23-page document, entitled 'GB Academy Programme'. One of the targets set for the new Academy, this document announced, was that by 2015 one athlete would have been accelerated from Academy level to the top World Class Programme.

Warr read this and phoned Seligmann. Good, she said, but don't you want much more? Where's the ambition? What's the Big Hairy Audacious Goal here? He had designed a programme to improve the status quo. She challenged him to go at it again but with a different mindset, not to improve the system but to fundamentally transform it, so that shooting could become a multi-medal-winning sport. This phone call – the permission to think big – was, says Seligmann, his lightbulb moment.

He then returned to the drawing board and drilled deeper into the problem. He studied foreign models. He analysed previous winners, how they trained, who they were coached by, how they competed. Increasingly, he became convinced that British Shooting did not have to live with the idea that 'anyone could win on the day', as if they were random investments that would occasionally produce a dividend. 'I was fascinated by that myth,' he says. As he saw it, by better managing their investments, shooting could dramatically improve, it could stop producing occasional success and deliver consistently. He also challenged current thinking that it required six to eight years to develop a world-class shooter; he didn't want to wait that long and evidence convinced him that he didn't need to. Again, this would allow smart investments to deliver a better – quicker – return.

Four months later, Warr received a second draft of Seligmann's GB Academy Programme document. This time it was 91 pages long. It contained depth, substance, evidence and showed intricate performance problem-solving. And as a stark indication of the rise of his ambition, he changed the target for the number of athletes breaking through into the top World Class Programme within two years – no longer one but three.

The contents of British Shooting's 60-second elevator test were the three coconuts that they set out to crack:

1. Training time. In training for London, Peter Wilson would be shooting some 1,000 cartridges a day. The other GB shooters were down nearer 250. That needed to change; they needed to match Wilson's workrate. There was also a culture that said that shooting was a seasonal thing: you'd hang your gun up for the winter. That had to change too.

2. Quality of training. The best athletes are produced by the best coaches, so let's employ the best coaches. British Shooting made three critical hires, one of whom was Sheikh Maktoum, who would work with Scott. Quality of training also requires an element of competition, so the 11 shooters on the World Class Programme would find themselves training with the kids on Podium Potential, the next level down. Just as was hoped, the kids snapped at the heels of their seniors, who were forced out of their comfort zones and responded.

3. Peaking at major events. It was essential to dispel the culture where GB shooters would compete regularly around the world

safe in the knowledge that, one day, they would come good. On average, they would compete at six major events a year. British Shooting narrowed the window of opportunity – not six events, now, but three – and challenged them to get used to peaking when it mattered rather than when it just happened.

To help with quality of training and peaking, other interventions were made. A psychologist, Paul Hughes, was taken on board. There was also a new focus on the performance environment. So, at the 2014 World Championships in Granada, for instance, there was, for the first time, a GB team tent. Not exactly a revolutionary invention – the USA and the UAE were already doing it – but traditionally, the shooters from the other nations would rattle around between events, waiting for their next moment to compete, in the same athletes' room. It was a bit dog-eat-dog in there and easy to become intimidated. In the GB tent, though, there were snacks, a water-cooler, a physio, in case of need, and comparative serenity. The GB shooters had never felt particularly special; one tent and that started the change.

They had not felt particularly united either, and Seligmann was convinced that there was a performance gain to be had here. 'I had come from a team background,' he explains, 'but I was convinced that the concept of "team" could be applied to an individual sport. Shooting can be a fractious environment, so we tried to stress that we were stronger if we were representing something together. I don't really believe you can do it on your own.'

There was another small but significant intervention at the Granada World Championships: a GB team handbook. They had never had one before. And it wasn't particularly special or revolutionary – with the standard mugshots and résumés – yet the athletes liked it, and it bonded them together, rather like their tent. And it may be mere coincidence, but there wasn't just one GB shooter who happened to come good and win a medal in Granada, there were three.

For all this to happen, the investment model had to be tweaked significantly. Seligmann narrowed the numbers down to just the mission-critical athletes; 11 centrally funded athletes were slimmed down to six. This freed up finance for the extra performance staff – physio, psychologist, coaches – and it meant that a more intense support programme could be built around the six athletes that remained.

Now the question was no longer whether British Shooting was transforming itself, but whether the effects would be felt in time for Rio.

When Headington said that he wanted to make heroes out of managers, Seligmann was one man that he had in mind. A year after joining as Pathways Manager, Seligmann had been promoted to Performance Director – in other words, he very quickly became the boss. Yet maybe the most heroic thing that Seligmann did, with the Games approaching, was to take one step back rather than another step forwards.

Ahead of Rio, Headington coined the phrase 'pivotal rookies'. He said that UK Sport, along with the British Olympic Association and Paralympic Association, needed to identify which of the leading management figures going to Rio were so inexperienced that they might be a risk to performance. Seligmann fitted into that category. He had never been to an Olympics before; by the time Rio came around, he would only have been the boss for two years. By everyone's assessment, he was learning on the job fast and impressively, but were the Games themselves the time to be learning? Every sport appointed an official team leader for Rio and it was generally the case that the performance director of each sport would, for the course of the Games, step up to become that team leader. For shooting, however, it was a very valid question: was Seligmann the right man? There was an obvious alternative: Phil Scanlan, a former shooter who had been team leader for London 2012. He had just retired from professional life as a director in Continental Tyres, so he wasn't a threat to Seligmann – it was not as if he wanted his job – but he was the other extreme, not young and thrusting, but senior in age, relaxed and experienced. He was also hugely popular with the athletes. Scott describes him as 'the dad to all of us'.

This information was presented to British Shooting. Seligmann then took the decision: Scanlan would be team leader. This meant that Scanlon got the accreditation, Scanlon lived in the Olympic Village, while Seligmann signed himself up as a B-list attendee at the Games, excluded from access-all-areas, excluded from official Olympic transport. Nevertheless, he got himself to the shooting venue every day; he wanted to watch, learn and ensure that he'd be ready for four years later.

You can never really know, for sure, what decisions helped athletes – or musicians, businesspeople, anyone – become successful, but we can have a pretty good idea. You can only put in place what you feel is the optimum environment for an athlete to give themselves their best chance to perform. The decisions shooting had taken were given a proper test. Two weeks before the Games, Scott split up with his long-term girlfriend. He was, he says himself, 'in a bit of a dark place'. So the decision to have psychologist Paul Hughes as part of the team in Rio paid off. 'He was a massive benefit to keep me on the straight and narrow,' Scott says. 'He kept my mind on track.' The decision to have Scanlan as team leader seems to have paid off too. 'He is so understanding,' Scott said. 'I'd call him a good friend of mine. We couldn't wish to have a better team manager.'

Thus, on Day Five, Scott found himself in the shoot-off for the bronze; not only were he and Kneale, his opponent, both Britons, they were also training partners. It was a wet and blustery afternoon, but Scott was immaculate. Out of 30 clays, Kneale missed just two; Scott hit them all.

That was GB's second medal. Turnaround complete? Well, no, not quite. But in Rio, they were ahead of schedule. They feel there is a lot more to come.

Chapter learnings by Chelsea Warr

This chapter is about breakthrough performance. It focuses on the need to look for future potential as opposed to current performance, and to be informed by the facts. Shooting was a dormant opportunity, stacked with medals and waiting to be systematised and positively stimulated via transformational leadership. This is a chapter about giving people the permission to think big and bold, and providing a safe environment to pursue it.

Understand your market and work with the facts. Then push your products into new markets.

Invite critique from other industries. This will cut through the noise, clean the problems and help you look for new solutions to old frustrations.

Peanuts v coconuts. When you're pushing through transformational change, find your top four or five really big things (your coconuts) as opposed to getting drawn into dealing with noise or low-impact items (your peanuts).

Selfless leadership. A lot of people would not have done what Steve Seligmann did, stepping back to let Phil Scanlan come forward in the most significant event of four years. Great leaders will know when to lead from the shadows and when from the front, always keeping performance and outcome at the heart of the decision.

9

Challenging the tyranny of the normal

The best bikes in Beijing

The way athletes and sports teams tend to progress is by making incremental gains: what was accepted wisdom yesterday tends to be handed down, repeated today and improved upon tomorrow. Most athletes and sports teams tend to improve bit by bit by carrying on doing pretty much the same thing but a little bit better. That is the normal way of things; this is a chapter about deciding how and when to break away from the tyranny of the normal.

To do something different, to embrace change, is a gamble but the rise of British Cycling was founded on the ability to tackle the question: why should we do it the way it has always been done? To tackle it successfully requires courageous leadership and fearless decision-making.

One of the daftest and most inspired things that Dave Brailsford ever did, when he was performance director of British Cycling, was to give a job to Matt Parker. Brailsford rang him at the start of 2007 and asked him to coach his men's team pursuit (TP) team for the Beijing Olympics. The TP job was a tall order because it meant chasing the Australians whose world and Olympic titles and numerous world records were evidence of how far they were ahead of the rest of the field.

At the Athens Olympics, the Aussies had set a record so outstanding that it was considered a freak ride. The record they broke was their own. And the record before that was theirs too. A British quartet had come second behind them in Athens, but they had not come close. When the Aussies set that record in the 2004 Olympic final, many thought it would stand for years to come.

Two-and-a-half years later, it still stood strong. That was when Brailsford rang Parker to say that Simon Jones, who coached the British team that couldn't get close to the Australian record-breakers, was leaving. Would Parker take over?

This might not have been such a strange call if Parker had been either a cyclist or a cycling coach, but he was neither. And he never had been. Parker was a sports scientist. The height of his coaching experience had been in age-group football.

Yet all the evidence suggested that if this team just followed accepted wisdom and carried on making incremental gains, they might never catch the Aussies. The hunch, therefore, was to try a new approach. By giving Parker the TP job, there was a guarantee in place that the job would not be done the way it had always been done, largely because Parker did not know how it had been done before.

Even now, Parker says his promotion was 'a ridiculous idea'. Yet he also relished Brailsford's willingness to question accepted wisdom. 'Dave took the bull by the horns and said if I'm going to crash and fail it's going to be on my own terms.'

Every so often, an innovation in sport arrives that completely changes the game. Dick Fosbury's famous backward flop in the 1968 Mexico Olympics high jump competition is the stand-out example of a radical change that encourages others to follow suit and ask the question: is the old way always the best?

At the end of 2010, the company Netflix did a similar thing. That was when they started streaming video, therein challenging customers to ask themselves: do we want to carry on renting from shops and mail-order companies, or shall we just stream it? This was a brave challenge to the norm, largely because Netflix was itself a successful business that distributed DVDs in the mail. In other words, the better the new Netflix streaming business, the more vulnerable was its own mail-order business. Netflix could have carried on the old way, could have continued growing the mail-order business – just as Blockbuster had carried on renting movies from their shops – but it decided to invest in innovation. 2010 also happened to be the year that Blockbuster went bankrupt.

Netflix today has a 10-digit dollar value and is held up as the ultimate case study of disruptive innovation. 'Disruptive innovation' is the trendy label in modern business practice, so much so that analysts now argue about what is disruptive and what is not. A disruptive innovation is one that creates a new market and, in so doing, disrupts an established one. This is what Fosbury did. When the Fosbury Flop came in, it put both the scissors jump and the old Western Roll out of business.

In sport, as in business, there is a vast difference between a long-shot gamble and a calculated innovation. Everyone throws a Hail Mary from time to time, sometimes you have no choice. The Hail Mary pass is a term from American football, meaning a late, long-shot pass where the probability of it coming off is so low that it requires divine intervention. British Cycling, however, generally prefers not to gamble with a long-shot tactic. Their innovations tend to be calculated investments. Like Netflix and the streamed video.

One of the other great innovators in the British Olympic movement is Peter Keen. He had – has – a belief in his convictions that is so firm and bordering on belligerent that he was twice the recipient of death threats. One was in the mail, composed of letter clippings from a newspaper. The other was delivered to his face, by the parent of an athlete, when he was at an airport leaving for a training camp. Happily, this second death threat was not carried out either, but retribution of a kind was exacted as Keen discovered when he returned from that camp to find that his house had been vandalised.

Yet Keen had reason to follow his convictions. His first success in coaching was with Chris Boardman, with whom he trained and innovated to a professional level previously unseen in British Olympic sports. Such was the detail with which he prepared for Boardman's world championship attempt in 1994 – in the fierce midday heat of an Italian August – that they worked out how long before he competed they needed to put a bottle of frozen water on the bike so that it melted just at the moment he would start racing. Every day they trialled and perfected their timing. They got it right eventually (answer: 20 minutes). And Boardman won two world titles. Boardman's frozen bottle may well have been British Cycling's first ever marginal gain.

Keen was the first Director of Performance at UK Sport. He was appointed initially, before the Athens Olympics, by Sue Campbell, the UK Sport chairwoman, as a consultant. Campbell had a model in mind that would allow athletes to be funded over an eight-year period before hitting their peak. Keen and Liz Nicholl, who was then the director of elite sport (now the CEO), were tasked with implementing Campbell's vision. Keen's job was to establish a model for how money should be invested in the long lead-in to the 2012 Olympics. In other words, he had to decide which sports would be well funded, which would not, and how much they would all receive.

In short, he became an overnight investment specialist. As he explains it: 'You've only got so much money, so if you're trying to win as many medals as possible, where would you spend that money? You'd spend it on the athletes who are most likely to win – that's your investment isn't it?' So far so simple, but as he says, 'That was hugely controversial.'

The idea, back then, that money going into sport would be regarded as a business investment that expected a return, was considered so distant from accepted sporting culture that the *Daily Telegraph* carried a column under the headline 'A flawed and inadequate scheme'. The column name-checked Keen as one of the crazy inventors of 'one of the most hare-brained schemes yet devised by the rulers of British sport', which it claimed was 'primed to virtually destroy a handful of summer Olympic sports'. The column said that the investment model was 'a bean-counting exercise in a straitjacket of almost comic proportions', and 'It beggars belief that such a flawed and inadequate method will now govern the success or failure of British sport over the next four years.'

Two of the sports that the *Telegraph* claimed were primed for destruction were gymnastics and triathlon. Both sports would win medals in London 2012 and golds four years later.

People who manage sports teams are used to the emotional fallout from making team selections. It is inevitable. When you introduce money, though, it is another matter altogether. Keen's view is clear: no passengers.

Before he ran UK Sport, Keen was the performance director at British Cycling. When Keen started at British Cycling, lottery money had just been introduced, and he was astonished when he discovered how it was being spread around – so thinly that to some it would make little difference, and in many instances it went to cyclists who weren't even doing Olympic sports.

His view was that, rather than share out the lottery booty so that lots of people were happy and had a little extra cash to make themselves a little better on the bike, you had to strictly prioritise, so that an elite few who had the potential to become world class were afforded a proper opportunity to fulfil that. 'You cannot take passengers with you,' he says, 'because it fundamentally undermines the culture, and again it's not about who is right or wrong it's about being honest with the nature of the business. The moment you stay in that space where you're selecting people who you know are going to fail at the level you're aspiring to, it's not just that they continue to fail, it makes it harder for everybody else too.'

'The crunch', as Keen describes it, came in 2002, when he was still in cycling. For the first time, he tried a detailed analytical approach to help him decide which athletes to fund. He worked out that his squad of funded riders could be no bigger than 38. Any more and the money would be spread too thinly. He then set out a matrix whereby each athlete would be assessed, by Keen and the coaches, against eight different factors. At the time this was both innovative and disruptive.

In Keen's matrix, there was one decision that stands out as the case study example of his brave new world. Previously, funding would have gone to Julie Paulding, a sprinter who had just won silver in the Commonwealth Games. Funding would have been seen as her rightful reward. Keen, however, did not put Paulding on the funded programme and instead funded someone Paulding had just beaten in those Commonwealth Games. That was Victoria Pendleton.

Paulding had just had her best ever season, but she was 35 and Keen's matrix told him that she was not going to make it. Pendleton was some distance behind Paulding at the time, but she was 22 and he believed that she had a genuine chance. The decision went to appeal but was upheld. Keen recalls that it was 'incredibly hard' on Paulding. Pendleton would go on to win two Olympic and nine World Championship golds.

In persistently trying to break new ground in British sport, Keen is confronted all too often by what he calls 'the tyranny of the normal' or, in other words, 'a desire to encourage you to stay in the pack – don't go too far away'. He has, he says, tried to breed 'a mindset that's willing to say why not, why not be world champion, why not win far more medals at Olympic Games than people think we can?' Yet, at the same time, he says, 'Virtually every corner where I've turned, you encounter an "are you sure?" resistance. When I look back on it all, it's just how it is and it never goes away.

'There's so much opportunity to innovate because an awful lot of what is traditional and dogmatic in sport is silly, doesn't necessarily make sense or could be improved upon. But the moment you start innovating in sport, even in elite sport, you upset traditionalists, you immediately create a tension between what is accepted wisdom and the way you do it. The moment you try and aspire to the very highest level, you're going to upset people, not intentionally and again it's not that they're wrong, but I think it's just a natural reaction to anybody wanting to break that far from the pack.'

Keen tried to break from the pack early in his days at British Cycling and he nearly came crashing down. The issue at hand was – of all things – his suggestion to change the team strip. Fair enough, his proposed colour was lime green – his detractors had a point. Yet Keen saw it as a point of principle: we have to be prepared to change. This was Keen versus the tyranny of the normal, all over a lime green strip.

The year was 1998. The track cyclists' strip at the time was a mish-mash of red, white and blue, but, exactly like the GB riders at the time, it was comparatively anonymous. During a bunched track race, there-fore, it was hard to pick out the GB riders. The lime-green certainly solved that problem, but Keen saw in it further value.

'It was a statement saying "We have changed." When you look back, it's sort of funny and embarrassing in equal measures but the mindset behind it was the right one: what stronger statement could you make to fundamentally change the traditional expectations of what the national team should look like?'

Predictably, the board of British Cycling said: No way. 'That is where it became a point of principle,' Keen recalls. 'My position was: "I'm ei-ther empowered to do what it's going to take to transform the way we think or I'm not."'

Keen conceded enough ground to win the day. The team settled on a slightly toned-down, slightly less unpleasant green. Yet the point had been made. Cycling would not tolerate the tyranny of the normal.

With Matt Parker coaching the TP team, there would be no tyranny of the normal. No chance. His own appointment to the job, which Parker himself describes as 'a ridiculous idea', is recalled by Ed Clancy, who was one of the younger riders in the squad, simply as 'a shock'. This is how Clancy saw it: 'We were working with Simon Jones, he was established and was seen as the benchmark. He had an aura as the super-endurance coach. So, yes, to discover suddenly that Matt was taking over – it was a shock.'

The riders knew Parker but not well. 'We were used to seeing him around across the road at the English Institute of Sport (EIS),' Clancy explains. It was at the EIS where the riders did most of their lab testing; from 2002, Parker had been employed there doing a lot of that testing. In 2006, he started working more directly with British Cycling as their performance scientist, feeding in specialist information to Jones. Yet he had not been a coach and he had worked little in the velodrome itself. That is why his appointment could have been seen as both a ridiculous idea and a shock.

As Parker acknowledges, 'I didn't know what I was doing.' But this can be a strength as well as a weakness. 'It made it a big risk but in some ways it made it easier as well.'

What Parker means is this: pretty much every child in every school class, pretty much like most professional people in most walks of life, knows what it is like to sit on a question and not ask it in fear that it could be regarded as a foolish inquiry. Because Parker was new to class, he had no fear of asking any questions, because he didn't know what was foolish and what wasn't. He just addressed his challenge with a straightforward question: we want to win gold, so what are the performance requirements to achieve that?

The first thing he did was set the team a target for the Olympic Games. In Athens, the Aussies had gone 3min56.61sec for their world record. The British quartet had hardly ever broken the four-minute mark. To win in Beijing, nevertheless, he decided to lower the target to 3min55.2sec. That was the time they would train for. A massive seven seconds quicker than they were currently riding at.

Why 3min55.2sec? Parker explains: 'One: because I thought it was achievable. Two: because it was massively ambitious. Three: because the Aussies might have done it again. Everyone was saying that Athens was a freak ride, but they had a lot of their good riders coming back and you couldn't rule out them showing that it wasn't a freak after all.'

Parker went on asking apparently straightforward questions. First, what gear do we need to ride on to go that fast? 'I had no idea what the gears meant,' he says. 'I had no idea what it was like to ride at those gears, but I did know we needed something bigger.'

As he did not have the answer himself, he asked the mechanics in the Manchester velodrome. For years, world-class TP teams had almost all ridden on a 98-inch gear. The mechanics' answer was that, to go at world record pace, they needed to push 102. Parker said OK. When the riders found out, a series of text messages quickly circulated asking a rhetorical question: what does this guy think he is doing?

Parker's view was this. The team had long been training in the vain hope that they would improve incrementally in order to get close to world record times. Why not turn it around? Why not train at world record pace instead?

So from day one, that is what they did. Parker was perfectly aware of the doubts of the riders, and to an extent, he doubted himself too. Yet he believed sufficiently that this was the right course. 'The first thing we did,' Parker explains, 'was get them riding quicker than world record pace – not for very long, but that's where we started. Only for about two of the four kilometres. We couldn't sustain it. The idea was that we would carry on at that pace but train to go progressively longer. So we just layered up the event as we went along, but Day One we just put a marker down – big gears, fast pace.'

Another of Parker's questions that no one else had asked was: why not make life hell for Man One?

Man One in the TP team was Ed Clancy. Man One's prime role is to lead off the team from the start; he has to be a power-rider because his number one task is to get them up to speed as quickly as possible before swinging up out after three-quarters of a lap, handing over to Man Two at the front and pulling in to draft behind Man Four at the back.

In a team pursuit, every time a team changes when its leader peels off the front, it loses a bike length and the equivalent of a tenth of a second. At the first change, just as the team has been gaining speed, it loses its momentum and therefore loses marginally more than a tenth. Parker asked, therefore: why not get Clancy to go more than three-quarters of a lap? If he could postpone the first change, he would get the team going faster earlier and less speed would be lost on that first change.

No pressure, then, for Mr Clancy, who was now being asked to break new ground. Please now start with a one-and-a-quarter-lap first shift.

'Matt had no respect for tradition or the way things were done in the past,' Clancy says. And: 'It's a bit scary when you try something like that for the first time.'

But he was only 21 and therefore less daunted than he might have been. 'I was,' Clancy says, 'crash-happy, happy to try things and go for it. It was more of an issue for the older riders who'd been doing it the same way year after year after year.' So Clancy gave it a blast.

The risks were clear. Physiologically, Clancy was different to the other three – Paul Manning at Man Two, Geraint Thomas at three and Bradley Wiggins at four. Clancy was more sprinter, less endurance athlete, incredibly powerful, but was so early in his development as an athlete that he struggled with the back end of the race. In a TP team, one rider is permitted to drop out before the finish, but the earlier a man drops out, the more it costs the other three who have more work to do. As Parker says: 'In many people's eyes, asking him to do more at the start was setting him up to fail. But in the overall plan for Beijing, if the rest of the team could accommodate Ed in the last kilometre, him getting us up to speed quicker would give us an advantage – which it did.'

To incorporate his plans, Parker flipped training. Usually, at the start of the year, the TP team would be doing road work in Majorca and then put it all together on the track; Parker insisted instead that they just worked hard on the track in order to work on the new gearing, the new start, the new Clancy. Nothing came easily. On occasional bad days, Clancy would fail on the one-and-a-quarter-lap start. Parker says: 'It made sense to start off with the elements of the race that would be the hardest and take the longest to develop. It's not hard to generate speed on the track but it's hard to be comfortable and be able to go 4km at speed. We were talking about going the best part of 64kmph for four minutes, two inches off the wheel in front. You can't do that by getting together for two or three weeks on the track.'

On 24 February, after less than two months under Parker, the team would face its first test, competing at the World Cup event in Manchester. Parker set them a challenge: to go under the four-minute psychological barrier – which they did in qualifying. They then beat Russia in the final.

As Parker says: 'Essentially, in a few weeks, we'd gone faster than we ever had done before in a World Cup and Ed Clancy went from being a team pursuiter who struggled in the back end of the race to being the only person in the world who was doing a lap-and-a-quarter start, so all of a sudden he became one of the world's best team pursuiters.'

And crucially, of the seven seconds they had targeted to save by Beijing, they had already lost two.

How would Parker go about saving the others? Largely by continuing to ask the same kind of questions as before: why is everyone else doing it the way they are doing it, and why not try something else?

Why, for instance, should we be riding the shortest distance around the track? The way everyone else had always done it was to hug the black line which marks the tightest line around the track, thus giving them the shortest ride. Makes sense, right? Not necessarily, thought Parker: 'When you go into a bend, the bike speed increases and if you take the corner too sharply the team expands because Bike One goes away from the next, when you come back onto the straight it contracts again which means that the power is going up and down because you're trying to regulate distance. So we just moved it out slightly which meant the turn into the bend was more progressive which meant the change in speed was less. Slightly longer distance, more progressive but the line was a lot smoother, recovery was a lot better.'

A month after Manchester, the World Championships were held at the velodrome in Majorca. And just like in Manchester, the GB team were fastest in qualifying and winners in the final. And they had dropped another two-and-a-half seconds.

The following winter, Olympic preparation started for real. And again, Parker changed the modus operandi. The team were used to doing long blocks of road work in the winter to get miles into their legs in order to improve their endurance, but now their road work became far more specific. Less mileage, more high-intensity efforts. As Parker explains, 'We were trying to use the road work to improve the track performance rather than use the road work to improve endurance performance.'

They would do their best work in Majorca on the Sa Calobra climb, 20 seconds' sprinting uphill followed by 40 seconds' rest repeated six times, with ten minutes' easy riding between each set of six and every sprint executed at a cadence of 120 revs-per-minute to make them TP specific.

Because he was not built for it, it was Clancy who really suffered. 'Even if somebody else was having a bad day,' Parker says, 'Ed was always having a worse day.' Clancy recalls days towards the top of Sa Calobra when walkers would go past him on his bike: 'There were some days I hated. It's a joke when you are by far the weakest guy there.'

Yet the training clearly worked. Five months before the Beijing Olympics, the World Championships were held in Manchester. 'By that point,' says Parker, 'we were pacing every kilometre to within a tenth of a second, so where rides previously had gone up and down, quicker and slower, we would go out fast and we would stay at the same speed kilometre after kilometre.'

In Manchester, they not only won gold again, but they beat the Australians' world record. Even amid all the celebrations, however, there was an awareness that, to hit Parker's target of 3min55.2sec, they were still a second short.

Five months out of Beijing, though, the GB team had a significant psychological advantage. The teams who got so comprehensively beaten in Manchester went away thinking: we need to do something different, to do more or train harder. Yet as Parker says, 'In those months before the Olympics, while other teams were trying something new, we knew exactly what worked for us and that is what we did.' On this occasion, something new or something different – which was the kneejerk reaction of their rivals – didn't work. When they got to Beijing, GB would be the only team who went significantly faster than they had done in Manchester.

They would hit their target in the semi-final, against Russia, when they rode 3min55.202sec and broke the world record they had set in Manchester. And better was yet to come when they were up against Denmark in the final and smashed their own world record in 3min53.314sec. So, in winning gold, they also got their third world record. And Australia did not make it onto the podium.

In making a number of significant changes, Great Britain's TP team had effectively opened up a new market. Previously, the event was an Australian market; now it had moved on. In the years that followed, other nations followed the British way. Like video hire shops and the old techniques of doing the high jump, the event had moved on and rendered the old TP world redundant. It took hardly any time before everyone had their Ed Clancy clones doing a lap-and-a-quarter start (now they often do more), and the 98-inch gear is long gone. The 102 has gone too.

Clancy now describes Parker as 'the best coach I've ever had'. As Parker showed, you need the right mind to challenge the normal. Disruptive innovations cannot happen any other way. And beware experts. 'None of us are really an expert at anything we do,' Parker says. 'As soon as you start thinking that you are an expert, your mindset becomes closed.'

Why on earth did Brailsford give Parker that job in the first place? Clearly he saw potential in him, but this is his explanation: 'If you're constrained by classical, conventional wisdom on appointments in recruitment you're never going to optimise the situation. You need people to bring different thought processes and challenge the system. You need a cognitive diversity. You never know if it's going to work or not, but if you're not brave enough to try then you're going to be limited.'

On the road to Beijing, the TP quartet got used to their novice coach making decisions that challenged the tyranny of the normal and they in turn would challenge him. Why? Why are we doing this? 'He wouldn't give you an answer straight away,' Clancy says. Instead he would wait and at the end of the day he would sit down after dinner and explain everything. Sometimes it would take him half an hour. Always there was a good reason. And quite often, it was something that had not been thought of before.

Chapter learnings by Simon Timson

Almost every child in a school class knows what it's like to sit on a question and not ask it for fear of appearing foolish in front of their peers. The workplace is often equally constraining for adults, and questioning the norm is not commonplace. However, Matt Parker was both curious and bold enough to do so, and this remarkable transformation in the men's Team Pursuit performance followed. Three principles drove this remarkable change in performance:

Successful innovators reject received wisdoms and traditions to challenge the norm. Never automatically accept the status quo and existing constraints in your environment.

Smart innovations are kindled from asking courageous questions. Successful innovators start by asking simple and fundamental questions like: how do we go faster? How can we do this better?

Innovation is brought to fruition with fearless and disciplined decision-making. Innovation should not be confused with gambling on a long shot. Questions need to be answered with rigour, and success follows courageous decision-making, calculated planning, and specific execution. Transformative change does not happen on a whim: the men's TP team would not have succeeded if Ed Clancy had not been prepared to reinvent himself and persevere.

Winning
Environments

10

How the mighty fall

The longest one-hundredth of a second of the London Games ticked by shortly before 8.30pm on Day Five of competition in lane four of the swimming pool. Lane four was occupied by the Australian self-appointed superstar, James Magnussen, and that one-hundredth of a second was the difference between him in silver medal position in the men's 100m freestyle and Nathan Adrian, the American, who touched ahead of him for the gold. In just that one-hundredth of a second, Magnussen would earn himself, in the words of one American columnist, the title of 'the biggest Australian flop since *Crocodile Dundee 3*'. Three days earlier, in the men's 4x100m freestyle relay, Magnussen – nicknamed The Missile – had led his team to a fourth-place finish which was itself described, in an Australian paper, as 'the biggest defeat since Gallipoli'. In the three nights between those two races, while Magnussen was haunted by irregular sleep patterns, the media stirred themselves for a competition for the most poisonous put-down.

Magnussen had come to London not only with the 100m world title to his name from the previous summer, but also a mouth that was happy to tell anyone prepared to listen that more and better was yet to come. He happened to be the lead actor in the blue riband event for swimming, which also, over many Olympiads, happened to have been his country's best medal opportunity. In other words, he was the face of Australia's Olympics. One-hundredth of a second faster and he would have been spared from becoming, instead, the symbol of Australian failure.

Long after that race, the Games continued to unravel for Australia. Even after they left London. The swimmers took home with them just one gold medal and returned to an official enquiry into the reasons for their collective underperformance. For Magnussen and his freestyle squad, it got to the stage where they were hauled before an Integrity Panel. There, they had to account for behaviour which included schoolboy pranks such as knocking on other athletes' doors at night and, more seriously, taking Stilnox, a sedative drug (not on the banned list), at their pre-Games training camp in Manchester, which they said they did as part of a bonding session.

Though Magnussen and his cohorts remained the focus, he himself was the pin-up face of national decline. At their own Olympics in Sydney 12 years earlier, Aussie swimmers had won five golds; in Athens four years later, they won seven, then six in Beijing, then suddenly in London just one. When you do a success-ectomy to a nation's single most successful sport, then, for that nation, the entire picture changes. They had finished fourth in the medal table in Sydney and fourth again in Athens, then slipped a little to sixth in Beijing, but suddenly in London they were down to tenth, behind countries like Hungary. Magnussen was the headline act of a fallen nation.

When you are flying as high as the Australians did and for so long, how can you know that you are actually on the path to decline? If you have scaled the mountain peaks of performance, what indicators might suggest that, a couple more steps forward and you could be falling off a cliff? In other words, could the Australians have seen this coming?

These are generic questions in sport. If you are still winning, how can you tell if you are heading in the wrong direction? The most dominant sportspeople and sports teams in history all eventually found their way onto the path to decline. The Liverpool team of the seventies and eighties did not realise they had found that path until the nineties; the West Indies cricket team of Clive Lloyd and Viv Richards dominated for more than a decade and then fizzled out, likewise the Australian cricketers from the Alan Border to Steve Waugh era. If we are still on top of the world, how can we recognise the signs if we are heading for a fall?

The All Blacks have long been in search of answers. Steve Hansen, the All Blacks head coach, went so far as to study the Spain football team, the world champions and double European champions, a stand-out example of sustained success. They became Hansen's model and he went to Spain to learn what kept them for so long ahead of the world. At the following World Cup, however, Spain opened their defence of their title with a 5–1 thrashing by Holland, and that was followed by a 2–0 defeat by Chile and the first flight home. Spain had tumbled too and they never saw it coming either.

How can you recognise the signs? Jim Collins asked this question in his brilliant analysis of rise and fall in the commercial world, *How the Mighty Fall*. By looking at huge companies – Bank of America, Xerox, Motorola – he determined to lay out what he called 'a roadmap of decline', from which he hopes that 'institutions heading downhill might be able to apply the brakes early and reverse the course'. He says you have to spot the signs of what he calls 'The Doom Loop', which come in five stages, starting with 'Hubris Born of Success' and ending with 'Capitulation to Irrelevance or Death'.

Collins uses Motorola to case-study Stage One of decline. By the mid-nineties, Motorola had grown in a decade from $5billion in annual revenues to $27billion and established itself as the number one mobile phone maker in the world. In 1995, though, the company launched their newest mobile phone, the StarTAC, which was the smallest in the world and had a novel clamshell design. The problem, says Collins, was that StarTAC was an analogue technology device put out at exactly the time when digital was entering the market. According to *Business Week*, a senior Morotola executive had no time for this new digital threat, saying: 'Forty-three million analogue customers can't be wrong.' Motorola were, apparently, so confident in their new product that they employed heavy-handed tactics with the phone stores, imposing mandatory stipulations such as the percentage of product in the shops that had to be Motorola and the special stand-alone displays that they insisted must be given to Motorola cellphones. That did not go down too well either. Four years after the great StarTAC launch, Motorola's market share percentage had plunged from nearly 50 per cent to 17.

There can be little doubt that, like Motorola, the Australian Olympic system reached Collins's Stage One of decline. You could argue, too, that Australia got all the way to the third stage of the five, 'Denial of Risk and Peril'. The surest sign of a nation's Olympic strength is not where it finishes on the medal table – which is determined by the number of gold medals each nation wins – but by the total number of medals won. Total number of medals won indicates broader strength, and from 58 medals in Sydney in 2000, Australia dropped to 49 in Athens. However, because their number of golds stayed strong (they actually rose from 16 to 17) they held their fourth place on the medal table. When still sitting in fourth, it was easy to deny the evidence that they had just had nearly a fifth of their medal count wiped out.

In *How the Mighty Fall*, Collins sifts through the twin fortunes of two of the great store chains in American retail history. Both chains had the same ideal of small-town stores selling low-price retail goods. Through the seventies and early eighties, momentum made them both massive, and the performance of one pretty much mirrored the other. One was Wal-Mart, the other Ames Department Stores. In the Fortune Global 500 list of 2014, Wal-Mart was rated the biggest company in the world with a revenue of $476.3billion. And Ames? Ames never bottomed out of the Doom Loop; in 2002, the chain went into liquidation.

Collins tells a story about a group of Brazilian investors who bought a retail store chain in South America and, in the late eighties, decided to educate themselves better on how such businesses were run. They wrote letters to a number of CEOs of big US companies, asking if they could come on a learning mission to visit them. Only one CEO replied and that was Sam Walton, the founder of Wal-Mart. Walton went so far as to meet his inquisitors off their plane and, after a couple of days of his hospitality, when Walton had been asking them question after question, they realised that this was not so much a case of them learning off him, but the other way round.

Walton never allowed himself the hubris born of success. For many years, the Australians were like him until they hit the heights of fourth in the world, at which point, crucially, they changed. When they were in the process of rising up the rankings, rival nations started to take notice and wonder out aloud: what is it they are doing? What is their formula for success? Some nations then took it further and got in touch. They were mostly interested, in particular, in the Australian Institute of Sport (AIS), the centralised high-performance centre in Canberra. Can we come and see it?

Like Sam Walton at Wal-Mart, the Australians would say 'yes'. They saw it as an opportunity. When you are in the bottom right corner of the world, and quite an expensive journey away from the other high-performance environments in sport, you have to take opportunities, especially when they come knocking on your door. So the AIS had a very straightforward reply to those asking to come and see: yes, of course you can come, but you have to be prepared to share. So guests who came to see what happened inside the doors of the AIS would be obliged first to give a presentation of what they were doing back home and how they were doing it. In other words, while sharing with their guests some of their own intellectual property – the workings of the AIS – the Australians leached every valuable gem of information they could glean from them all in return.

One of the leading lights in the rise of the Australians was Wilma Shakespear. She was ten years a head coach within the AIS, and then, when the system was so successful that it started to regionalise, she got the job as founding director of the Queensland Academy of Sport. It was her academy that provided so many of Australia's successes at the

Sydney Olympics. Like so many, though, her value as a player in the global sports market rocketed with every home medal in Sydney, and by 2001 she had been recruited to the UK to set up what was hoped would be a British version of the AIS, the English Institute of Sport.

Shakespear recalls the day, not long after her arrival in the UK, when she was sitting in a London office, astonished, reading a press document from the AIS which announced that their approach to interest from the outside world had changed. They were now shutting the doors. They thought – at least so it seemed – that they had all the answers and needed no more.

'I remember sitting there thinking: "You are kidding me,"' she says. 'Once you start to close the door in this world, there is only one way and that is down.'

Even before Australia closed the doors, they had let a lot of their knowledge go. Shakespear was just one of a number of Aussies recruited by the UK. Bill Sweetenham, the Australian swimming coach, was recruited to run British Swimming. Paul Thompson, the Aussie rowing coach, came in to be head coach of the GB women's rowing. Matt Favier came in as a senior athletics programme manager. David Moffett, who had been running the National Rugby League in Australia, came to England to run Sport England. And that is just to name a few.

Maybe the price-tags round these people's necks made their departure impossible to stop, but instead of seeing an opportunity and taking advantage of it, Australia just closed ranks further. All of a sudden, there were a large number of Australians working abroad, understanding how high-performance systems worked in other countries. Like Sam Walton, the AIS could have seen that as a chance to stay in touch and ask the relevant questions: what have you learned? What are these rival nations doing? Yet they elected to do the opposite.

'I think they were panicked by the number of us that were recruited offshore,' Shakespear says. 'They didn't understand that it was an opportunity for them to play it smart, to keep in contact, to keep the information flow going. They chose to seal off. You have to be careful, when you are successful, that you don't think: I am so clever. You always have to have your eye on the world. I think they paid very dearly for it. I think they looked at their navels when they should have been looking at the world. I could never understand why they didn't keep the communication open. At times, we were made to feel like we'd jumped ship. No one at the AIS ever once asked me to come in. No one ever asked: "Tell us what you've been doing and how you have done it."'

After six years in the UK, Shakespear returned to Australia, by which time Australian Olympic sport had also been hit by a decline in funding. Two years later, in 2009, Shakespear went to a conference of the sporting institutes. She was speaking at the conference herself but, she says, she wanted 'to listen and to get a feel' of how people felt about the health of the national Olympic sports. And her reaction? 'I was horrified,' she says. 'It was almost like: "We are so clever here, of course we can take on the world – we don't need all the money." I just shook my head and thought: "Surely you don't believe this." But they did.'

The Olympic world has now been turned upside down. Just like the Aussies used to, it is now the Brits who receive regular requests from international rivals asking to come on a learning mission and see the system. And just as the Australians once did, the answer is usually 'yes', but there is a caveat: you have to show us something in return. The Australians have at last moved on and wised up too. They no longer assume they have all the answers, indeed they are very much in search of them. In 2012, a very significant appointment was made: Matt Favier was going back to Australia as Director of the AIS. And he was going to bring a lot of the answers back from the UK with him.

Having all the answers, however, does not necessarily mean that you win all the medals. In Leipzig in Germany in January 2015, at an elite, private convention, this is what became clear to Simon Timson and Chelsea Warr. They had been invited to The Institute of Applied Training Science with a number of their peers from a small number of leading Olympic nations to take part in the event. To get the invitation was a compliment, because it suggested you had intellectual property worth tapping. To accept the invitation was essential, because it meant you could tap everyone else too.

A number of nations gave presentations at the Leipzig convention, each of which was intended to provoke debate. Does money really buy medals? What does money buy, and what does it not buy? How to deal with failing sports? How to identify talent in Generation Y when football and X-sports are increasingly the magnets for the top talent?

Timson addressed the question 'What is the actual effect of being an Olympic host nation?' In his presentation, he noted the challenges: the fact that a home Olympics is seen by many as the end of an era, so that some senior athletes resist retirement until after a home Games, thus clogging up the pipeline for the next generation; and that there is a danger of a post-home Games brain drain because coaches are far more susceptible to new job offers once the home Games are done.

The presentation that Warr gave was the one on failing sports. How do you turn around a sport that is not delivering medals? At the end of her presentation, she threw open the floor and asked for ideas and contributions, but the response she got surprised her and Timson. Some nations hadn't thought about it that way, and were treating all sports the same – when, clearly, they aren't. They were at the stage of working out the challenges rather than working out how to solve them.

The overall conclusion from the convention, says Warr, was this: 'It was a great opportunity to benchmark ourselves against the rest of the world in a more intimate setting. Simon and I concluded we were ahead of the game, but needed to keep the system future-focused and not get complacent. Success can breed safety – and we can't play it too safe. Simon and I thought the best guy was the guy from the Netherlands. He was closest to where Simon and I were in thinking about what really good high-performance environments should look like. With him, I definitely thought: you're really on it.'

Timson put it another way, slightly more bullishly: 'I don't think we were scared of any nation.'

All of which could be interpreted as coming dangerously close to Hubris Born of Success.

Timson and Warr may well not have been scared of any single nation, yet they were certainly scared of the Doom Loop. It was not just Australia which showed them where successful Olympic nations can go wrong, but also Jim Collins, whose text on corporate failure they knew so well. They were continually looking over their shoulders for signs of Hubris Born of Success.

Leipzig may have persuaded them that they have a system of unrivalled sophistication, but the other prime thought that they took home was this: so what? As Timson put it: 'If our system is more mature, why isn't this translating?' Or as Collins would put it: if you have the best-run company, why isn't it running up the most profit?'

Inevitably, in Leipzig, conversation had turned to medal predictions for Rio, and no one thought GB would get anywhere near the 66 Olympic medals they had targeted. Indeed, they seemed to rather enjoy giving their damning verdict. The consensus was that GB would be nearer 50.

Of course, before their peers, Timson and Warr shrugged this off with as much nonchalance as they could summon. Deep down, though, they couldn't disagree. Every time recently that they had done the maths, their own projections, from within UK Sport, were telling them pretty much the same thing.

One of their real worries was cycling. Yes, cycling – cycling, which was as important to GB as swimming was to Australia.

After the glory of London 2012, British Cycling had lost to retirement its top male sprinter, Chris Hoy, and its top female, Victoria Pendleton. In London, between them, Hoy and Pendleton had won three golds and a silver; in their entire Olympic careers, they had amassed eight golds and two silvers. If British Cycling was to sustain its success, it would depend considerably on how well they replaced these two icons.

While the men's sprint team had some depth, the women's did not. This was a problem that had been seen miles off – way before London

2012 – and with that in mind, a Talent ID search had been launched to fill the gaps. Back in 2009, when the broad Olympic talent search programme called Girls4Gold was launched, at the top of the wish-list was a troop of sprint cyclists. The search went well; a good, strong group was identified. Most interesting was a young farmer's daughter who could put out immense power. The coaches raved about her in particular, but the whole cohort that was pushed towards cycling was widely perceived to be one of the strongest groups ever to come out of a Talent ID programme. Happy days.

A few months down the line, however, British Cycling pulled the plug on the whole programme. They insisted it wasn't needed, and the group of women who had put weeks of effort into it, who had spent time with the programme at the Manchester velodrome, were quickly and quietly cut. Strenuous efforts were made to persuade British Cycling to change their mind, but they were not for turning. Among other reasons, they had a great young talent called Becky James coming through. Maybe the search for the next Pendleton had already been completed.

Or maybe, without realising it, British Cycling had quickly and quietly moved on to Stage Three of decline: 'Denial of Risk and Peril'.

There was actually another factor that really scared Timson. Hunger. Are we still hungry? When he gave that presentation in Leipzig with its somewhat vanilla title 'What is the actual effect of being an Olympic host nation?', what he had really wanted to call it was 'Home Games: blessing or curse?'

When you get the home Games, you get the home crowd. You probably get the odd home team judging decision going your way too. The sum total of everything that home advantage confers on the team can therefore create a mirage that suggests you are better than you really are. More than anything, though, the home Games creates a unique hunger.

'In London, people were hungry for success, more than they normally would be. They would have run through brick walls,' Timson explained. 'And so the question is: are they still as hungry now? You have a load of people who climbed Everest, and now there's nothing higher. They are going: what now?'

This very subject had been the topic of discussion between Timson and Dave Brailsford only two months earlier. In November 2014, a group of British sports leaders had met at the Pennyhill Park Hotel in Surrey. Their meeting was an informal forum for the sharing of experiences and the exchanging of ideas, and after an evening's good dinner and discussion, Timson and Brailsford returned to their rooms and had one of those hotel corridor conversations that never seem to end. It was there that Brailsford confessed his fears for Team Sky: after two successive years of winning the Tour de France, had his team lost their hunger? And how was he going to get it back?

For around 90 minutes, they kicked the subject around and, for Timson, much of what Brailsford said resonated. As he recalls: 'I was thinking: am I seeing elements of what Dave is saying here in the Olympic sport system? Because I am also scared shitless that what's worked before is not going to work again.'

Timson would not have to wait long for his fears to be realised. Three months after Pennyhill, one month after Leipzig, cycling's World Track Championships were held in Paris and the results were the stuff of nightmares.

At the London Olympics, as in Beijing four years before, GB's ultimate success had been in the velodrome. Of the ten gold medals available in the track cycling in London, GB had won seven. They had also won a silver and a bronze and they might well have won an eighth gold in the tenth event but for a marginal mistake resulting in a disqualification. But two-and-a-half years after coming away from London with those the seven golds, GB returned from Paris with zero. And no, Becky James didn't win a gold, a silver or anything because she was injured, and had been for over a year, and the medics were beginning to wonder if they would ever even see her on a bike again. Without her, no British female sprinter got on the podium. The cutting of the 2009 talent cohort was looking shortsighted in the extreme.

Paris was the first time since 2001 that the GB team had failed to win a single gold. It was a fall from great heights far more dramatic than the Australian swimmers at the London Games. That they were on Jim Collins's roadmap of decline was undeniable. The question was how far down it they had gone and, of course, whether and how quickly they could execute a U-turn.

The day after the cyclists returned from Paris, Timson and Warr were pondering their failure and the reasons why. On a whiteboard in the UK Sport offices, Timson wrote down the names of Dave Brailsford, who had been performance director but had left to concentrate solely on Team Sky, and Steve Peters, who had been the team psychiatrist but had also left to pursue other work. Underneath their names he wrote Chris Boardman, the Head of Research and Development, who had left after the Olympics in order to run his own business. And underneath Boardman he wrote Scott Drawer, who had occupied a similar role to Boardman at UK Sport and had effectively been Boardman's partner in many of the brilliant design projects that had contributed so significantly to the team's success. Drawer had left to go and work for England rugby. Then, under Drawer's name, he wrote Matt Parker and Dan Hunt, two more senior figures on the coaching staff; one had been recruited to England rugby, the other to the Premier League. He stood back and shook his head. The evidence was there on the wall. Then he thought a little further and carried on writing names. In total, he worked out that, since the London Olympics, 17 people had left the management of British Cycling.

If you lose the people who know how to win, you lose the ability to win. 'Jesus,' Timson sighed with resignation, 'why were cycling not talking to us about this?'

The result of GB's outrageous success in cycling over successive Olympics Games was that it had prompted the biggest brain-drain since – well – probably since the Australians after the Sydney Games. Every departure from British Cycling, every job offer from the world of commercial sport had been well deserved. And everyone who left had gone with their best wishes. But no one had put all this together and registered the scale to which the most successful British Olympic sport had allowed its IP to be wiped out.

In Jim Collins's book, you can follow the Doom Loop like Ames Department Stores all the way to stage five, 'Capitulation to Irrelevance or Death'. Or, like Motorola, you can bottom out. Like both Ames and Motorola, and the Spanish football team and Liverpool and all the rest, British Cycling had been a stand-out model of success who had not recognised the crisis towards which they were hurtling.

For Timson, this was a crucial moment. Eighteen months ahead of Rio, it was confirmation of a deep-set fear. 'This is where we are now,' he said, his hands gesticulating, describing a low point. 'We need to recognise this; this is a significant point. It's either the low point from which we bottom out. Or we are crashing. But we are pulling back on the joystick hoping the nose is going to lift up again.'

Chapter learnings by Chelsea Warr

One of the most significant messages in this chapter is about building in early warning signs within your organisation to alert teams if they are on a trajectory towards the doom loop. Knowing and understanding the early warning signs enables one very important thing to happen – it earns time to make disciplined action to revert the downward trend. In a high-performance environment, that can be a deal-breaker.

Learn your early warning signals. This is not easy. Self-awareness and honesty are key.

Success is not an entitlement. Never be arrogant enough to think you've got all the answers. Do not erect precious professional boundaries. Never stop challenging yourself.

Invite opinion. Never think you know enough. Reach out to new industries and networks to help you solve the perennial problems that your organisation faces.

Succession planning. Any high-performing organisation understands the importance of identifying and growing talent to fill business-critical positions in the future. This is something that was overlooked in British Cycling. I've always believed that under every senior leadership role in an organisation there needs to be two individuals waiting in the wings who have the potential to do the role with even greater insight and innovation. Who is that in your business?

11

How to be a high-performance parent

BECKY JAMES, BRYONY SHAW

Project Becky James didn't begin after the failure of the 2015 World Track Cycling Championships in Paris. As with every Olympian that ever lived, the project began years earlier. As with all of them, it began at home.

In Rio each day we were lauding Olympians and also their coaches. Well done the coaches, we'd say. Masterful coaching. Clever tactics/preparation/intervention/psychology. Whatever. Take your pick. Yet here's the thing: high-performance coaches are trained in the art of high-performance coaching. But no one ever taught parents how to be high-performance parents. And it doesn't necessarily come naturally.

David James, Becky's father, will tell you how he became a high-performance parent and he is searingly honest in the way he tells it too. He learned the hard way. He is that rare parent who admits he got it wrong.

Part of it is the sacrifice, though pretty much every parent of an Olympian will understand the sacrifice side of things. David James can recall the monster days behind the wheel of the car to get to competitions: Abergavenny to Dundee and back was one. Abergavenny–Preston–Abergavenny–Manchester in one day, that was another; he slept that night on Becky's couch and drove back the next day. Dave is blessed – though some might challenge the use of the word 'blessed' here – by the fact that Becky is not the only elite athlete in his brood; she has four elite siblings, all of whom, at various times, have competed on bikes at a high level. So take the miles he has done for Becky and multiply that by five.

There is a sixth sibling, too, who has never been on a bike and never will. That is Bethan, who was born with hydrocephalus (water on the brain) and is severely handicapped, has never been able to feed herself and never spoken. So the way they have handled the responsibilities is that David does the lion's share of the driving and Christine, his wife, tends to spend more time with Bethan at home. They never leave her, though; Becky and their other children have competed around the world, but the parents do not get to travel. They have never been outside the UK to see them race. That is the time-consuming, self-sacrificial bit. But that's the deal you might choose to accept as a parent. Many do. It is hard but straightforward.

David is especially interesting on the subject of the psychology of parenting a high-performing child: how much do you push your child? How do you talk to a wannabe world champion, when you were never a world champion yourself? How do you know what to do? Well, you probably don't, that's the bit that's not straightforward, and here is where he is so honest.

Becky's brother Gareth is older by only a year and a half. Crucially for her, he started competing at junior level before she did and he found himself in elevated company among the best young riders in Wales at the time. His peers included Luke Rowe and Alex Dowsett, who would become professionals. He trained with them and raced with them. David and Christine were new to the competitive cycling world then and wanted the best for him and, as you do, they found themselves at start lines and finish lines exchanging information with other riders' parents. Some of them, David remembers, would say 'he should be doing this, he should be doing that, he should be training X amount of hours a week'.

This is how David sees it: 'We started off on the wrong path. That's because we were learning from others. After a race, we would ask Gareth: "Why did you do this? Why didn't you do that?" We focused on negatives. We were emphasising the wrong things. He was training hard and not quite getting the reward, and we didn't help by criticising him. He was still getting high finishes, but we never gave him the credit and I think he resented that. I don't know if you are a bit harder on a son than a daughter, but we were not as intelligent as we should have been. You have to instil self-belief and we didn't do that with Gareth. For three years, we were too hard on him and that put him off it.'

So Gareth walked away from it – and his father blames himself. This is a brave and painful contemplation. He believes Gareth could have made it professionally. 'He could have done. We made mistakes.' He loves the fact that Gareth later rediscovered his love of the bike, but cannot help thinking of what might have been. 'Gareth knows I feel this way,' he says.

If anyone benefited from this, ironically, it was Becky. 'We learned,' David says. By the time Becky came though, they were equipped to meet her requirements.

He recalls her first national race, when she was 13: 'She came last and got lapped, and we said, "You did brilliantly, you finished!"' He remembers, too, the girl that won that day. 'We thought she was amazing. Her parents were pretty vocal, too. They had three talented children. None of them are riding their bikes any more.'

How many more kids aren't riding their bikes any more? How many more might have been Olympians were it not for low-performance parenting? And this isn't just an Olympic thing or a sport thing.

'The distance between support and pressure is short, and for parents, it can be equally difficult for them to manage their expectations and ambitions.' These are the words of Nicolas Chisholm, for 22 years the headmaster of the Yehudi Menuhin School. He has countless tales of low-performance parenting: 'I shall never forget a young boy who played pretty well in the end of year concert, better than I'd expected, and afterwards his parents berated him for playing badly. You could see this child withering under this parental onslaught and I just thought this is awful. I did say, "I'm sorry, you're wrong, you can't speak to your child like this. That was a fantastic effort, it was wonderful, the children are still learning." But the parents wouldn't take it. How children survive that psychological pressure, I don't know. In my view, it's psychologically damaging.'

Chisholm wrote a paper about it, entitled, 'The pressures of growing up as a musically gifted child', in which he writes, 'How often have I heard the cry: "We have given up so much for you to have music lessons"? The emotional blackmail of cries like this puts a child under huge pressure. It is hardly surprising that this pressure can be one of the hardest for a gifted young person to bear.

'The desire of parents for their offspring to enter music competitions is another area of intense pressure in which the parents often live vicariously through their young child's successes … Winning can be as difficult to manage as losing, and so much of a child's self-esteem can depend on the attitude of parents towards this. The tunnel vision of parents can be as damaging to a gifted child and the child's own approach if it results in the devaluing of all other pursuits in a child's life.'

For David James, there are now some clear, defined guidelines. 'One thing that doesn't work is PUSH,' he says. 'If I tell my girls to do something, they'll do the opposite. It's about support, taking the worries off their shoulders. And this is a key factor. You are in it for the long game.'

He tells a story about Becky, aged 15. She had just won four national junior titles and, thus, simultaneously, quite a reputation. Not long afterwards, she was competing in an omnium in a track event in Newcastle-under-Lyme and she was suddenly a name people had heard of and were interested to see. However, she had been doing some heavy gym training, so physically she was not fresh, she hadn't tapered, and so she finished sixth. After the event, she heard the comments: other parents saying, rather too loudly, that she was 'not all that she was cracked up to be'. Naturally, she was very upset. For David, there was a lesson in this:

you can't win every event and it doesn't matter if you don't. This is a long game; it isn't always about winning tomorrow's race.

These are the kind of experiences that he will share when asked. In November 2015, the Welsh Rugby Union (WRU) launched an initiative for the parents of their top young players; it was called High Performing Parents and James was asked to come and talk to them. It was the opinion of the WRU that, since it is the parents who provide the environment for their players, who are their supporters in chief, sometimes their detractors and very often the major influence in their lives, why assume that they innately know how best to nurture the outlier in their midst? Research shows that, after a game, children playing sport at this high level would rather travel home with their grandparents than with their mother and father. Parents are desperate to talk, desperate to discuss the game. Those car journeys can be painful, particularly after a defeat. With grandparents, they are more relaxed. Being a parent is hard.

'These are extraordinary kids,' says Gethin Watts, the WRU national performance manager, who put the programme together. 'They have extraordinary lives, but live in ordinary homes and go to ordinary schools. Our coaches go on these amazing courses where they learn how to create the right environment for high-performance athletes. No one tells the parents.'

The first batch of parents that the WRU put through the High Performing Parents programme were the parents of the Wales under-20s team. Although of course no one can tell for sure that the two things are related, that Under20s team then went straight on to win the Under20s Grand Slam. Either way, the WRU were convinced that High Performance Parenting had to remain.

Of course, it makes sense to work closely with the athlete's parents. In March 2012, UK Sport held a two-day symposium on the subject of High Performance Parenting. One of the coaches asked to speak was Toni Minichiello, Jessica Ennis-Hill's coach. His view was that parents can be 'a source of great support or a power of great destruction' and, therefore, 'why would you not want to engage with someone who has that much influence?'

The British sailing team became convinced of this long ago, so convinced that they have a regular programme to help their parents. They are convinced that parenting can be a performance gain and when they put it like this – 'Nearly all athletes are on the podium because of their parents' – then it seems pretty obvious, doesn't it? You can help and you can hinder. 'The parents that most effectively get their heads around this give their kids the biggest chance for sure.'

These quotes are from Mark Nicholls, who is Youth Racing Manager, which means he runs the programme which teaches parents how to parent a wannabe Olympian. As he puts it: 'The parents obviously have the biggest impact on the child because they have the most contact time with them. We are not interested in how they can be better parents – that's not our business – but better *performance* parents, how they can help provide results. If you make all the parents 1–10 per cent better, you can make a real difference.'

Nicholls has witnessed all the horror stories. The loud, shouting parents 'who treat their kids as if they're adult performers,' he says, 'can be really damaging.' Likewise parents who struggle to contain their disappointment when their children don't win, or simply underperform. 'The kids are pretty good at letting go of disappointment very quickly,' he says, 'whereas parents hang onto it for a long time.' Even the wording of a press release can be controversial. Sometimes children's names are left off a release in order to lighten the pressure on them. 'But if we don't include all the right sailors in the press releases, the parents will start shouting at us. The smarter among them understand it if we're leaving their kids out.'

The car journey after an event is a well-established problem. 'The sailor hasn't done that well and you are in the car afterwards – what does the parent do? Nearly always the first question the parents ask is: "How did you do, did you win?" That's about the least helpful thing. A lot of the time the parent will push the kids for information, but that's often about what the parent needs. They need some sort of affirmation that they've spent all of their money and time wisely. But what the kid needs to do is different: what the kid needs to do is think through their racing; work it out in their own time.'

The area of greatest sensitivity is, of course, selection. Or rather non-selection. 'You're essentially telling them their kid isn't good enough,' Nicholls says. 'Failure is normal in sport, everybody fails all of the time, but people are really uncomfortable with the idea of it. I think the athletes are good at it but the parents aren't. You take it personally if your kid doesn't fulfil all of your expectations. Nearly always the answer from us is that on this occasion they weren't good enough. But you then try and move it onto what they can do next, so that they've got something to work on.'

Nicholls empathises with the emotional burden of the parent in all of this. 'Most of them genuinely want to do the best job that they can do,' he says. The programme he lays on for them involves two sessions a year plus a series of 'webinars' and other online resources. Much of the message is about a child's ability to learn and improve, about differentiating between winning today's race versus fulfilling long-term potential. Often he refers parents to Carol Dweck, one of the established global authorities on child development, and a TED Talk she gave on 'The Power of Yet'.

This is how Dweck opens her 'Power of Yet' talk: 'I heard about a high school in Chicago where, if students didn't pass a course, they got the grade "Not Yet". I thought that was fantastic. If you get Not Yet, you understand you are on a learning curve, it gives you a path into the future.' And then she asks the question: 'Are we raising our children for *now* instead of *yet*?'

Too often, parents are focused on now. This is one of the essential issues Nicholls tries to challenge. 'Sailing is a decision-making sport and there's an element of risk about it. So we need sailors in the programme that can make intelligent, risk-based decisions all the time; they need to be able to think on their own. We need parents that can support that, but parents also like to give their kids the best opportunity in life –

that's only natural, isn't it? – and that can confuse them. They might organise extra tuition for them at school, extra coaching, some are still effectively organising play dates for their kids when they are 18.

'One of the big areas is to help parents to understand that pushing all of the barriers out of the way isn't going to help their children because they can't do that for them on the racecourse. If you tell your children what to do then they are not thinking for themselves. There's a point when they're in the 17/18/19-year-old group when they need to transition into the Olympic classes and you're looking at some of those parents and thinking: yeah, you've made it pretty hard for your kids.'

How to deal with disappointment is a part of the learning. Massaging bruised egos is fraught with danger. Tell a child they were unlucky or played well when, actually, they didn't, and the bullshit can be smelled instantly. 'It's never a good idea to build confidence where there's nothing underneath because the kids will just see straight through it,' Nicholls says. 'And don't pretend you know what you're talking about if you don't, because they already do. Think of the number of hours they put into it; they are already effectively experts.'

How should a parent handle those tense car journeys post-defeat? 'One of our players,' Gethin Watts says, 'told us: "I tell my parents I'll speak about it with you when I am ready."'

Nicholls's advice is not dissimilar. Don't push conversation; let it happen. 'The trick for parents,' he says, 'is to ask questions and to not think about the outcome and to try not to lead. Focus on effort and endeavour more than anything else. And: it's fine to not be good enough, as long as you follow it up with *yet*.'

Even if your child does fulfil their dreams and gets to the Olympics, it doesn't get any easier. Probably harder. Your child experiences Olympic disappointment? That conversation that you want – What happened? Are you OK? How do you feel? – might just never happen.

In 2008, Hazel Shaw travelled to Beijing to support her daughter, Bryony, a windsurfer, and the advice to her and the other parents was loud and clear. 'You are not encouraged to talk to the athletes,' she re-calls. 'They know where you are. They know how to find you if they need you. But you basically leave them alone.' Shaw recalls the one race in that Olympic regatta when Bryony was disqualified, when she didn't speak to her afterwards and 'the agony' of the distance, emotional and physical, between her and her daughter was so great she went back to her apartment and hit the bottle. Bryony phoned her at 11.50pm.

A sailing competition goes on for over a week. At the end of it, Bry-ony won bronze. 'It's very, very tough,' Hazel says. 'They were the ten worst and best days of my life.'

When the British sailing team want an experienced parent to come and talk to the new parents, as part of their parent education programme, it is often Hazel Shaw they turn to. Shaw's advice is clear: 'Don't push. Don't think you know better than them. Don't be a helicopter parent hovering over them. Let them take responsibility for themselves.'

If required, she will tell them the whole Hazel/Bryony story. She will recall the early years in junior competitions when she said to Bry-ony: 'This is your sport, you have to nag me, it's not going to be the other way around.' And Bryony was fine with that. They would travel to events in a camper van called Girtie, and at the water's edge she would hear other parents saying to their kids: 'Get out there and kick arse!' And she would just say: 'I love you.' And: 'Have fun.'

In her hardest months, when Becky James was injured, she never knew if she would ever be able to ride a bike again. From February 2014, she was out for 18 months, a period when she had cervical cancer, shoulder surgery and a long-term, apparently irresolvable knee problem. She be-came, in her words, 'an emotional wreck'. David, her father, recalls the attitude he and Christine took at the time: 'We never said: "Maybe you should knock it on the head." But we did say: "If you don't want to do it, don't." That way, the onus was on Becky.'

When her body did eventually allow her back to train again, it did not give her much time. Rio was close; too close, some worried. She would be able to do the speed work, but the endurance training that requires months and years – that was beyond her. Nevertheless, in the first week of August 2016, David and Christine boarded a flight to Rio. Becky was fit, her Olympic dream alive, so David and Christine decided that, for the first time, they would leave home to watch one of their children competing. They organised 24-hour care for Bethan. 'Leaving her,' David says, 'was very hard mentally.'

The Olympics was the big stage, but his feelings now, he said, were no more heightened: 'It doesn't change. The more you get into it and the higher the level, I don't think you are more worried or want it more for them. My big worries were that she would get injured or not do her best. Obviously there is a part of you that wants her to get a medal, but that was secondary. I wanted her to give it a go, do her best, to put on a show. I was more nervous for the semi-finals. I knew she'd be disappointed if she wasn't in the final.'

By the time they had arrived, Hazel Shaw was already in the Olympic city and Bryony had started competing. Hazel's agony had begun. Rio was not a good Olympics for Bryony. In one race, a plastic bag became caught around the fin of her boat. In another, she saw some debris in the water ahead of her, manoeuvred to miss it, hit a log and fell in. Such is the random misfortune of an Olympian, especially if you are out at sea in the Rio regatta.

The velodrome was in the Olympic Park, an hour and a bit across town. On Day Eight, Becky James was in the keirin and having a better time of it. She won her first round in commanding fashion. The semi-final was a different matter: with less than a lap to go, there was a loud clatter as one of the riders crashed down onto the pine track. It seemed as if David James's fears had come true – but Becky was fine, Becky was strong again, it was Sarah Lee Wai-sze of Hong Kong whose dreams were dashed.

An hour later, it was the final: a hard race. Elis Ligtlee, the Dutch rider, hit the front early, James jostled for position but, with one lap to go, she appeared to be shut out at the back of the pack. So she did put on a show – just as her father would have wanted. She did it the hard way, up the banking, and backed her power. From her position on the banking, her height then gave her speed coming down. She nudged towards Ligtlee at the front and only by three-hundredths of a second did she not get there.

As she stood on the podium to receive her silver medal, David and Christine rushed round from their seats on the other side of the velodrome. They wanted to share the look of joy on her face.

'It was a great race,' David said. Yet, after all the miles and all the years, his real joy was not the medal. 'It was just to see her there on the start line. I was loving it for her.'

Three days later, in the women's sprint, it was same again, silver medal, this time behind Kristina Vogel of Germany, and again David and Christine bustled round the velodrome to soak up the moment on the podium. No one could know what she might have achieved had she been fit for all four years of the build-up and not just the fourth, if she had had a bit of endurance to see her through the gruelling Olympic schedule; some couldn't help wondering either, certainly not Becky. That is how the competitor's mind works.

In between Becky's two silvers, Bryony's Olympics came to an end. She had finished ninth. That night Hazel joined her and some of the other sailing families for dinner and, no, she wasn't allowed the intimate reflection that any parent would have wanted: are you OK? How are you feeling? 'No, no serious conversations,' she recalls. 'It's not the time after a bad event.'

A month after the Games, I spoke to Hazel and it was still the same. 'Maybe a couple of months down the line,' she said. 'She knows that if she wants to talk to me, she can. Until then, I'll button my lip.'

Chapter learnings by Chelsea Warr

Parents are a key part of the elite athlete support team; ignore them at your peril. The best elite sporting programmes recognise this and embrace deliberate strategies to engage parents early on the performance journey. Parents are a valuable asset to performance if supported, educated and engaged.

Help train the support team. Most parents' intentions are right but often they just don't know how to channel them – and that's not their fault, it's because we've failed to engage with them about their role in the journey. Just as athletes have a curriculum of development, parents need to be given this opportunity to develop in their role too. How can we expect them to know how to behave and support if we've never told them or taught them?

'Praise the effort, not the talent.' These words from Professor Carol Dweck, the lauded psychology professor from Stanford University, are to be treasured. Parents and coaches should praise effort and resilience and avoid singling out intelligence, smartness or talent.

The value of independence. We should be seeking to develop independence – and remain very aware of how easy it is to impede that process.

12

The power of empowerment

ALISTAIR AND JONATHAN BROWNLEE, NORWEGIAN
CROSS-COUNTRY SKIERS

Every self-respecting book of this genre deals with the subject of nature v nurture. As in: were you born a champion or did circumstances turn you into one? There are entire tomes given over to the subject. At the very least, we are obliged here to give it a chapter – and here it is. It is about the Brownlee brothers, Alistair and Jonny. They are the two best triathletes in the world, so you would conclude that it has to be something in the genes. Well, you would, wouldn't you? Mother Cathy swam for Wales as a junior; father Keith ran for his county one time. So there is some decent DNA in there, no?

Alterntively, you could put the question to Keith. How did you end up with two Olympic medallists in the family? And he answers, smiling and bemused: 'To be honest, I ask myself that same question all the time too.'

Or you could start with Alistair's first ever race. The first signs of greatness? Hardly, as Keith recalls: 'When I first took him to a cross-country running race, it was a schools race, Saturday morning, he was nine years old. There were about 450 kids across all age spectrums; Alistair came about four hundredth. It was a very mediocre but gutsy performance.' He remembers in particular the sight of his young son, all red-faced, puffing his way up a hill. And also this: 'In the car on the way back, Alistair said: "I really enjoyed that. But I think if I am going to get good at it, I need to be not quite as chubby as I am. I am going to start eating potatoes and stop eating chips, and for puddings I am going to eat fruit." The remarkable thing is that he did.'

This was the mark of young Alistair. 'An interesting, driven character,' is how Keith describes him. For his A-levels, he did maths and the three sciences, but taught himself further maths as a fifth A-level at home. 'He had to do everything. He qualified Grade A singing, played the flute. Even as a tiny child, with reading and stories, he wanted more and more. If he fell asleep while you were reading a story, he could tell you exactly where you were in the story the next day. And when he was tiny, he couldn't be in the house. Otherwise he'd squall. So he was always on the go. We'd pander to that, give him more and more opportunities. That's middle-class parents for you.'

Aged ten, Alistair decided independently that, to get better, he needed to get up early for a run before school every day and Keith insisted that he couldn't go alone and that he should join him. Soon Keith started to sneak into Alistair's bedroom when he had fallen asleep, to turn off his alarm clock. Not long after, Alistair started hiding the alarm clock.

From everything that we know about Alistair and Jonny, if there is anything innate, in-born that stands out, even from those days as a toddler, it is not excellence of performance at all, but a determination.

In their races as juniors, they were good but not outstanding. In Alistair's first triathlon, aged nine, he fell off his bike four times. He didn't win but, more to the point, he made it to the finish. In his first 800m race, aged 12, for the Bingley Harriers, he came last. Their times, as younger teenagers, were so unexceptional that the Talent ID experts of today would not be impressed and would probably exclude them from any early junior elite training groups. This was in part because they suffered from the biological happenstance that affects many teenage athletes: they matured late. The other part was simply that they were not *that* naturally blessed.

According to Malcolm Brown, who has been their running coach since their early teens, 'They weren't the best talents in Britain in triathlon in that time. There were others better in their age group in the UK and definitely the world. They were good but they weren't the best. They had races where they performed poorly. On measures of speed over 200m in the pool or 3,000m on the track, there were others who you would say were more talented athletes.'

This is Jack Maitland, who has been their long-term swim coach: 'They have great characteristics, but they are lacking in other areas. Like speed; neither of them was particularly fast. When they started with Malcolm, they were one-paced animals.'

The boys themselves argue that maybe being slightly second-best in their junior years was instrumental. 'I wonder about the thing about us not being that good,' says Alistair. 'Does that instil something in you? It doesn't come easily, so you really have to work for it. It's because you are not that physically mature, you don't win things easily so you have to work for it – that carries on through. The guy that was physically mature and had more natural advantage, when he gets to 18, doesn't have that natural advantage any more, and he hasn't spent his years working and trying for it.'

As Jonny says: 'For some to whom it came too easily, they can get to the point where they realise: I don't want to work for it.' In other words, they didn't care to nurture what gifts nature had given them. As for the Brownlees' own gifts, the nurturing never stopped.

In one sense, they didn't *work* for it, not work as in hard grind. But, almost without meaning to, they found themselves on a unique training programme. They cycled to school, Bradford Grammar, every day along a canal tow-path; that's ten miles there and back, 40 minutes each way. Younger brother Ed went on the school bus and got the job of carrying their schoolbags. Then, at school, there happened to be a long-developed and well-coached running club, so they would go out running at lunchtime every day. The school coach would put on races most weekends, they would also run for Bingley Harriers and, on top of all that, their absolute passion was competing in a series of fell races on the Brontë moors. Even to this day, they still insist on competing in the annual Auld Lang Syne race on New Year's Eve – cold, wet, muddy – and they certainly never did it for the prizes; one of Alistair's first trophies was a balloon-making kit. To this day, Dan Salcedo, one of their early triathlon coaches, says that the Auld Lang Syne race is, for the Brownlees, 'their Disneyland'.

If you add to all that their swimming club (they both swam for their county) and the cycling club, which allowed them to join the regular long 100-mile Sunday rides into the Dales, you can see why the early advice from British Triathlon was: you are over-training. But they quite liked what they were doing, so they took on board the advice and ignored it.

They also thought nothing of defying the modern mores of child safety. Well, they were children, so they would, wouldn't they? This is Keith on the subject, which he discusses with a faintly embarrassed giggle: 'From a child protection angle, it is all a bit frightening. At 13, Alistair would disappear saying, "I'm off for a ride." I'd say, "Where are you going?" He'd say, "I don't know." "Will you take a mobile phone?" "No, it weighs too much." Six hours later, he'd return after a 90km ride. I felt a lot more comfortable once they were doing it together.'

Let's cover off a couple more angles. Are they the product of pushy parenting? 'We don't think we are responsible,' is Keith's answer. 'There is a very fine line between encouraging, facilitating, financing and push-ing somebody. In all honesty, I think we were on the side of facilitating. I've had far more conversations with Alistair about reining it back, do-ing less, and I can't think of any about doing more. Even now, I'd say the majority of conversations I have with him is: rest, don't do as much.'

And what is their response to being told to rein it in? 'Like any teenage child to any parents, it's "You don't know what you are talk-ing about." Al would say, "You don't understand. To be a professional athlete, you have to do the most you can to be the best you can." He feels he knows better than I do. Remember, I am a medic, but he's probably quite right.'

There was one topic that parents and child debated hard: Alistair's Cambridge University career. In 2006, the Beijing Olympics were a goal on a not-so-far-away horizon and yet his A-levels were good enough to win him a place to study medicine at Cambridge. Keith says: 'I am absolutely of the opinion that children have to want to do what they do. If they don't, they can always blame someone else. And they won't commit.' Nevertheless, on the subject of Cambridge, they were uncharacteristically firm. 'His mother and I said, "You have to give Cambridge a try, it is an opportunity you cannot say no to." So the conclusion was: go to Cambridge, see if you can fit the training in around your studies. If it doesn't work, reassess at Christmas.'

So he went to Cambridge and his parents started receiving 5am phone calls saying: 'I am running up the A14 on the hard shoulder.' In other words, he had left the best training paddock in the world – the Yorkshire moors that were outside his front door – for a Cambridge A-road. 'It just didn't work,' Keith says. 'Wasn't compatible. He saw his potential career diminishing.' So, as planned, they reassessed at Christmas and Alistair left Cambridge.

Is their success due to the sibling thing? Absolutely. There can be no doubt whatsoever that this has played a massive role. Between them, Alistair and Jonny long ago mastered the act where they josh around about it and share amusing tales about falling out over holiday games of crazy golf. The truth is more raw and uncomfortable. In the year before the London Olympics, they devoted a reasonable portion of their rare hours away from training to giving long interviews for their joint autobiography, *Swim Bike Run*. We should bear in mind that, for much of that time, Alistair was injured and therefore frustrated, a state of mind that wasn't helped by the fact that, because he and Jonny were housemates, he had to endure the sight of his training partner and rival going out training every day, getting ahead when he was falling behind. That is just some of the subtext behind what is one of the more brutal chapters of any sporting autobiography, a chapter called 'Brother on Brother' where they are both toe-curlingly honest about what they really think about each other. In this chapter, they acknowledge the basic premise – the fact that the brother-brother dynamic has always been governed by Alistair being two years older – and reflect, with painful candour, on their personality differences: Alistair the free spirit, Jonny the cautious one; Alistair who never doubted himself, Jonny innately insecure; Alistair the leader, Jonny the follower.

This is Alistair: 'I wonder if our personalities have developed in opposition to each other. The big difference is that while triathlon is what I love doing – there is literally nothing else in the world I would rather do – I've never got that impression with Jonny. He does it and he does it brilliantly; but the motivation I get from pure enjoyment is something he doesn't share; he is motivated by an obsession for doing everything right, and on time, and by the book. He has to be on time for sessions because that is what motivates him to do it, not because he desperately wants to do things.'

And: 'Jonny would deny it to the core, but I think his entire life has been about trying to compete with me. Trying to get level with me, and then beat me.'

And: 'He once asked me, "Have you ever seen a result of mine and wished I'd done worse?" I was genuinely shocked.'

Jonny explains, 'We have learned not to make so much of the tiny goals within a goal. It's essential for our self-preservation. If we were competing over every single repetition in every single session, we would have killed each other two years ago.'

And: 'Our relationship has evolved in the last year. I feel less like the little brother now. I stand up to him now … I am sure part of it is that he doesn't want me around him all the time now I'm his biggest rival.'

However, Jonny's willingness to accept the role of number two is acknowledged in an anecdote he tells of a training session on the track they did together a couple of months before the London Games.

'I knew I could drop him at any point,' he says. 'If that situation had been reversed he wouldn't have thought about it at all – he would have just gone. Bang. But I was running round thinking: Alistair is struggling. I could drop him at any time – but he's my big brother and if I do, he'll get in a mood.'

It's all very Yorkshire. Extremely blunt. And yet extremely powerful.

Sporting siblings are no novelty. There are, for instance, three pairs of Russian brothers who compete with the Brownlees at world level triathlon. Talent studies tend to show that second or third siblings are better positioned to be high performers. These are generalisations but the pattern is straightforward: the younger sibling instinctively chases the elder; the elder sibling instinctively tries to stay ahead. What is fascinating is the dominance hierarchy and how that dynamic can mould world-class athletes.

Was it hard to watch as parents? 'We were desperate and continue to be desperate that they don't fall out over it and continue to be friends,' Keith says. 'That competitiveness has had a sharp edge to it at some points in their training when they were younger, but as they've grown older, and particularly going through the Olympics together – that was absolutely massive – they've actually become closer and more supportive.'

Nature v nurture? If it was nature, then what happened to younger brother Ed? Alistair and Jonny say Ed is probably the most naturally gifted swimmer of them all. He has played rugby at a decent level too. But he was five years Jonny's junior, too young to try to chase him and too far behind to get locked into this intense sibling competition. When Alistair and Jonny were cycling to school first thing in the morning, Ed thought they were mad and was just delighted that there was a bus option instead.

Nature-nurture is not a riddle that requires a book to answer it. Here is the answer in one sentence: it is not either-or, not one or the other, it *has* to be both. Sure, the Brownlees are blessed to have been genetically gifted; but they are also blessed to have been able to open their front door onto as good and uplifting a triathlon training paddock as you will find anywhere in the world; and they are blessed, too, to have been born into this exceptionally advantageous sibling bond that is both so competitive and so supportive. Nature, good, yes. But have any athletes nurtured their talent quite as successfully as these too?

In November 2012, in the downtime after the Olympics, from which Alistair had emerged champion, Brown, his coach, organised for him to go on a short trip to Addis Ababa for the annual Great Ethiopian Run, a mass participation event for around 35,000 competitors. The event founder was Haile Gebrselassie, arguably the greatest distance runner of all time (though that is another debate altogether) and certainly an inspirational figure. Brown thought that going to the event and meeting the great Haile would be good for the soul.

'One of my concerns,' Brown reflects, 'was: how would the Olympic victory affect Alistair? Would there be any doubts about him losing his grounding?' Brown pauses momentarily, smiles and then continues: 'Well, there shouldn't have been any doubts at all. Winning had no effect whatsoever. He still loves training. I've hardly seen him happier recently than on last New Year's Eve at that dreadful Auld Lang Syne fell race. There was snow on the ground, bitter cold, Yorkshire moors; he got all his tri mates to run, and he was just so comfortable.'

So Alistair didn't need Africa as the reality-check experience that Brown had intended. Nevertheless, he loved it. 'Incredible, fascinating,' he says. 'Those East African distance runners, it is clear there is a genetic component there: right shape, skinny ankles; there is an environmental factor there too, the fact they live at altitude. We also went out of the city to where they train, when you see 200 of them training in the fields; that is incredible. The thing I really enjoyed was just seeing the enthusiasm for running. That was really hammered home.'

The similarities here are stark: a combination of genetics, environment and passion – as in Ethiopia, just so in Yorkshire. Alistair also saw kids running to school in the morning and then running back. This is the very platform of Gebrselassie's success: the 10km thereand-back that he ran throughout his schooldays, a huge accumulation of base training. And that is the Brownlees for you too: cycling to school every day, running at school pretty much every day. Are there any other schoolkids anywhere in Britain in a position to accumulate so many miles and lay down such a base? Without ever having sat down to plan it, the Brownlees had turned themselves into Great Britain's Africans.

Over dinner with Alistair and Jonny, we are discussing nature v nurture and they themselves are deeply engaged in the subject too. They want to understand how and why they have become who they have become, and not just because they both have a lively intelligence, but because they believe that the very process of understanding is crucial. Thus, I believe, we stumble upon something that is absolutely fundamental to their success.

They have made it completely their responsibility to see how far they can push themselves. They flirt with excess training and sometimes therefore injury, and if you look at their injury record, you would conclude that too often the flirtation has gone too far. But they believe that it is their job to understand knowing where the line of 'too far' lies. Alistair talks about 'seeing how much you can do without going over the edge, then trying to recognise the edge before you go over it'. He says: 'That is a real skill. Pushing it hard isn't that difficult. The skill is in managing it and knowing when to do less.' Then he chuckles: 'I'm not sure I've really cracked it, to be honest.'

This is Jonny: 'There is a maximum amount of training you can do before you get injured. But while you might not able to do more, you can always go harder than you think – there are sessions when you can go harder and faster.'

Both of them recognise that while their lives are dedicated to harder and faster, there are dangers inherent in their personalities that prevent them from backing off. Alistair has this more in him than Jonny. Together, though, they are educating themselves on where lies that edge between hard training and injury and how close to it they can go. Here again the sibling thing works. Two people's learnings are far better than one.

'It's a really interesting dynamic,' Alistair says. 'You want to push each other on by coming up with new ideas. One of us could think of a way of doing something, the other could see if it works or not; that way you could progress twice as fast. You have to balance that with the fact that you are not playing one-upmanship. As soon as that happens, the relationship breaks down and you cannot train with each other.'

For instance, when Alistair started doing an extra run on Wednesday nights, Jonny watched, saw that it worked and followed. Likewise, at the start of 2015, when they were in a period of heavy training, Jonny started getting fatigued, so he adjusted his sessions, making them shorter and sharper. It worked; Alistair followed.

You wonder, then, where the role of the coach is in all this. When I put that question to Brown, he rolls his eyes and chuckles. This is his answer: 'In an ideal world, I'd send them a training schedule which they'd follow every minute of the day and they'd then win everything and say "It's all down to Malcolm."' But this is not an ideal world. Brown is relaxed about the world they do inhabit, because he has also worked very closely with Paula Radcliffe and Kelly Holmes, so he knows what best practice looks like and he knows that the Brownlees look like that too. But when he is asked, for instance, how often he does lab-testing with them, he laughs because the answer is pretty much never.

'We like to empower the boys with decisions,' he says, knowing that there is really very little alternative. The boys empower themselves. There have been times when he has used other older runners in their running group as his inside eyes and ears. 'They would feed back to me what the conversations with Alistair and Jonny were,' he explains, 'and I would get certain influences into Alistair and Jonny through them. That way it isn't all about Malcolm telling them all the time.'

The bottom-line deal is that Brown sets them three sessions with him a week and they attend them religiously. Yet, as Brown, says: 'The person who knows most about triathlon in the world is not me, it's Alistair Brownlee.'

Alistair says: 'The people around us realised early on that neither of us, and probably particularly me, wanted to be told what to do. Instead, they take on an advisory role. I think that was important.' There are two clear reasons for this, he explains. One: 'When something goes wrong, there is constant feedback. I am immediately thinking: what is it, this or this? Rather than saying "There's something wrong today" and then telling the coach and then the coach trying to work it out, you are more accountable.' Two: 'When you stand on the start line, you want to be completely responsible for that performance. I am standing there thinking, if anything goes wrong it's my fault. Not the coach's. That is really powerful.'

'I used to hate athletes who would say, "It's my coach's fault,"' Jonny says. 'I never ever want to be like that.' He adds that there is a definite streak of strong Yorkshire belligerence in their attitude. Alistair acknowledges that, at times, his I-know-best approach is plain arrogant, but he still values it and would rather it that way than putting himself more in others' hands.

Where does this fit into the nature-nurture debate? I am not sure to what extent this attitude – their Yorkshireness, if you like – is natural or is because of their Yorkshire environment. But without doubt, it has brought the best out of what nature gave them. Many athletes have their hands held from an early age, they do what their coaches say, train when their parents drive them to training, so they are reliant on others and are the product of other people's decisions. Maybe that is why all those kids who would beat the Brownlees when they were young are no longer competing at the top. But if a performance plan really comes from the self, if it is self-driven and self-owned, then that, as Alistair says, 'is really powerful'.

In the eternal search to solve the mystery of success, there may be no more comprehensive attempt to crack the code than in Trondheim,

Norway. Cross-country skiing is the Norwegian national sport; two-fifths of the population have ski tracks within ten metres of their front door. The cross-country skier Petter Northug is quite possibly the most celebrated man in the country. Northug has had his own TV reality show (called *Circus Northug*), he is great tabloid fodder, has had roller-coaster highs and lows, and likes to poke fun at Swedes; but more importantly, he has won more world titles (13) than any other male cross-country skier ever. So he occupies as much newspaper space as the Norwegian royal family. When athletes like Northug are winning medals, then Norway can feel good about itself.

In 2006 at the Turin winter Olympics, however, Norway suffered a sporting disaster. Norway is accustomed to finishing top of the cross-country medal table; in Turin it came seventh. It is accustomed to winning four or five golds; in Turin, zero. In a very straightforward Nordic way, two questions thus arose in 2006: why were we successful before? And: why are we not any more?

The ends to which they went to find the answers were brilliant and exhaustive. They put together a team of physiologists, psychologists, historians, former athletes and their coaches. They started by interviewing the current athletes and the coaches: what are you doing? What does your training look like? What is your lifestyle? What is the role of your parents? What do you believe influences success and failure? And then they started retracing their steps and tracking down as many former champions as they could find and started asking them the same questions. They went all the way back to Oddmund Jensen, the 1959 Norwegian national champion, who became coach of Oddvar Bar, winner of two world golds in 1982.

In all, they interviewed 30 former champions. To their advantage was the meticulous nature of so many of their interviewees, who had recorded and kept training diaries. Jensen still had diaries from the 1950s. In Vegard Ulvang, who won three Olympic golds in Albertville in 1992, they found a treasure trove of information. A fiercely intelligent man, Ulvang would go from success on skis to starting his own mega-successful clothing company. And he still had, the researchers discovered, extraordinarily detailed documentation of what got him to those three golds. The data from Ulvang et al was then filtered into a central pool and the analysis team would gather every second month to sift through it together.

This then became the ultimate success manual, a book called *Den Norske Langrennsboka* ('The Norwegian Book of Cross-Country Skiing' – a title so brilliantly Norwegian and logical). It just so happens that in 2007 Northug won his first world title and, at the Olympics in 2010 and 2014, Norway came top of the cross-country medal table again with five golds at each Games. No achievement was greater than that of the Norwegian team at the 2015 world championships in Falun, Sweden, where they won gold in nine of the 12 cross-country events.

How did they achieve this? What was the miracle code to success? What was in the book?

With these questions in mind, in March 2015, a group of British Olympic coaches paid Trondheim a visit. Trondheim is one of Norway's elite performance centres, and it is also home to the National Centre of Elite Sport Research where the work on *Den Norske Langrennsboka* was done. And it is responsible for producing a very large percentage of Norwegian Olympic success; if the Trondheim area alone had competed at the Sochi Olympics, it would have finished fifth in the overall medal table.

What did the British visitors learn? First, that because the Norwegians now have such a distinct understanding of how cross-country has developed as a sport over the long sweep of its history, they feel that they can analyse competently where it is going to go next. In other words, the masterminds behind Norwegian cross-country try to set the trends, to get ahead of the game rather than follow it. For example, there are, essentially, two styles of cross-country: the skating technique and the 'classical' technique, which is propelling oneself using double-poling. A phenomenal amount of research has been done on the advantages in ski design that can be gained by only using double-poling.

And that is reasonably interesting, yes. But the science of double-poling was slightly lost on the GB crowd.

This, on the other hand, was not. Because cross-country requires a lot of training and a lot of long distances, 80 per cent of the work has to be done solo, or away from the eyes of the coach. Whereas swimming coaches can watch the athletes trawl up and down a pool, and track coaches can observe trackside, cross-country coaches have to let their athletes go and just trust them. In the new, post-*Den Norske Langrennsboka* Norway, then, every bright young athlete is obliged to record a training diary, just as Oddmund Jensen had done over half a century earlier. These diaries are recorded online, a massive feedback system which means the national federation will never again be short on information.

More significantly, the young athletes themselves are encouraged to understand and interpret their own training data. In other words, because they effectively self-train, they are encouraged, as far as possible, to self-coach. There is evidence that one discriminatory factor between those who are and who are not successful is their ability to do this: to understand, to self-train, to think for themselves, to take ownership – in other words, to be most like a Brownlee brother.

As we know, you cannot just pitch up to a high-performance centre like Trondheim and expect to walk off with all their intellectual property. You have to give back in return. Thus, when they were in Trondheim, a presentation was given to a group of elite cross-country coaches by Salcedo, the coach who had worked with the Brownlees in their early years. Salcedo also worked in GB boxing during its highly successful London 2012 phase and he is now back with triathlon again as one of the head coaches. The presentation he gave was largely about athletes as leaders, and he also talked around the Brownlees, putting up a slide of the pair of them on their annual Auld Lang Syne race.

Salcedo recalls: 'The bit about the Brownlees really struck a chord. The ownership of their programme, the way they dialogue with their coaches – the Norwegians saw immediate parallels with their skiers.

The geographical circumstances are not so different either: exercise on their doorstep, all those Norwegians living ten metres from a ski track, the Brownlees with the Dales outside their front door. And when I spoke to the coaches afterwards, they said that Alistair Brownlee epitomised the profile of Petter Northug.'

On the face of it, Alistair Brownlee and Northug could not be much more different if they tried. Brownlee has no great appetite for publicity or celebrity. He is not known as an *enfant terrible*. He has never brought out a music video. He does not have his own TV channel. He has not had a drink-driving incident splashed across the newspapers. What he does have, though, is an absolute determination to control his own destiny – this is what he shares with Northug and is fundamental to both men's cracking of the success code.

If the Brownlee brothers were a business, they would be Adobe, the global tech company. Every year, *Fortune*, the business magazine, publishes its list of 100 Best Companies to Work For and every year Adobe is on the list. The 2016 list was Adobe's sixteenth consecutive appearance. Adobe was also in *The Huffington Post*'s 2015 'Best Places to Work' list. In 2010, *The Business Insider* did a '25 Best Tech Companies to Work For' list and Adobe came second. In India's Best Companies to Work For in 2016, as rated by *The Economic Times*, it was twenty-first. *The Economic Times* made comments about the Adobe environment, like 'trust leads to innovation' and 'there are no fixed timings and the company does not believe in micro-managing the work process of its engineers'; and it noted 'a work culture of free-spirited innovation'. All of that sounds very much like the Brownlees. Give your employees, or your athletes, trust and ownership of their output, and they respond with better output. At Adobe, all employees are entitled to stock options, so ownership is literal, it is not a concept. Likewise, the Brownlees do not like the idea of being owned, or their programme being owned by their coaches; they own it themselves.

In 2013, Adobe started a programme called Kickbox designed to mobilise a massive workforce in a way that would encourage innovation and ideas among all employees, no matter how senior or junior. Kickbox was just that: a box, a red box. The boxes contained instructions for how to pursue an idea; crucially it contained a credit card with a pre-paid $1,000 to build and test the idea; and it also contained a Starbucks gift card and a chocolate bar because, according to Mark Randall, whose job title was 'Vice President for Creativity' and who came up with the Kickbox concept, 'Sugar and caffeine are, to my experience, two of the four major food groups for innovators.' The box contains instructions taking its owners' ideas through six stages of development, of which the fifth requires testing of the idea with over 100 users, and the sixth is presenting and selling the idea to management. If you are successful after stage six, you are moved on to a blue box. The blue box is personalised according to your idea and intended to push the project on to the next level.

Within two years, over a thousand red Kickboxes had been distributed and some of the ideas had gone all the way to completion. An article in the *Harvard Business Review*, in February 2015, described these $1,000 investments as 'little bets'. 'The brilliance of the Kickbox,' it wrote, 'isn't that it gives employees a magic box, it's that it gives them permission. And often, that's all that's required to unbox creativity.'

This is how the Brownlees have come to operate. They took permission. On a micro scale, that allowed them to innovate, for Alistair to try out the extra Wednesday night run, for instance. On a grander scale, they don't look for a manager or a coach to deliver them to Olympic success, they don't want to be a product; they want complete ownership themselves, which is so much more powerful.

On Day 13 in Rio, at the men's triathlon on the Copacabana seafront, we saw both nature and nurture. The Brownlees' plan was simple: to swim hard and then kill off their major rivals on the bike. The bike ride involved eight laps of a loop up some punchy climbs; if there was anything that the topography of Yorkshire had given them, it was the ability to excel on climbs of this exact kind. That was nurture.

Very quickly, the run was a three-man affair, two Brownlees and Vincent Luis, the Frenchman, and they dropped him quickly too. At that point, you knew that gold and silver were going to the two brothers; it was just a case of who got what.

With 4km to go, Jonny made his one mistake. He thought they were pushing on too hard and said to Alistair, 'Relax.' That one word told Alistair that Jonny was struggling more than he looked and Alistair immediately attacked. That was nature. There, on the world stage, the instinct kicked in that had been with him since they were tiny boys – to stay ahead of his brother.

Alistair took gold, six seconds ahead of Jonny, who took silver. Nature and nurture had both done their work and taken them to the podium, and so had their complete ownership of their campaign to get there.

Chapter learnings by Simon Timson

Maximising 'discretionary effort' has occupied the minds of corporate leaders across the globe, and is the focus of a myriad of approaches to performance management in business settings. Discretionary effort is the maximal level of effort people could give if they wanted to, well above and beyond the minimum required. Typically, it is not something the coaches of elite athletes like the Brownlees and Norwegian cross-country skiers ever have to consider. They are used to working with highly motivated, persistent and self-determined people. So what lessons can be learned about how to create environments that promote such self-motivation and high performance?

Psychologists explain the impact of these environments through Self-Determination Theory, some of the principles of which are evident in this chapter:

Make people feel competent, in control of outcomes and their success by giving them the responsibility to make important decisions. Creating decision-rich environments will help develop people's strategic thinking, tactical acumen and the agility to respond to new challenges.

Give autonomy. Empower athletes (employees) to push the boundaries and let them make mistakes. Failure is an essential part of learning, development and innovation.

Brave leadership. This chapter gives a number of examples of athletes who are self-determined and a group of coaches that enabled and facilitated that. It would be natural for a coach to resist handing over any control; Malcolm Brown adapted his coaching to the individuals in front of him.

13

Moving the goalposts

Dave Henson

On 13 February 2011, Dave Henson, an officer in the Royal Engineers, was leading a patrol in Helmand province, Afghanistan. He was a 26, in charge of a team responsible for the planning and conducting of Improvised Explosive Device (IED) search operations. Afghan families had been displaced by the years of fighting; the intention of the patrol was to make safe an area that they could return to. Henson, however, stepped on a bomb. His first recollections of the incident are of getting himself seated, looking down and seeing his legs in pieces.

His life was saved first by the aid he was given by his team and then by the fact that, within 37 minutes, he was on an operating table.

Two extremely challenging years later, Henson was being driven to Sheffield, by Jayne Kavanagh of Help for Heroes, for a Talent ID day. He was a double leg amputee. Maybe he would make it in the Paralympics. A pathway had been created: the British Paralympic Association, together with Help for Heroes and the English Institute of Sport, had created a new programme that they called Front Line to Start Line, the intention of which was to help injured servicemen and women convert into Paralympians.

In theory, it sounds great, doesn't it? You provide those injured at war with a new purpose, a new direction. And you also know that they are already an elite group: they have reached high levels of fitness, they are highly trained, highly trainable. Everyone wins.

But any such assumptions should be shelved. If ever there was proof that talent spotting is not as straightforward as sifting numbers, sticking up tape and doing a few physical exercises, Front Line to Start Line is it. Turning talent into champions does not work that way.

Here are two basic truths about the military.

One: in the military, there is no room for mavericks; your allegiance is to your team or your unit; you work as a group, you leave no one behind, you move at the pace of the slowest man. To be a Paralympic champion, however, the state of mind could hardly be a more polar opposite. Champions need a cut-throat, me-first approach, especially those in individual sports. You want to be the fastest, not move with the slowest. Kavanagh saw this all the time with her Front Line to Start Line cohort: 'They were used to operating as a team and they find it very hard to think: what do *I* need? So they can struggle with the values of high-performance sport where you clamber over other people to get to the top. How do you develop that selfishness in someone that's spent their professional lives working for a collective?'

Two: soldiers are experts at taking instruction. That is what they have been trained to do. Conversely, the best athletes learn to think for themselves; they want to understand their coaches' thinking, but challenge it if they think it is wrong or could be improved upon; they contribute to the process. In attempts to convert military servicemen to high-performance athletes, that contribution rarely happened, if ever. They had been trained to accept instruction, not to challenge it.

However, there was in all this an element that went far deeper.

At the London 2012 Paralympics, Jon-Allan Butterworth won three silver medals in paracycling. He had been in Basra, Iraq, in 2007 with the Royal Air Force when a rocket attack cost him his left arm.

He started riding a bicycle in 2008, was later put into an elite paracycling programme and then, in London, appeared to be a poster boy for the whole concept of talent transfer for injured servicemen and women. The truth, though, was very different. Butterworth's success was more the exception to the rule. After London, rather than congratulating itself for the success that had been achieved with Butterworth, the British Paralympic Association was mainly asking questions such as: why were there not more successful military converts? If they were indeed these ideal athletes – fit, strong and trainable – why hadn't more of them transitioned better? Why did a number of them take a break from the sport the minute the Games were over? Why did so many of them flit from one sport to another? Could we have done this better? And if so, how?

After London, then, the whole process was stripped back and reviewed, and after extensive feedback from the athletes themselves, some basic truths became very apparent.

Kavanagh explains: 'None of them had ever *wanted* to be a Paralympian. None of them had ever watched a previous Paralympics and thought, "Yes, that's what I want to do." They wanted to be a soldier, not an athlete. They'd wanted to be a soldier and that had been taken away from them. They had been through experiences that we simply couldn't imagine, and we were saying, "Yeah, sport is great!" They were learning how to walk, how to use a catheter. Their focus wasn't: how do you become an athlete? A lot of them said, "I don't want to be that disabled person that people look at." So, rather than be prescriptive, saying, "We all know how to develop talent, crack on!", we had to understand better what we were doing. For instance, we'd thought any snipers from the military would make good Paralympic shooters. Well no! Getting behind the weapon again is not necessarily what they need. One guy said to me, "We thrive in the crappest places on earth. When we are tired and hungry, we have people shooting at us. Now we have the best gyms and the best running tracks. Sport is the opposite." I had to get to understand that.'

Everything that Kavanagh was learning was pretty much what Henson himself had experienced. He recalls, 'When I got injured it was 2011, the year before London 2012, and there was a lot of talk about military athletes going into the Paralympics. We were highly trained, highly trainable, motivated people. But for me, it was not something I necessarily wanted to do and the reasons were very psychological. To count yourself as a Paralympic athlete was about accepting your disability, accepting that it's happened and you are moving forward with it. Yes, I certainly made jokes about having no legs, but deep down, it wasn't something I accepted, not for a long time. You can go off and do military sports competition, but that's fine, that's an environment where you are comfortable and familiar and everyone knows your situation. Exposing yourself in the public eye was not something I necessarily wanted to do.'

That was very much what he had in mind in Kavanagh's car on the way to Sheffield. When he got there, the sports scientists liked the look of his long arms. They prescribed for him a future as a rower, or a wheelchair racer, or a thrower – anything that involved using those long levers. Yet Henson did not want any of that. He wanted to be a runner. He had got his running blades and quite liked them. He had never been a sprinter before, but running – jogging – was what he used to do pre-injury, it had been his way of escape. So, as an athlete, he just wanted to run, and when he said that to the talent testers, he was informed that getting him to world class would require a six-year journey.

'British Athletics were saying to me, "You've probably got a six-year pathway, you are looking at Tokyo 2020," and that, to me, was far too long away. I wasn't willing to commit to that. I was happy going to military competitions, keeping myself fit and just getting myself quicker.'

In other words, his approach to paralympic sport fitted the pattern. He wasn't desperate to be a Paralympian; he wasn't interested in taking advice and maximising his chances of success in paralympic sport by rowing or throwing, or doing whatever anyone said would be best for him. As an ambition, the Paralympics didn't really register.

By this time, the Front Line to Start Line programme was beginning to be embedded and, after the post-2012 review, Kavanagh was confident that she knew what needed to change. To get the best out of the injured servicemen, it was not going to be as straightforward as prescribing sport as a kind of happy medicine. Elite sport is hard and demanding, and Talent ID schemes are generally no different: you put a series of challenges in front of people and you see who can adapt, who can survive. That wasn't going to work here. The goalposts had to move.

'*We* had to be the adaptable ones,' Kavanagh says. 'The programme had to be individualised. We had to find out from each of them what they *wanted* from sport. Their sport, we found, worked as a secondary thing. It isn't: sport is everything. It's more: sport is a good way to show they can succeed again. The goal has to be set around their recovery. For instance, it can be proving to themselves: this injury will not stop me. Or: I want to show my kids I can still be a role model.'

Lifestyle and psychological support was the key. Rather than drive them all on as a group and insist that they work at a set pace, Kavanagh got to know them all individually in order to understand what would work for them.

For Henson, the priorities were clear: 'Sport for me was rehab first and success second.' Nevertheless, his approach changed in 2014 after the Invictus Games. Until then, he had competed only in the relative familiarity of military competition; Invictus was another military event, but it was out in the public eye where Henson had not been before. And he found he didn't mind it. He was also struck by what Dame Tanni Grey-Thompson said in her TV commentary: that if he really applied himself he could make it to Rio. After thinking hard about it, he thought: OK, then, I'll take you up on that.

As far as was possible, he then tried to fast-track his development. He entered any race he could, not just disability races. He had to learn fast too. For his first race in 2015, he forgot his shorts and had to run in pants. ('Crazy. I'd been training every day, day in day out, and I'd never forgotten my shorts, but add in the stresses of a race environment and suddenly I was forgetting stuff.') For the World Championships in Doha in 2015, his biggest event to date by quite some distance, he was thrown by the 'call-room' experience – when athletes are called to an air-conditioned room to wait for their race. ('I hadn't eaten enough and I was cold. Coming out and trying to perform on the track, I just couldn't do it.') The business of mastering his event, the 200 metres, was another challenge altogether. Running in blades is a real skill, running the bend even more so. If you hit the bend too hard and too fast, you lose control, you can easily lose your balance and fall. The skill is finding the edge where your pace can be pushed to the limit without going over it.

Henson also experienced the philosophical challenges of the transition from the military and being a team player to elite competition and being obliged to be selfish. He would be asked to make appearances at charity events, give talks at schools, etc., and he would say yes to everything, persuading himself that he could fit in his training around it all. 'It took me a year and a half to get into the mindset where I'd say, "Sorry, no, I am training." It felt like I was being selfish and not putting other people's needs first.'

It was when he got to the European Championships in Grosseto, Italy, in June 2016, that he recognised how much he had reassessed: 'I realised how far I had come psychologically, how much I had developed as a person, healed and redefined myself. Suddenly I was a GB athlete, I was part of the team; I wasn't a wounded soldier any more. I had redefined myself.'

Three months later, he was in the Rio athletics stadium, lane seven, preparing himself for the start of the Paralympics 200m final, class T42. Though he had reached the final, he was still relatively inexperienced; the final was only the thirty-sixth race he had ever run. He was wary, too, of what had happened in the semi-final: he had hit the bend too fast and started to lose control. 'I had to take that into the final, thinking: how are you going to be different to get the result you deserve?' That was a mental challenge in itself: there were two other athletes in the final, Richard Whitehead, the experienced, much-garlanded Briton, and Ntando Mahlangu, from South Africa, both of whom had consistently run better times than him. Should he chase them? How hard should he go out to catch them, given the danger of losing control in the process?

'You want to be right on the edge,' he recalls. He also acknowledges that when the gun went and he hit the bend, he wasn't anywhere near close enough to finding that edge. 'Rather than running too fast,' he says, 'I actually ran in the safety zone.' As a result, he came into the straight further back than he should have been; of the field of eight runners, he was eighth. He had a lot of work to do. 'I turned on the gas,' is how he described what happened next. Only when he straightens up does Henson really hit his speed, and here it started to take him through the field. Gold and silver were the unchallenged rewards for Whitehead and Mahlangu. Henson went through the back of the field but struggled to catch Shaquille Vance, the American. Only in the last five metres did he nudge ahead of him. He had the bronze.

Of the Front Line to Start Line cohort, Henson's was one of a number of successes. Seven were selected for Rio, six of them representing GB, one representing Ireland. Of the seven, two won gold medals, Henson's was one of two bronzes, while two finished sixth and only one failed to reach his final. As a programme, Front Line to Start Line had exceeded hopes and the targets it had been set.

It may have redefined Henson but it still didn't completely change him. With her understanding of military talent and military minds, Kavanagh knows that as well as anyone. After bronze in Rio, is Henson hooked on the sport? Is he tunnel-vision focused on one thing, on going all the way to the top of the podium, eyes dead set on gold four years later at the Tokyo Olympics? No. He isn't at all. After Rio, he said, he knew he might target Tokyo; it was certainly a tempting option. But it wasn't what his life was all about.

'I am doing some quite important research in London as part of my PhD,' he explained. 'I think it is important for me to contribute to society by being the best I can in my biomechanics research.' The PhD, specifically, is on amputee biomechanics, understanding the amputee's body and using that knowledge to create better therapeutic interventions, better prosthetics, better implants, better surgical procedures or rehab programmes.

In other words, taking on the 'me first' attitude of an elite athlete still sat awkwardly with him. Winning medals is a secondary goal. The better we understand that, the better equipped we are to help deliver it.

Chapter learnings by Chelsea Warr

Creating a talent pathway for injured ex-servicemen and women should, in theory, be fairly straightforward. These are men and women who are highly trained, trainable and disciplined – surely sport would be their saviour after a career-ending injury? Dave Henson and Frontline to Startline were a success because certain people had the wisdom and humility to recognise that actually it wasn't straightforward, that they needed to stop and start again after London 2012.

Troubled transition. Transition for people who have lived the dream and had it cruelly snatched away is probably the hardest journey of all. The programme of transition has to be tailored exactly for them, no one size fits all. The key learning here, for anyone, not just for military, is understanding people's motivation for success. Once that is established, success can be better pursued.

Individualism. The military teaches above all else that team work is essential, you never ever leave anyone behind. You never question, you comply. To succeed in high-performance sport you leave everyone be-hind, you do what you have to beat the opposition and you question and challenge. Breaking this ingrained value set is key.

Selfish for success. Sometimes we have to give ourselves permission to be selfish if it means we can give ourselves the best chance of achieving our dreams. This can be hard but has to be understood.

Performance

14

How to deliver on the day

JESSICA ENNIS-HILL

At your home Olympic Games, the enormity of the event, the distractions and the pressure can derail anyone. Before London 2012, for instance, Jessica Ennis-Hill could have been distracted by the fact that her image had been painted onto a field near Heathrow to greet foreign Olympians coming in to land. 'Welcome to our turf' was the message writ large next to the image that was so big that it covered the equivalent of 15 tennis courts and required over 600 litres of paint. No pressure, Jess.

No one ever asked Ennis-Hill if she wanted to be the 'face of the Games'. It was not exactly an ambassadorial role that she applied for. She just found herself becoming public property. 'I am,' she writes in her autobiography, *Unbelievable*, 'just an ordinary girl from a run-of-the-mill street in Sheffield and yet I have been plucked out of that normality and plunged into this melting pot of hopes and dreams and fierce competition.' On 2 August 2012, the day before she would compete, she read a post on Twitter from a 20-year-old boy on the Olympic Village cleaning staff who had declared excitedly that he had just been in to clean Jessica Ennis-Hill's room. That is how public she had become.

That night, she looked out from the balcony of her room to the stadium, all lit up, as if it was within touching distance. The building of the stadium had been completed 15 months earlier but, in that time, she had refused to go there. Sponsors wanted to take shots of her in the stadium, but she said no. Many other athletes had gone simply because they wanted to see the place and get a feel for it, but she stayed away. She wanted her maiden experience to be of an Olympic Stadium that was packed and buzzing; she wanted to walk in the next morning and be hit with as much of an adrenaline shot as was possible. This was just another part of the plan to answer the question: if you are the face of the Games, if it is you above everyone else that has been plucked out of normality and has the eyes of the Olympic world upon you, then can you deliver?

This is a chapter about delivering, about how to get it right, and it is framed around Ennis-Hill because there are not many Olympians who do this better. To win a medal, you have to get it right. To win a heptathlon medal, you have to get it near enough right seven times in a row. Ennis-Hill had become so good at getting it right that, in the four-year build-up, she won a medal in every major multi-event competition she entered. For two years of that, she only ever finished first. In all that time, she never finished below second.

That night, the eve of her London Olympic campaign, the last thoughts she allowed through her mind were the hurdles, the first event she would face the next morning. Visualisation of this kind is commonly used by sportspeople. She tried to picture herself hurdling with a perfect technique. As she put it, in *Unbelievable*, 'My mind wandered and I fell, so I tried again. When I cleared all the obstacles a few times, I drifted off to sleep.' The next morning, in the hurdles, she broke the British record. That was a pretty good demonstration of delivering. Indeed, her whole seven-event gold-medal performance was a masterclass.

Nearly four years later, 21 weeks before the Rio Games, I am in exclusive company in the confidential Olympic planning room in UK Sport's offices in Loughborough: this is the war-room, the room containing the famous Medal Tracker Board.

The board contains exactly 200 names or teams, split into their different sports. These are the 200 possible Rio medallists. There are 31 for athletics, for instance, six for shooting, 19 for swimming, etc. The predicted medal range is between 44 and 71. The top figure is up by three from the previous quarterly medal tracker meeting because another cycling event has been upgraded to medium confidence, as have Bryony Shaw, the windsurfer, and James Davis, the fencer, both of whom have had good recent results. Some 60–100 people – coaches, performance directors, sports scientists – have fed in their information to give the most accurate possible picture of the current health of the GB team; the amount of information on this board is extraordinary. Other medal predictor models have been less generous than the 44–71 prediction given here. Infostrada Sports, the Dutch sports stats company, arguably the most respected business of its kind in the world, has just put out its six-months-to-go predictions and has GB on 49 medals. That is a low-end forecast, but the information in this room makes for an infinitely more accurate glimpse of what will play out in Rio.

Next to each name, beside their medal confidence status, are a number of other categories: the number of medal opportunities for that athlete, whether they have actually qualified yet, their performance trajectory, the probability of injury/illness, any other risks, a summary, and then supporting actions. Fifteen names on the board have an asterisk next to them. This indicates they have missed one out-of-competition drugs test. There is one athlete with two asterisks by her name. This is Lizzie Armitstead, the cyclist. We discuss Armitstead and how she can be managed in order to prevent her missing another. A third missed test and she would be suspended from the sport. Action has therefore been taken, we are informed: a performance manager in cycling has been specifically detailed to help her. Everyone understands how galling an own goal it would be if she did miss another. As Chelsea Warr, the chair of the meeting, says: 'That would be really tragic.'

There are four others in this meeting. Two more from UK Sport, one from the British Olympic Association and one from the English Institute of Sport. Over a whole day, the meeting will go through each name and each sport individually. We discuss some broader topics: 'What should the final week before the Games look like to get a team to over-deliver?' And 'Whose heads are going to go? Whose are going to be right?'

We drill down into the minute detail too. We discuss a rowing coach with a sick parent; is this a concern? There is a cycling coach whose wife will give birth close to the Games, so he might travel out late; is that a concern? The gymnasts at Lilleshall need a refurbished landing pit; that is an urgent priority. When do the women's K4 canoeists get their new boat? And what is the latest on the health risks for the sailors in Rio? Is that not a problem? Apparently not, was the answer: because the GB team are so well prepared, 'we should be better equipped than others to cope'. There is a real feeling here that, because of the expertise of those delivering the GB team to the Games, the worse the conditions in Rio, the better it is for GB.

Yet there is a bigger conversation that dominates the entire proceedings. Winning medals is primarily about the athletes, but from 20 weeks out, the focus in here is not so much 'How can we help the athletes?' but 'How can we help their leaders?' 'Enabling the enablers' is the precise term used in the room. This close to the Games, most of the athletes' work – the training, the hours, the toil – will already be done; but when it comes to delivering a performance, the influence of their team leaders is regarded as a crucial make-or-break element.

So Warr puts the question to the floor: 'How can we create an environment that empowers and frees those in the driving seat to do what they need to do?'

One answer, which is what we are doing here, is to identify which leaders can be left alone, which might need close monitoring, and which will probably need assistance. As an entire group, the support staff for the team are inexperienced; of the 312 coaches, physios, medics and sports scientists who will go to the Rio Olympics, 90 per cent have never worked at an away Games before.

When they are actually in Rio, these leaders will have to perform as never before. Take swimming, for instance: Chris Spice, the team leader, will have 28 athletes to manage, plus 16 accredited support staff (coaches, medics, physios, sports scientists). That is like being the CEO of a small to medium-sized business, except most businesses are judged on their day-in, day-out performance; the success of this company hangs entirely on whether the 44 employees in Spice's company can perform to their optimum in this one tiny window in the four-year calendar when the pressure is greater than it has ever been before.

So, 21 weeks out, the Medal Tracker meeting is sifting the system, probing for weaknesses. It is trying to pre-empt problems, trying to help the team over-deliver. The accepted, achievable medal range is 49–71; this is all about pushing for as close to 71 as possible.

How can you prepare a leader to perform in the pressure cauldron of an Olympics? One answer was: teach the leaders to fly. This was called Project Icarus.

At a flight simulator in Heathrow, a number of team leaders were booked in for flying lessons. They would go in pairs. A pilot would give them an intensive short course in how to fly and then put them in their pairs into the pilot and co-pilot seats. They would take turns in each seat and they would have to land their (simulated) plane at a number of different simulated airports. The idea was to make the scenario as lifelike as possible. This wasn't a fun video game. It was a way of replicating extreme stress in an environment different to the one they were used to, and then to see how they operated under pressure. Sometimes the (simulated) flights were rigged to increase the stress levels, the plane would bank excessively left or right, for instance, and the pilot team would have to react clearly and precisely. The point was not to see who was good at flying, but who was good at pressure. More to the point, it was a way of holding up a mirror to each person so they could recognise what they looked like under pressure and how they could handle it better.

From when Spice was in the simulator, for instance, he saw how he could become gripped by frustration, he recognised exactly the kind of information he wanted from his co-pilot – short and concise – and he recognised that he was very visual in the way he operated and would tend to use his eyes to land the plane rather than trust what he was being told by his co-pilot. He therefore crashed the plane four times at Heathrow and JFK. That didn't ease his frustration. The stress levels were very effectively cranked up in the simulator, he said afterwards. The learning experience had been outstanding.

John Norfolk, the head coach of GB Paracycling, and Jon Pett, the programme manager, both recognised that they could benefit from this kind of training. They were the joint leaders in GB Paracycling together, but on the same level, and that can cause tension. They are also quite different personalities, which they recognised. 'I like to get my head down and concentrate on the detail,' Norfolk explained, 'but I might get short and snappy. And John likes to solve everyone else's problems as well as his own. We sort of knew all that but it was good to have it confirmed.' When Pett was piloting, for instance, he was also trying to read the dials and do Norfolk's co-pilot job at the same time. It was helpful for them both to see that.

And did it work? 'As soon as we were under pressure in Rio, we shared a little smile at each other, recognising that we knew what happens here, we've been here before. We knew how we needed to work.'

How do you perform? How do you over-deliver? An answer of a kind was provided a decade ago by the Michigan Health and Hospital Association. Michigan hospitals were inspired by Peter Provonost, a critical care specialist at the Johns Hopkins Hospital in Maryland, who decided to simplify process by giving his doctors and nurses a checklist. He started on just one single problem, common to all hospitals: central line infections. He created a specific checklist itemising every tedious step as to how central lines should be applied and managed; he then demanded that his doctors follow the list step by step, and he empowered his nurses to intervene if the doctors missed a step. Big yawns all round; everyone knew how to apply a central line. Yet Provonost insisted. And his belligerence was vindicated, because the infection rate plummeted. The results were then monitored over 15 months, and this showed, when compared to the hospital's normal pre-checklist infection rate, that 43 infections had been avoided and eight deaths saved, along with $2million in costs.

All this is brilliantly documented by Atul Gawande, a surgeon and author, in his book *The Checklist Manifesto*, which is subtitled, appropriately, 'How to get things right'. Gawande follows the story from Maryland to Michigan, where Provonost's success had been noted. Michigan hospitals were understaffed and under-funded, and here too there was a feeling that doctors and nurses were stretched enough anyway without having to complete a checklist for every central line. Nevertheless, the decree went out that this would be the new system for central lines throughout all Michigan hospital Intensive Care Units (ICUs). The results, again, were astonishing and were trumpeted in an article in the December 2006 edition of the *New England Journal of Medicine*: infections from central lines in Michigan hospitals went down by 66 per cent in three months. On a longer-term basis, Michigan ICUs outperformed 90 per cent of the ICUs in the county and, over 18 months, more than 1,500 lives were saved along with $175million in costs.

Gawande finds his Checklist Manifesto holds true for investment banking, for jetplane pilots, for the construction of skyscrapers. When Chelsea Warr read it, she was convinced that it applied to Olympic preparation as well. There was already a programme underway, by the name of 'Rio Ready'. That had a checklist too.

The British Olympic Association (BOA), for example, made its first reconnaissance trip to Brazil in 2010. It sourced a training camp in Belo Horizonte where the facilities caused so much envy that the Brazilian media were asking: how come they got it and not us? That was the first tick on the list.

Another crucial one was the hotel it booked near the Rio seafront. David Tanner, the rowing team leader, had a very specific rule of thumb: 'bed to boat', as he puts it, has to be under 45 minutes; anything more than that requires a long and sometimes stressful bus journey with athletes never completely knowing that they will arrive on time. In Rio, the journey from the athletes' accommodation in the Olympic Village to the rowing lake was billed as 48 minutes but was invariably longer – so, by Tanner's formula, not good enough. Yet it wasn't just the rowers for whom this was important. Going by the medal count in London, 24 per cent of GB's medals would come from the cluster of events held at or near the Copacabana seafront: not just rowing, but sailing, triathlon and flatwater canoeing. So when the BOA managed to book out the Ipanema Inn, one block from the beach and, more crucially, eight minutes from the rowing lake, it was tactically a triumph. It wasn't exactly posh; outside of Olympics, a room in the Ipanema Inn costs £110 a night. Yet it clearly had potential as a performance gain. Another tick.

In the lead-up to the games, every sport worked on its own Rio Ready checklist. The canoe slalom leaders, for instance, decided that their best chance of delivering was by spending as much time as possible on the Rio Olympic whitewater course. They therefore took a radical decision: to select their Olympic team in autumn 2015, straight after the 2015 World Championships, a full ten months before the Olympics. All their competitors did the opposite; they picked their teams in the weeks and months immediately prior to the Games – which gave them the benefit of picking on form. The GB team were picked early, instead, so that they could be a tight number and therefore maximise their budget for flying to Rio and training there. In the six months before the Olympics, they were in Rio six times for training camps on the Olympic course and, therefore, when they got there for the Games themselves, they knew the water as well as anyone. Another tick.

And how to best manage the swimmers? The Olympic swimming programme was held late at night, often right up to midnight, which meant the swimmers would be getting back to the Olympic Village late. They therefore needed to sleep in late, which, in the Village, is easier said than done. The solution: in the GB accommodation block, they were billeted at the top of the block (so they wouldn't be disturbed by the sound of the lift in the morning), on the west side (so they wouldn't get the morning sun) and had black-out blinds brought over for them from the UK (just to make sure). Another tick.

Arguably, no part of the preparation was executed with quite the mastery of the team's arrival at the Village. First in was Mark England, the team's chef de mission, on 18 July, six days before the first of the athletes, the canoe slalom team, which was 13 days before competition started. When England arrived at the GB accommodation block, he stress-tested the entire building, turned on every single tap and every single light and, before long, had identified a list of 118 problems, 70 of them relating to plumbing. Clearly, the place was not fit for purpose. So England and his BOA staff went to work to get it right. The shortcomings were not exactly unexpected, and he had brought with him a team of five electricians and plumbers (tick); he also had access to a small army of plumbers and electricians provided by the Rio 2016 organisers, but they were being dragged from pillar to post because absolutely every new arrival needed them. So he contacted the British Consulate and drummed up as many maintenance workers as they could find too (tick). By the time the canoeists arrived, the GB block wasn't yet completely fit for purpose, but there were enough rooms that were. As the work continued, the Australians made jarring press statements; they said the accommodation was sub-standard (it's not good to criticise the organising committee – a cross), and that they would have to spend a few days in nearby hotels instead (athletes do not like moving around – another cross). Conversely, the GB team were ready, and then even helped other nations with their problems (tick, tick).

On Day Seven in Rio, Fran Halsall was queuing at the bus stop at the Olympic Village for her ten-minute bus ride to the pool for her 50m freestyle semi-final. There were two buses; she couldn't get on the first so she got on the second, which left ten minutes later. When that second bus set off, however, it got on the motorway and headed, instead, to the athletics stadium, which was 50 minutes away from the pool. This was a driver error, not Halsall's. She was on the right bus with the wrong driver. Two other girls in her semi-final were on the same bus. They tried to explain to the bus driver that he needed to turn round, but they didn't know any Portuguese and couldn't make themselves understood.

Here, immediately, was a test of Spice's crisis management skills. He had to find a Portuguese interpreter to speak to the driver and a transport manager to get him to turn round. He also had to locate the Olympic swimming programme manager to postpone the race because the girls would be late and wouldn't have their usual pre-race warm-up time. This wasn't popular with the team leaders of the girls in the other five lanes: they had already begun their warm-up preparation and, if they had to warm down and then warm up again, this would be detrimental to them too. He therefore had to work with the other two nations who had girls missing to lobby with him (the Danes were particularly helpful), and he used one of the team's communications officers to try to persuade NBC, the hugely influential American broadcasters, that they wouldn't want to be showing a race with three empty lanes – so could they lobby for a postponement too? None of this was easy, because the evening's swimming had already started. Spice therefore also had to manage Halsall's coach, James Gibson, who had another swimmer, Ben Proud, in action in another final that evening and needed to be focusing on him, rather than be distracted worrying about Halsall. Most importantly, he had to manage Halsall, who was sitting on the bus, wondering if her Olympics was over; so he directed another swimmer who was in the stands and not competing that night, her friend Aimee Willmott, to be Halsall's point of contact, to be receiving her calls and sending regular texts to reassure her that all would be OK.

The situation was eventually resolved with an interpreter using Willmott's phone to call Halsall, and Halsall then putting her phone to the ear of the bus driver, who was finally persuaded to turn round and head to the pool. In all, 11 staff (and Willmott and a transport manager) were involved in the operation. The bus did eventually arrive, the race was postponed by 30 minutes, Halsall got 30 per cent of her usual warm-up – and she then won the race.

Question to Spice: was the Heathrow flight simulator responsible? 'I can't say for sure, but it certainly helped.'

'Ultimately, you can't turn a lamb into a lion.' This is the gospel according to Tony Minichiello, Jessica Ennis-Hill's coach. 'If they haven't quite got that last little bit then I'm not sure there's a huge amount you can do.' That last little bit is 'what Jess has always been: uber-competitive'. Maybe, Minichiello wonders out aloud, that comes from her mother. 'If Jess could throw a ball 10 metres, her mum could throw it 11. Her mum is very competitive, not in a nasty way, but if they played Monopoly as kids, her mum played to win.' Besides instinctive competitiveness, there is another aspect to Jess's temperament, Minichiello says, that was ideal for a multi-event competition: 'She's able to let things wash over her and move on. So if she has a bad event, bad high jump, for instance, she'll go, "OK, I'm really pissed off, that's shit, I'm really hacked off about that. But now I've got the next event, the shot, what do I need to do here?"' He says he's never known anyone as good at that as she is.

Yet Minichiello couldn't just wind her up and send her out to perform; there was a series of processes and checklists required to help her deliver. Not visiting the London Olympic Stadium before the London Olympics was not, for instance, a quirky superstition; it was because, while a lot of people tend to shrink away when there are big crowds, for Ennis-Hill, it was a case of the bigger the crowd the better, so they wanted the full Olympic crowd to smack her in the face.

Part of all this is knowing the athlete, recognising their behaviour and adjusting accordingly. Ennis-Hill, for instance, would go through what Minichiello came to call her 'bubble wrap period' before competition, two or three weeks before competition, when her anxiety arose and she didn't want to train for fear of getting hurt. While she wanted to be bubble-wrapped, Minichiello needed her to go through a proper taper. The solution? 'You negotiate your way out of it,' he says. He would therefore write her long training sessions knowing that she would see them and go 'No way!' and that they'd then reach a compromise where she would do about two-thirds of them; that way he was happy with the taper and she felt happily bubble-wrapped.

Part of it is having competition day immaculately prepared. There are always time lags between morning and afternoon sessions for the heptathletes, but in Rio these were eight hours long. That is a long time to kill, but they did the maths: you can go back to the Olympic Village to eat, but that requires 50 minutes sitting upright in a bus before you go through security when you get there, before you have to walk to the food hall and then to your apartment block before you can settle for a sleep. By the time you've got the bus back, and got through all the security checks again, you might have spent three hours travelling and moving around. Alternatively, you can stay in the athletes' room at the Olympic Stadium, find a mattress in a quiet corner, pull out the blanket and pillow you have brought with you and be resting within 20 minutes. That is what she did.

And part of it is consistently putting the relevant information before her. Minichiello keeps spreadsheets of all her performances and split times in training in the weeks before a major event. Looking through the spreadsheets, she is reassured of how good she is in training, her anxiety fades and a confidence grows that she can be that good in competition too.

When it comes down to the very process of performing, Minichiello and Ennis-Hill use checklists too. As Minichiello puts it, the seven events in a heptathlon are seven sets of movement patterns. 'In the heat of battle,' he says, 'once the gun goes off, it's all about: can I control myself? Have I got the movement pattern? For example, if you try too hard you can create tension and over-stride or under-stride.' Delivering is all about controlling those movement patterns in spite of the stress of the Olympic occasion, so rather than have Ennis-Hill focus and worry about putting out a good long jump, for instance, he will have her go through the checklist. 'You can hold certain amounts of information in your head,' he says. 'Some people can manage seven things, but I try and boil it into three things because then it's easy.'

The checklist has to be worked out with the athlete so the language makes perfect sense. With Ennis-Hill's long jump, for instance, the checklist starts with 'Don't let the shin escape'. Minichiello explains: 'Imagine the thigh parallel to the ground and the shin then vertical below the knee. Letting the shin escape means that it goes too far in front, therefore you start to over-stride.' Point Two on the checklist is 'Control your chin' – because 'in the last three strides she tends to lift her head, and when she does that, she drops her knees, she's not running all the way to the board, she starts leaning back at the board.' Point Three, when she is in the air, is 'Squeeze', which means 'just holding her body upright and long. Squeeze and hold the position in the air.'

The long jump is the fifth of the seven heptathlon events, with the javelin and the 800 metres to follow. By the time Ennis-Hill had completed the long jump in London, she was well on the way to gold. By the time it was done in Rio, she was in second place and struggling to reel in Nafissatou Thiam of Belgium, who was leading. This was one she would be scrapping for right to the end.

***

You can only plan to deliver and sometimes the plan just doesn't work. For all the help put in around Lizzie Armitstead, she would still go on to miss a third out-of-competition drugs test. After launching an appeal and successfully challenging one of these tests, she managed to get the three missed tests reduced to two and she therefore avoided a suspension and was allowed to compete in Rio. The glare of public attention was so strong, however, that she never got close to the podium and could not get out of Rio fast enough.

Sometimes the plan works rather better. Those slalom canoeists had four boats in Rio and won two medals from the four: a gold and a silver.

As for Ennis-Hill, she never quite caught Thiam. So she failed to become the second woman ever to win successive heptathlon golds; she became, instead, the first to get Olympic heptathlon gold and silver. Perfection may have eluded her but delivering a performance did not. Seven weeks after Rio, she would announce her retirement. In seven years, she had competed in five world or Olympic heptathlons and she had won gold or silver in every one.

Chapter learnings by Simon Timson

Good corporate governance demands that senior executives and directors establish and regularly review a risk register. The goal of corporate risk management is to increase the likelihood of success by reducing the impact of uncertainty on performance. Deficits in information, knowledge or understanding in relation to performance strategy generate uncertainties. The aim is to detect threats to the company's success, plan mitigating actions and deploy them to facilitate performance and make the organisation resilient. Successful sports teams, athletes and coaches like British Sailing, Jessica Ennis-Hill and Toni Minichiello understand this is also the key to being resilient and performing under intense pressure in the Olympic cauldron. This chapter highlighted two key principles that enable people to be mentally tough:

Early threat detection and 'what if' planning. Systematically ask yourselves what could go wrong on the day? What pressures will we face? Then plan methods to manage the threats and ways to cope with your physical and mental responses when things go wrong.

Build belief through enactive mastery. Simulating the performance environment in order to practise coping is the most effective way to build confidence and promote resilience. If someone has been able to do a job successfully in the past, then he or she will be more confident to be able to do it in the future.

The art of resilience

KATHERINE GRAINGER, GILES SCOTT, CHRIS HOY,
MEN'S RUGBY SEVENS

On the morning of Tuesday 26 July, three days before the rowers were due to fly to Brazil, Steve Redgrave, rowing's famous five-time gold-medallist, gave an inspirational address to the team at their training base in Caversham.

The address was intended to raise the hairs on the back of necks. 'I had a great time competing,' was how it began, 'and now it's *your* time. *Your* Games ... You are world champion for one year, you are an Olympic champion for life. Dream big. Take that chance, make it happen. Your time, your place, your Olympics. Take the success that you deserve.'

As a spirit raiser, Redgrave's pep talk did the job for most. For Katherine Grainger it did not. In his speech, Redgrave went through all the boats that would compete in Rio, one by one, extolling their virtues and explaining why each had a chance of a medal. When he came to Grainger's boat, though, he explained that, because of the tricky year they had been through, of all of the boats going to Rio, it would be the biggest surprise if this one was to win a medal. At least that was how Grainger interpreted it. Redgrave was a man she admired hugely and he had always been supportive, so to hear this, she explained, was 'initially, obviously, very upsetting. Hearing someone you respect talk about your boat like that makes you realise how rock bottom you are.' So she went up to speak to him afterwards and, even then, given the opportunity to lighten the message, he elected to stick with it. 'He said: "Well, you wouldn't bet your house on a result, would you?"'

Thank you, Sir Steve.

Grainger was rowing royalty, but she didn't seem very regal at the time. She was a four-time Olympic medallist and the reigning Olympic champion in the women's double sculls: the most decorated British female rower of all time. She had quit after the London Olympics and made a comeback two years later, yet never in those two years on the comeback trail had it looked a smart decision. She was back in the same boat, but never had she and her new sculling partner, Vicky Thornley, produced convincing podium results. Thornley, remember, was one of Paul Stannard's Talent ID finds – the one who kept falling out of her boat (see Chapter 3). Here she was now, on the eve of Rio, one of the most accomplished oarswomen in the Olympic team, yet the partnership wasn't quite working. It still looked as though Grainger should have kept her account closed after London.

Grainger took on board Redgrave's opinion and, actually, she knew it was the opinion of many. She knew what others were thinking and the media were saying. Some just wanted her to be able to get in and out of Rio and through the experience without any kind of humiliation. Yet Redgrave's comment, so loud and clear, was, as she called it, 'a slap in the face of reality' and maybe a good one at that. 'Yes, we all have dreams of the Olympic Games but actually the reality is sobering,' she would explain some time later. 'I needed to accept that but still have the fight in me to think: that is the truth and that is where we are, yet there is enough there that we can bring something out of this.'

This chapter is about Grainger and Thornley and how they proved Redgrave wrong. It is about resilience, their resilience and the resilience of others. It is about that key ingredient. You don't have it? Then you don't compete – not in many walks of life, certainly not in the Olympics.

And it comes in many ways. You need resilience to get to the top, and you need it to stay there. And you may be one of the best in the world, but that doesn't earn you a place on the podium either; to deliver on the day of the Olympic final, the biggest day of your life – you need another kind of resilience for that too.

While Grainger and Thornley were scrapping their way through the early rounds in Rio, Michael Phelps was doing the same thing but six times over. Six events, six medals, five of them gold. There has maybe never been a more resilient Olympian ever. To do it over four consecutive Olympics, 28 medals, 23 of them gold – that is resilient.

There are some who would assume that resilience is innate. Yet, as we saw earlier, in Chapter 5, 'What the super-elite look like', resilience is built largely on life experiences – and life experiences can be contrived. Bob Bowman, Phelps's coach, had an understanding of this and, from Phelps's early years, he sought to engineer it. For instance, when Phelps was competing at a World Cup pre-Christmas meeting in Melbourne in 2003, Bowman deliberately trod on his swimming goggles. Phelps found the broken goggles. 'Hey, someone's stepped on my goggles,' he complained. 'Oh well,' Bowman replied, 'you're just going to have to go without them.' Likewise once, when Phelps was 14, when he was competing in a meet where competition took place late in the evening, Bowman had a word in their driver's ear before departure. 'Can you ensure we arrive back at our hotel ten minutes late?' It meant that Phelps missed dinner. That way, Bowman would explain, the kid just had to deal with it. He had to learn to be resilient.

Many nations use different triggers to encourage athletes to perform, of which money is the most common. For its home winter Olympics, in Sochi in 2014, the Russians handed out nearly $US6million in total to its 68 medal-winners. The €113,200 cash prize that was the windfall for Russian gold-medallists, however, was nowhere what Kazakhstan was offering: €250,000 for a gold medal. There were no Kazakhs who won gold, though, so the highest bonus-earners from those Sochi Games were the three biathletes and two skiers form Belarus who pocketed €150,000 each for their gold medals.

Most leading nations give medal bonuses. At those same Sochi Games, France offered €67,800 per gold, the United States offered €25,000, Canada €17,900 and Australia €13,000. Great Britain made no medal bonus payments at all and never has done. Norway do not pay medal bonuses either. Joergen Graabak, the double gold-medallist in Nordic Combined, would have made half a million euros from Sochi if he had been Kazakh, but he is Norwegian, and when asked about this he replied: 'I'm not really envious of the other nations. If money is the great motivator, you have already lost. You can earn much easier money with other things than by winning Olympic gold.'

Does the incentive of money drive success? No doubt, there are cultural differences here. When eastern European coaches work in the UK, they find it extraordinary that their athletes are expected to be motivated to win without a cash prize on offer. Conversely, most surveys of the bonus culture in western society businesses suggest that bonuses do not incentivise performance. Why do City firms pay those infamous annual bonuses? Because everyone else does and you need to in order to retain your best employees, not so those employees will work harder. In 2003, a survey of more than 200 senior executives in more than 30 countries, by Harvard professors Michael Beer and Nancy Katz, showed that bonuses had little or no effect on company performance.

Why are there no medal bonuses paid to successful Olympians in the UK? Not because British athletes are, in any way, less materially driven. Lord, no. But because there is no proof that the stimulus of financial rewards would bring in any more medals. Were Grainger and Thornley more likely to upset the odds in Rio if there was a pot of money waiting for them on the podium? No chance. If you have money, spend it on winning medals, not rewarding them.

Before the Rio Olympics, one group of players who were widely written off as no-hopers were the GB men's rugby sevens team. 'Odds stacked against Britain's men' was the boldly negative headline in *The Times*, along with the commentary: 'No one could possibly suggest that this would be the right way to plan an Olympic campaign.' No, of course they couldn't.

Most sevens teams going to the Olympics had been training and competing as a group all year. The GB team did it another way altogether: they trained and played as a group for just 10 weeks. For most of the year, there was only opportunity for them to play as separate entities – England, Wales and Scotland – and it was only in May that they were able to come properly together. In that short space of time, they had to re-educate players who had come in from the 15-a-side game to play the 7-a-side version, they had to find and hone a gameplan for the Games, and then they had to whittle their squad down from the initial 27 to the group of 12 who would be selected to go to Rio to play it. That is not a 10-week task. Realistically, there was no way they should have been contending for the medals, yet this squad had something powerful in their tool kit – a mental toughness that gave them an edge and helped them create conditions for success.

Before they left for Rio, they did one group session with head coach Simon Amor and Katie Warriner, the sports psychologist working with the team, at which some cut-out headlines from negative newspaper stories were handed around for discussion. The question was then put to the players: what do you think? What do you think are the reasons you shouldn't win a medal in Rio? The conversation started, appropriately, with the acknowledgement that the 10-week plan was hardly ideal, but then it began to turn as the players rejected the reasons against them and instead started to promote those in their favour. This is how it went: because of the circumstances, the pressure to perform was not from the outside, the pressure to perform came from within, and if it was coming from within, then they could do something about it. Warriner then educated them about how the brain works under pressure and together they agreed on ways to help each other to keep everything in perspective.

Warriner explains: 'The 27-man squad and the management came together to define what they considered to be their "gold-medal attitude". They focused on what they could control, on making the most of each opportunity and staying calm under pressure. It became a powerful source of resilience.'

One of the eternal truths about the Olympics is that it is not always outstanding performances that win medals; very often the medals are actually lost by those who wilt under the pressure and underperform and are claimed instead by those who can survive it. To this sevens team, resilience would be a powerful tool.

Can you actually train resilience and mental toughness? An answer to that question had already been provided by Warriner's boss, James Bell, the National Lead Psychologist for the England Rugby Football Union. The subject matter of Bell's PhD, that had been based on four years' work with the England and Wales Cricket Board (ECB), was: identifying the personality characteristics of mentally tough cricketers and developing a mental toughness development programme for the up-and-coming elite. From the ECB, he went to work as Director of Psychological Services for the Cleveland Browns in the NFL, and from there, he moved back home and into rugby. His philosophy throughout his journey remained the same: that the brain responds to reward and punishment very differently, and that if you want to help an athlete to be more resilient, though they may respond to rewards – like medal bonuses – they have to learn to deal with threat, or punishment conditioned stimuli too.

As he explains, 'If you want to perform at a very high level in a very pressurised environment, which is what an Olympic Games is, then our evidence suggests that you have to train in environments which are very challenging with lots of threat. You can be as creative as you want; the point is athletes need to experience what pressure feels like and that can be achieved through exposure to negative consequences. Political correctness says you shouldn't use the word punishment but, in psychological terms, that's how your brain processes it. This isn't to say we didn't do any reward, but the focus for me was around threat and punishment because that's more impactful and our evidence found that the characteristics of tough people were that they were often more sensitive to punishment conditioned stimuli and more capable of detecting threat early and therefore more able to deal with it.'

What sort of punishments? This is the sort of thing Bell did with cricket. You might have to collect the water bottles, for instance, for dropping a catch. You might have to do a set of press-ups. You might have to clean up after everyone (they called it 'waitress service'). One effective punishment, Bell found, was when someone drops a ball, the rest of the team had to suffer (do press-ups, for instance) for it; that really emphasised the concept of letting down your team-mates. The brain-training this way had to be managed; for starters, you do not make every training session high pressure and orientated around punishment. The idea is not to break anyone. The theory is that if they regularly train under pressure, in sessions when there is a genuine fear of failure, then they get used to surviving and performing in such an environment. They practise resilience.

With the sevens team, Warriner tapped into some of Bell's philosophies and principles. She did not have to engineer punishment-type consequences because there were some very natural ones that they faced every day: the 27 men were going to have to be reduced to 12, competition for places was tough, the players knew they were being assessed daily. The ultimate punishment was missing the cut. Yet success on the Olympic stage involves an intricate weave of the tapestry of the mind. Transforming a team against the clock requires transformational leadership – in this case from Amor. It was the inspirational delivery from Amor that combined with the players' passion and mental skills to produce a unit that would leave for Rio with real self-belief and a determination to shock the world.

Sure enough, when they got to Rio, there were some teams who had trained together, played together and won tournaments together all year, yet when it came to the Olympics, just could not perform together.

New Zealand were the worst offenders. They were second favourites, behind Fiji, but they lost first to the minnows, Japan, and then to a slightly bigger shoal of fish: Great Britain. Conversely, GB continued to defy belief and, crucially, holding their nerve against arguably better prepared and more talented teams, they found themselves in a quarter-final against Argentina.

Here was a great test of their resilience. Sevens is often a high-scoring game; this one was not. It was 0–0 at half-time and as the full-time whistle approached, still no one had scored. The slightest defensive error is generally punished in sevens; in this quarter-final, neither team would budge and the big test was yet to come: with full-time approaching, James Davies, the GB forward, was yellow-carded, and his team then had to hold out one man down. The final whistle heralded an extra period of sudden death and in their huddle before it commenced, they took stock of the facts and tried to turn the situation to their advantage. Here, the captain, Tom Mitchell, led the discussion; they talked about resilience, keep calm, trust ourselves, trust each other and play the clock until we get Davies back on. Here they faced the most intense pressure, a true Olympic test, yet they survived until Davies was back on, then they won a scrum, launched an attack down the right and scored the match-winning try.

They would go one win further in their semi-final against South Africa and then on to a date in the final with Fiij, where they were beaten. Yet that wasn't a gold medal lost – a medal of any sort was a resilient, unforeseen triumph.

Maybe the best example of learned resilience was Chris Hoy's first ever gold, in Athens in 2004. Yet to understand Hoy's gold, you have to go back another four years to Jason Queally's in Sydney.

Queally's and Hoy's gold medals were in the same event: the kilo. The kilo is four solo laps of the 250m Olympic velodrome, against the clock. It is the two-wheeled version of the 400m on the athletics track: an exercise in emptying your tank and then surviving the pain when you have nothing left. The mind games for the kilo start earlier, though. The riders are ranked and they ride in reverse order, the lowest-ranked riding first, the highest last. In theory, then, the times should improve gradually throughout the competition, which in turn means that the tension rises for the last of the riders, the favourites, as they endure the long wait to perform. During their wait, they watch their rivals; they see exactly how fast they need to be to beat them. As the pressure on the later riders builds, the drama can be excruciating.

In Sydney, Queally was the thirteenth rider of 16 and he posted a personal best to top the leaderboard. Two riders followed, Stefan Nimke of Germany and Shane Kelly of Australia, but they could not better his time. The last man to ride was Arnaud Tournant, the awesome Frenchman, the reigning world champion. The broad expectation was that Queally would now finally be eclipsed.

However, even before he got on his bicycle, Tournant had lost himself the gold. On seeing Queally's time, he went straight to the French team mechanic and asked him to change his gearing to a harder gear. In other words, after all those months of trialling, testing, training and preparation for these Games, during which everything he did was directed towards the one, single goal of going as fast as possible on this day, right now, here in the Sydney velodrome, somehow at the last minute he believed he had come up with another way of going faster. And he hadn't trialled it; he hadn't tested it.

And so his error played itself out. His first two laps of the track were sensational and gave him a serious lead, but the harder gearing inevitably started to tell and soon his legs struggled to sustain the power output required. On the third lap he slowed, on the fourth he struggled so badly he could almost have run round faster. He didn't even get among the medals. He had been emotionally hijacked.

You might have thought that Tournant's mistake would be a lesson to all. But if you did think that, you would have changed your mind three years later.

At the World Track Championships in Stuttgart in 2003, the very same scenario played itself out, only this time it was Hoy who was the defending world champion, the favourite, the last man to ride. With Hoy watching and waiting, Nimke, the local man, posted a time that was a sea-level world record – and Hoy's frazzled response was similar to Tournant's. In a rational frame of mind, he would have concluded the following: this is a fast track and it is warm in the velodrome; that is why Nimke went so fast. Instead, under the pressure of the moment, Hoy decided the smartest response was to change the gameplan he'd worked on for weeks and months. He did not go as far as Tournant, he did not have his gearing changed, yet what he did was to jettison his gameplan, and instead attack hard from the start of the race and, in his words, attempt to 'blow it to pieces'. That decision caused the same result. Like Tournant, Hoy started fast, couldn't sustain it and failed to get a medal.

Hoy, like Tournant, had been emotionally hijacked. There was now a year to go to Athens to ensure that it wouldn't happen again.

Yes, resilience is very much in the mind. So Hoy started working with Steve Peters, the team psychiatrist. In an interview in Richard Moore's book *Heroes, Villains and Velodromes*, Peters recalled that process. He describes Hoy as 'the ideal athlete to work with'. Peters wanted Hoy to learn to control the part of his brain that flooded his mind with emotional thoughts. Emotions are irrational. Peters trained Hoy to switch off that part of the brain and, instead, to engage the part that deals in logic. 'In a nutshell,' Peters explained, 'you've got to switch from using one part of your brain to another. You learn the skill of controlling that. That's what Chris did.'

On 20 August 2004, two hours before the Olympic final, Peters went through a last mental dress rehearsal with Hoy. And Hoy would need it. The final could not have presented him with a greater test of his new skills and mental disciplines. The final came down to a familiar group of five riders. Hoy would go last. He described himself as 'like a kitten trying to act like a lion'.

First of the five was Shane Kelly – who went into first place by posting an Olympic and sea-level world record. Next up was Stefan Nimke, who bettered Kelly's time. Theo Bos, the Dutchman, then failed to better Nimke's time. However, the last rider before Hoy was Arnaud Tournant, the mighty Frenchman looking to set straight what he had messed up four years earlier – and he did beat Nimke's time. So that was three world records in succession. Three rides to play with Hoy's mind.

This time, though, Hoy stuck to the plan. He figured: it's a fast track, we have perfect warm conditions, and I have trained for a world record too.

He had trained himself to be resilient. So he did get his world record. He did win his gold.

If Giles Scott hadn't been resilient, he would have been nowhere near Rio. He would have walked away years earlier. For a number of years, he had been established as one of the best sailors in the Finn class of boats in the world. His problem was that the Finn was the boat sailed by Ben Ainslie, who was *the* best Olympic sailor in the world. In 2008, Scott was the young up-and-comer and he went to the Beijing Olympic Games as a training partner for Ainslie, to help him prepare. With that experience behind him, he was determined to knock him off top spot for London 2012; he won bronze in the World Championships in 2010, gold in the Worlds in 2011, so by 2012 he was absolutely ready to dominate Olympic competition. But Ainslie beat him in the trials and was selected ahead of him again.

At that point, you would seriously consider walking away, wouldn't you? The thought never crossed Scott's mind. It was only after eight years of trying that he finally got to compete in an Olympic Games.

His own story of learned resilience is fascinating. In that Ainslie generation, there was a triumvirate of great mates: Ainslie, Iain Percy and the late, much-loved Andrew Simpson. Percy and Simpson would win gold together in Beijing, in the two-man Star class boat. At the Athens Games four years earlier, though, it was Simpson who had played the

Scott role: he had lost the Finn trials to Ainslie and then gone out to the Games as Ainslie's training partner. So he understood what Scott was going through, and in Beijing he and Percy were full of advice for him; they told him not to accept second-best to Ainslie, to compete with him, to go hard. Scott recalls: 'They were effectively telling me to man up and take Ben on more. They were amusing conversations but quite odd really, because the three of them were very good friends but they also wanted each other to be pushed as hard as possible. I went away and thought about it: yes, actually they're not wrong.'

In 2008, Scott was thus obliged to toughen up against Ainslie. In 2012, he fulfilled the cliché of learning the hard way: his punishment stimulus – like the players in the GB sevens squad – was to miss selection. He says he learned ruthlessness from Ainslie too. 'There was really no better person to learn from. Without him, I think my resilience wouldn't be as good, my approach to training, competing, campaigning wouldn't be as professional. My sailing skill-set wouldn't have been developed as well. I mean it.'

After 2012, Ainslie retired from the Finn class and Scott was more than ready to take over. He won gold in the World Championships in 2014, 2015 and again in 2016. When they got to Rio, nothing was going to stop him winning gold there too.

Grainger and Thornley's Rio Olympic build-up was so average that, at one point, it completely derailed. After a poor winter, in the spring of 2016 they stopped training as a double and tried instead to break into the women's eight. That didn't work too well either so, with 50 days to go, they reunited in the double scull. Last chance saloon and all that. No, not ideal. Like the men's sevens, this was not the textbook way to prepare.

Grainger: 'It's very uncomfortable because, at the time, you think: fairy tales don't always happen. We both had those thoughts in our heads. How do you come into an event when everybody, even the experts, were saying "This is not possible"? The hardest thing is figuring out how you can come into the Olympics confident even when there's not much evidence to be confident with.'

What was her answer? Ignore the bigger picture, ignore the goal that, from 50 days off, could, if you allowed it, be so intimidating. 'I broke it down and took it in lots of little steps. We had exactly 50 days until the Olympic final, that's 50 little sections. What makes it easier is that that narrows the focus so sharply. There's no time for worrying about anything extra. Vicky and I would have little conversations, practically, about what we could do to make a difference, where we could grow the confidence. As long as there was something we could find every day that was moving in the right direction, it was going OK. Of all the crews out there, we knew we could develop the most.'

Grainger also had a shrill voice of confidence talking to her from within. She'd been in four Olympics and won four medals; she knew that showed a certain mental toughness. 'I trusted that to date I've delivered when it's come to the Games. I do think it brings out the best in me. I don't think every athlete is comfortable in that environment but the athletes who are will generally perform when they need to.'

With that self-belief and the 50-day plan, she and Thornley started to get stronger. In their heat in Rio, they set out confidently, but were reeled in by Lithuania to finish second – that was OK, only OK. The semi-final was better, they finished second to Poland by just under two seconds, but here was an example of the Olympics punishing underperformance rather than rewarding extreme excellence. The Australian pair, who were the world record holders, finished fourth behind them and failed to qualify for the final. Even more of a surprise was the fate of the Kiwi pair in the other semi; they were reigning double world champions and they failed to qualify too.

On the eve of the final, Grainger, Thornley and their coach met and talked practicalities, about raceplan and timing and the schedule for the following day, and they were just about to part for the night when Thornley said, 'Are we going to leave it there?' And then, Grainger recalls, 'we went onto the next level: emotional, heartfelt stuff of why we felt this was our chance to do something for ourselves and we were both ready for it.' That night, for the first time in 50 days, Grainger allowed herself to look at the ultimate goal and she found she genuinely believed they could do something special. 'What everyone in the Olympics is doing is taking on that challenge and living it. It is what makes you feel alive and it is horrible and uncomfortable, but I thought: this is possibly my last chance to go out there and see what we could do. I remember that night just thinking: I genuinely feel lucky. I don't know what's going to happen tomorrow and I could be heartbroken but not many people get this opportunity.'

Taking on the challenge. That was Grainger and Thornley's response the next day and, for a stretch of the race, it even seemed that they would win gold. They soon hit the front; by the 1500m mark, three-quarters of the way through the race, they were still leading. The race had already become a duel: GB versus Poland. GB were 1.25 seconds ahead but the Poles were timing their finish to perfection. With 150m to go, GB could hold on no more. Poland won gold; the boat that Redgrave wouldn't have bet his house on: silver.

'They had the strength of mind to believe they could do it,' Redgrave said afterwards. Indeed they did.

Chapter learnings by Simon Timson

Arguably we all have inner strength; we just have to choose to use it. Of course, some people are more naturally confident than others, but the lesson of this chapter is that resilience is not innate, it can be learned, practised, developed.

Psychologists refer to situation-specific confidence as self-efficacy, which is underpinned by four factors: previous accomplishments, vicarious experience, arousal control and verbal persuasion. Previous accomplishments in similar circumstances have the most significant bearing on our confidence in any given situation. This chapter demonstrated two key ways in which Olympic champions tap into their inner strength to perform confidently:

Gradual exposure to increasingly difficult environments promotes successful coping. Develop mental skills, test them, reflect and learn, test them in a more difficult situation, reflect and learn again. Throughout her career, Katherine Grainger had been constantly challenged to learn and develop in conditions of increasing psychological hardship. This bred an acceptance of, and confidence in the pressure cooker environment of the Olympic Games.

Confidence can be drawn from other people's performances. In other words, positively perceived vicarious experiences make people feel more confident. Grainger had a deep-ingrained belief, built up over four Olympics' worth of evidence, that if the other boats are going fast, then hers should be going fast too. Thornley then drew confidence from Grainger: I know I can do it because I know I am as good as her.

Sustaining Success

16

The art of leadership

DAVID TANNER, ROWING

Of all the venues at Rio, the no1 beauty was the Lagoa Rodrigo de Freitas, a natural lagoon hemmed in by Copacabana, Ipanema and Rio's Corcovado mountain, with Christ the Redeemer perfectly placed on high to adjudicate any photo finishes.

On Day Eight of the Games, on the Lagoa, in the last race of the Olympic rowing regatta, the GB men's eight swept to gold. They had been preceded by the women's eight, who won silver. Collectively, the GB rowers won three golds and two silvers, which made them the top rowing nation, so none of them, naturally, wanted to peel themselves away from the Lagoa, from the scene of success, from the glorious setting. Yet on the evening of Day Eight, when Jessica Ennis-Hill was waging her campaign in the Olympic Stadium across the other side of the city, and when his rowers were finally out revelling, David Tanner, the long-time boss of British Rowing, was making a quiet exit and boarding a flight for Rotterdam. This was typical Tanner: he had so much to celebrate over so many Olympic Games, yet it was never his style to be toasting triumph; his attention always remained belligerently focused instead on where the next triumph was going to come from.

The minute the Olympic regatta was over, the Rotterdam regatta had become more important to him. Rotterdam would host three events rolled into one: the World Championships (for the non-Olympic categories), the Under-23 World Championships and the Junior World Championships. Collectively, the three GB teams competing there amounted to 111 athletes. For Tanner, Rotterdam was all about the succession plan: which of the 111 would be his next Olympic champions? Who would help him sustain the success?

Winning is one thing, but winning again and again and again is another altogether. Tanner had been leading GB rowers to the podium since Sydney. Rio was his fifth Games and his teams had won 12 Olympic golds in total, with one powerful thread running through all five of them: at all five Games, his men's four won gold. At every Games, the crew of the four was changed; just as Alex Ferguson would reinvent his Manchester United team over the generations, so would Tanner change his men's four. No single rower ever kept a seat in the boat for more than two Games before being replaced, but always at least one rower from the four would straddle consecutive Games. The handing down of the intellectual property, the pride in the boat, the competition for a seat within it – all combined to make it a masterpiece of succession management.

'When you run any organisation, you have to look as far down the road as you can.' So wrote Ferguson in his book, *Leading*. This has been Tanner's great art: a vision far down the road, the skill of sustaining success.

When you meet David Tanner, he does not come over as your obvious leader. He is not relentlessly front-of-house, like Ferguson. He is not the face of the team, like Dave Brailsford. He is not bursting with follow-me charisma, like Jurgen Klopp. He eschews any kind of cult of personality. He does not see himself as a general inspiring his troops into battle, a wartime Winston Churchill, or like Jim Telfer, the infamously rousing former British Lions rugby coach. In 1997, in South

Africa, on the eve of one of the Lions' greatest ever victories, Telfer gave a speech – his Everest speech – that has become immortalised. 'This is your fucking Everest, boys,' is the line in the oration for which he is forever connected. It is hard to think of a line less likely to come from Tanner's mouth.

There are ways and means of leadership, though, and Tanner is very specific about what works for him. He is not Churchill – never could be, never wanted to be. Tanner is a former history teacher and the political leader he really admires is Clement Atlee. 'I would tend that way rather than to your noisier ones,' is how he puts it. He sees Atlee as a visionary with a strategy to drive through his vision; good with people, good at enabling people. Without quite saying so himself, this is how he would like to be regarded.

He recalls a trip he once made to Anaheim in the United States to visit a school friend who worked for Disney Imagineering, the development arm of the Walt Disney Company that creates theme parks and attractions. His friend invited him into the management team meeting and asked him afterwards: 'Did you spot the CEO?' Tanner said not and, when asked to make a guess, he got it wrong, twice. 'Exactly!' his friend told him, and then explained: part of the culture in Disney is that the big cheese isn't always required to be visible. He or she can lead without any cult of personality. Tanner liked the Disney model. 'I've carried that with me a bit,' he says. 'I think leadership is setting strategy and direction and then enabling other people to get on and deliver what you've set up.'

He is quite starchy, and has no interest in being mates with the athletes. In fact he has a very headmasterly air, which is hardly surprising because he spent his last nine years, before becoming performance director, as headmaster of a massive Middlesex state school. With 200 members of staff, that was quite a grounding in how to be a good leader.

One of the previous schools where he taught was Ealing Grammar School; that was also where he started coaching. He taught a year group of 30 pre-O-level children to row and, four years later, a crew of four of them (with one outsider) went with him to the Junior World Championships. They finished behind East Germany and won silver. They became known as The Ealing Four and, five years later, with Tanner still their coach, and just one change in the boat, they went to the Moscow Olympics together and won bronze. That was his first Olympic medal. To build a system which produces medals by design, rather than by curious, one-off brilliance, was another matter altogether.

How do you achieve success and then sustain it? How do you go from 'Good to Great' – the title of another bestseller by business analyst/superstar journalist Jim Collins. Collins began by analysing 1,435 good companies and whittled his focus down to 11 companies who, by his definition, became great. In a 2001 article for *Fast Company* magazine, he summarised part of his analysis: 'Companies that make the change from good to great have no name for their transformation – and absolutely no programme ... There was no miracle moment. Instead a down-to-earth, pragmatic, committed-to-excellence process – a framework – kept each company, its leaders and its people on track for the long haul.'

This very much describes Tanner. There was no miracle moment. No light bulbs switched on in his head. There was no change of direction. There is of course something in 'the long haul' approach too. Ferguson was the longest-serving top-flight manager of his generation and won by far the most trophies. Likewise, the three most consistently successful GB Olympic sports, cycling, rowing and sailing, have the best continuity of leadership: Tanner has done five Olympics; Brailsford did four (three as boss); Stephen Park, the team leader of the sailing team, did four too.

This is also from Collins: 'There is a direct relationship between the absence of celebrity and the presence of good-to-great results. Why? First, when you have a celebrity, the company turns into 'the one genius with 1,000 helpers'. It creates a sense that the whole thing is really about the CEO. At a deeper level, we found that for leaders to make something great, their ambition has to be for the greatness of the work and the company, rather than for themselves.'

This very much describes Tanner too. As the performance director, he is not a coach directly interfacing at the riverside with the athletes, he is the 'conductor' – to use his words – of a team of coaches and support staff (doctors, physios, sports scientists, etc.) that he recruited. As he observed from Disney, 'The big cheese isn't always required to feel visible and obvious.' Every autumn, he takes his senior staff away for three or four days for a debrief on the season just past and to plan the year ahead. At one of these, he recalls an under-23 coach asking him directly: 'What have you done this year?' To which he replied: 'Alright, I'll answer this in an obtuse way. My philosophy is that if I'm doing my job well, every one of you in this room would be able to do the job that they're doing better than I would be able to do it myself. My job is to conduct the orchestra; I don't need to be the lead violinist to be able to do that.'

Maybe Tanner could have led one of Collins's 'great' companies. His own passions, though, are his sport and seeing young people excel. How did he do that? Arguably by following another Collins dictum: 'Leaders of companies that go from good to great start not with "where" but "who".'

As Tanner says: 'If we were to carry on relying on our traditional luck of getting people out of rowing clubs then we'd never have enough people to build.' When he took over, after the Atlanta Olympics in 1996, he knew, for sure, that he didn't have enough women coming through. In fact, GB rowing didn't have any record with women rowers at all. Women were first admitted into Olympic rowing competition in 1976 and, since then, GB had won 12 rowing medals – but not one of them was won by a women's boat. In 2001, then, Tanner employed Peter Shakespear. The man who had over a decade's experience of finding female Olympic rowers for Australia would now come and work for him. As Tanner explains: 'I'm not shy to nick other people's ideas.' This was an idea that really worked.

Shakespear would build a programme that attempted to talent-spot potential star rowers in schools across the country. Male and female. This programme was called Start. Of the ten GB Olympic champions in London, five came through Start. Of the Rio champions, five again came through Start; four of the ten Rio silver-medallists came through Start too.

Ferguson, in *Leading*, says that he 'always wanted to know what the pipeline of players looked like for the team we would select three years in the future'. Tanner is the same, not looking ahead in sets of three years, but in Olympic cycles. Just as he would leave for Rotterdam straight after the Rio Games, the day after the London 2012 rowing was finished, instead of soaking up either victory or champagne, he was at the GB rowing headquarters in Caversham working with the under-23 team. 'It was a way of sending a signal out that we have to invest in the next cycle of athletes,' he explains. From those 2012 under-23s, four would be in finals in Rio four years later.

At the end of the Sydney Olympic regatta, at which two GB men's boats won gold, Tanner had been asked, in a media question, if that was something he intended to build on. 'Not really,' was his answer, because GB had just won their first ever women's rowing medal, silver in the women's four, and that was his priority. Now he wanted a first ever women's gold and it was a target he set for Beijing 2008, two Olympics down the line. He would miss the target in Beijing, when his women's boats won two medals, a silver and a bronze. However, he hit it with some style four years later in London with not one women's gold but three.

His next ambition, after London, was to win a medal in a quad. GB had never been strong in sculling, but four scullers in one quad? That had been beyond him. 'That,' he said, 'is the one I've been working at for quite a long time.'

Did Tanner take British rowing all the way from good to great? That is a matter of opinion. In his first four Olympics, the number of medals won rose solidly – three, then four, then six, then nine. That is good to great. Yet in Rio, it went back down to five. That is not. GB still topped rowing's Olympic medal table in Rio, yet the medal target they had been set was six – so they missed that. One whole department – the lightweight boats – failed to get on the podium. Not everything works.

What makes the job hard? What is it, in particular, that makes success hard to sustain? Tanner's answer is a fascinating modern dilemma.

The hard part, he says, is the transition from juniors and under-23s to seniors. In other words, the hard part is when most of his athletes go to university. In particular, it is hard with American universities buzzing around the hottest talent and offering them scholarships. You can't tell a child to say no to the experience of an American college education, but it's hard to avoid being concerned that they are not being developed exactly as you would wish. As Tanner says: 'They are outside our say-so for three or even four years.'

This was a theme picked up by Clarissa Farr, the headmistress of St Paul's Girls' School in London, one of the highest-achieving schools in the UK, in an interview in the *Sunday Times* in 2015. Farr said that the modern employment world raised questions over the relevance of university education.

'Fast-moving firms like Google recognise that conventional education is not at the moment keeping up with the requirements of the modern workplace,' she said. 'They are throwing out a challenge to schools to be much more imaginative about what it is that young people really need to know. If you listen to employers like Google, they need more people who can work in a team, think creatively and take educated risks. They will be trying to encourage young people not to mark time at university when they could be moving into an exciting world of employment where their training will continue but in a way more attuned to a modern way of thinking.'

That is, increasingly, becoming a decision for the school leavers: do you join the 'university of Google' or the university of Oxford or Cambridge or Bristol or Leeds.

Indeed Deloitte, for instance, have a BrightStart programme where they seek to recruit bright school leavers rather than pick them up three or four years later when they have been through university. Many big employers are increasingly working on the same theory: that three years of their own education and training can accelerate learning and develop an employee's thinking more appropriately than a university.

Tanner's scourge is inadequate education at some universities – for his purposes, inadequate coaching. To that end, he has made an investment, part-paying salaries of coaches in selected universities in order to raise the standards. He does not, for a minute, believe he could change culture sufficiently, so that rowers didn't go to university – nor does he wish to. Yet utopia for him would be to have all his 19- to 23-year-olds in one place. The university of British Rowing.

In the meantime, though, he continues to push his rowers towards greatness. In Rio, the men's quad, in which he had invested so much hope and energy, did not reach the podium. They suffered unfortunate circumstances: one of the four dropped out with sickness on arrival in the Olympic city, which meant the crew had a last-minute change. So now Tanner intends to see that project come good in the Tokyo Olympics in 2020. One of the gold medals won by the under-23 team in Rotterdam, where Tanner went from Rio, was achieved by the men's quad. Looking to the next Games, the view already looks good.

Chapter learnings from Simon Timson

It is no coincidence that the best-led programmes in Olympic and Paralympic sport are the most successful ones. There is no single defining 'leader personality', though the fundamental principles that have made successful leaders and delivered sustained success are very similar:

Articulate an inspiring vision. Team members need to understand the destination they are following you to.

Set very high performance expectations for everyone, and role model them. Tanner demands excellence from himself, and in everything from neatly kept physiotherapy rooms to having the most high-functioning portable preparation and recovery areas at international regattas.

Make ruthless decisions and manage them compassionately. Tanner's high expectations are accompanied by transparent and unforgiving selection standards.

Trust. Sometimes he is unpopular. A leader must acknowledge that they have to be. They have to make hard decisions and hold a hard line, but Tanner's staff and athletes all trust him and that is why they accept that. There are three aspects of trust: Credibility – do you do what you say you're going to do? Reliability – do you do it when you say you're going to do it? Intimacy – do you do it in a way that is sensitive to the people around you? Tanner lives those three qualities in the way that he does things.

17

Research and innovation as a global arms race

Something extraordinary was happening on Day Six in Rio and the story spread fast round the Olympic Games. It was news from the velodrome, where the track cycling had just begun: 'Have you heard? The GB men's team sprint team, in qualifying, have just broken the Olympic record!' This was followed a little later by more news from the velodrome: 'Have you heard what's happened now? The GB women's pursuit team, in qualifying, have just broken the *world* record!' And then, finally, as evening set on the Olympic city, we were all alert and tuned in for the extraordinary culmination to an extraordinary day: the final of the men's team sprint, Great Britain versus New Zealand. Gold to Great Britain.

This was the same men's team sprint team that had come sixth in the World Championships just five months earlier and eighth in the World Championships the year before that. At the start of that day in Rio, they had been fifth favourites at odds of 15–1. This was also the women's pursuit team who had come third in the World Championships five months earlier. And, yes, rewind a year and a bit or a few chapters in this book and you will recall that this was the same GB track team that had appeared to be cycling off a cliff, following the Doom Loop to disaster. This was the bubble that many thought had burst.

What we were just starting to discover, on Day Six in Rio, was that they had bottomed out spectacularly. Another way of looking at it is to quote Arie de Geus, the luminary Dutch businessman: 'The ability to learn faster than your competitors may be your only sustainable competitive advantage.' Hold on to that; that quote is the key.

Day Six in Rio was just the start. For the next five days, the other cycling nations would watch sour-faced as GB rose again to rule the velodrome and they could barely contain their envy. Yet they, too, might have heeded the lessons of the previous two Olympics, because GB had been the fastest learners at Beijing in 2008 and London in 2012, and here they were again. They were masters of staying ahead of the game and their learning had kept them there. In so doing, they were among a tiny elite; only Chinese divers and Jamaican sprinters over successive Olympics maintained a competitive advantage over their corner of the market to the level that British Cycling did.

That de Geus quote, incidentally, is a one of Scott Drawer's favourites. And there may be no one who helped GB learn faster than Drawer.

Drawer joined UK Sport in 2000. He came from Loughborough with a strong statistical and analytical background and a PhD in injury risk in football. Within four years at UK Sport, he was head of the Research and Innovation (R&I) department. If you want to know how and why UK Sport toyed with using military missile-tracking technology to help their archers shoot arrows straighter, for instance, or why they toyed with Darth Vader helmets to help their cyclists go faster, it is because of Drawer's restless mind. Those were ideas that didn't quite come off, but they show the right kind of mind that filters out a lot of great ideas that don't work before alighting on those that do. Drawer discovered, for instance, that you are aerodynamically more efficient on a bike if you cross over your hands on the handlebars – interesting but not very helpful. He discovered, too, that you can design the most aerodynamically efficient race helmet in the world, but if Chris Hoy finds that it covers his ears, he will refuse to wear it. Hoy requires the full use of his hearing for spatial awareness on the bike, it turned out. So what do you do? You redesign the helmet.

Here, though, are some examples of what he did that really did work. He used Formula 1 technology to help build winter Olympic bobsleighs and British Aerospace technology to build the skeleton sled on which Amy Williams won gold in Vancouver. He found a way of using sensors for swimmers to perfect the tumble turn. He helped pioneer 'hot pants' for cyclists to wear to keep their muscles warm between races, and he helped pioneer the liquid repellent that coated the spray skirt of Ed McKeever's canoe in which he won gold in London. For the London Games, his department helped deliver 140 R&I projects across 25 different Olympic and Paralympic sports.

So, yes, he sounds like the ultimate lab-coat boffin, but he isn't; what he is good at is identifying people with good brains and creating an environment where they are encouraged to think for him. He didn't actually invent the sled or the pants or liquid repellent himself. Instead, he executed what was, in effect, his own Talent ID search – not for the best athletes in the country but for the top engineers and scientists.

It helped that the UK is so brilliantly stocked with such expertise. Eighty-five per cent of F1 engineers, for instance, are British. The UK is one of the world's leading nations in scientific engineering. Thus, after the Athens Games, Drawer set out to find high-quality people in science, medicine, engineering and technology who might have the right skills and the motivation to help. He researched academic lists and rankings, and visited some 30 academic establishments. 'Curiosity,' Drawer says, 'was one of the talent selection criteria.' His vision was that, by bringing together smart minds from related worlds and applying them to Olympic sport, innovation would naturally and quickly occur.

Eventually a group, some 20 of them, convened in a meeting room in Sheffield. As Drawer recalls: 'I still look back and think, "Shit! How did we make that happen?" But, at the time, it was the right thing to do. We didn't know anything different. This wasn't necessarily the best group of people in terms of academic expertise, but it was the best in terms of creativity, people who would listen, be curious, want to explore. The naivety was a real strength. You need people who want to go random. Sometimes we say: forget the rules. When you get people in a place with a good environment where people can think like that, you can be amazed where it goes. It was like a marriage: matching those people to a sport that was ready.'

The sport that was ready for this was cycling. A key member of the group was Chris Boardman, British Cycling's director of research and development. He was able to guide the group towards the central mission: to challenge contemporary thinking to build a faster bike. 'In effect,' says Drawer, 'we created our own F1 team for track cycling.'

What was in it for all these experts? Drawer started issuing small contracts – 'Here's £10,000, now go away and see what you can do with that' – but it wasn't the money. Not *that* money. 'Part of it,' he says, 'was because they were interested and intrigued by engineering or science in Olympic sport. And they genuinely thought they could have an impact. You find with those sorts of individuals that they think they can change the world. That was their reason and motivation for being there.'

By the time that Chris Hoy et al arrived for the Beijing Games, their kit – bikes, suits and helmets – were made up of 250 newly sourced or designed components. Only the pedals, shoes, sprockets and chains remained unaltered. By the time they had left Beijing, three weeks later, out of the ten events in the velodrome they had won seven golds.

The challenge of a cyclist is to propel the bicycle at speed through air. Ninety per cent of a track rider's energy is spent moving air, therefore much of Drawer and Boardman's intellectual energy was devoted to making their bikes and their riders more aerodynamic. They spent a lot of time with their riders in the wind tunnel at Southampton University, and they tapped into the best experts in Computational Fluid Dynamics that they could find. Their time was well spent.

The helmet they produced for the riders in Beijing reduced aerodynamic drag by 2–3 per cent, which meant that, over the 4km of a pursuit race, it was worth a time-save of approximately half a second. The whole package – bike, suit and helmet – represented a time-save of approximately two seconds. When Steven Burke qualified for the bronze medal race (which he would win) in the individual pursuit, the margin by which he got there was less than a second. In the team pursuit, in qualifying and the semi-finals, GB twice edged out New Zealand, first by 2.2sec and then by 2.3sec. The improvements made by Drawer and his team were not just marginal gains, they were medal-winning ones.

What Beijing proved was that they were taking the research and design of sports equipment to a level where few others were even attempting to compete. Research and innovation – of bike components, hot pants, liquid repellent and sleds – is like a product, and Drawer and his team were like a small start-up company who had found a gap in the market. They started with a budget of £200,000 and, as the market grew, their budget grew with it, but to make the money stretch they had to work it like a business too. They fund-raised simultaneously; by London 2012, they had secured match funding, or funding in kind, so that every £1 from their UK Sport coffers became £3.

In Beijing, they realised that no one else was doing it the same way. The Germans, for instance, had actually started doing it decades before. In the old East Germany, in 1962, they opened the Institut für Forschung und Entwicklung von Sportgeräten (Institute for Research and Development of Sports Equipment), which was still running, so they had a 40-year head-start and, in theory, should have been decades ahead with their product. The difference was that they employed their own people and did it all in-house; they didn't use the network, they didn't go out to find the best minds, they just exhausted those that they employed within. As Boardman explained in an interview with *The Times* in 2008: 'Once you know all about the sport yourself, you're knackered, you are self-restraining. Our German competitors, for instance, don't talk to anyone outside their team, so they've limited their thinking.'

After Beijing, the next challenge for Drawer was: how to keep their thinking from becoming limited. For the Beijing cycle, there was low-hanging fruit to be picked – faster bikes, more aerodynamic equipment – and because no one else was picking it, it was an easy gain. But what do you do thereafter? When the others have seen what you are up to and start properly chasing you? How do you stay ahead of the game?

A brief recent history of R&I in Olympic sport in the UK looks like this: up until Athens in 2004, it hardly existed, then there was a big step up for the Beijing 2008 Games; it was all about equipment, stuff that you could see, stuff that could help you go faster, like Hoy's helmet. For the London Games, there was again a lot of equipment, but the big gains in equipment had already been made, most of the low-hanging fruit had been picked, so it became more about understanding perfor-mance, training and allowing coaches to coach better and athletes to perform better. The hot pants, for instance, were a classic product of their time, as was using sensors for the swimmers' tumble turns. Then, for the Rio 2016 cycle, it had swung much more towards understanding performance than designing equipment; the low-hanging fruit had all gone and all the very bright people who had feasted on it before were now required to stretch a bit in order to bring in another harvest.

By the time the Rio cycle really swung into operation, Drawer had left UK Sport and Boardman had left British Cycling. Tony Purnell, the former principal of the Jaguar Formula 1 team, took over from Board-man and continued to embrace the smartest minds he could find – only he found them rather more easily, among the engineering students he taught at Cambridge University. They were, to use his words, 'our own version of Bletchley Park'. Their challenge? The same one he inherited: to find ways to make the bike go faster.

That was all very well, but in the spring of 2015, it seemed a long way off. The GB team had just returned from their disastrous World Championships in Paris, the first since 2001 in which they had failed to win a single gold medal. The performance was so poor that it had the positive effect of completely refocusing the leadership. A number of big game-changer plans were put into motion. One of those was to attempt to bring Mark Cavendish back into the track team in time for Rio; another was Project Becky James. James's injury had been misdiagnosed and she was now in a race against time to be fit and competitive for Rio; Project Becky James was all about ensuring that she would be.

At that stage, although Purnell's 'Bletchley Park group' were already in harness, the intelligence which would sustain British Cycling's competitive advantage was a long way from kicking in. Collectively, the drive for better, faster equipment was called Project Gump – a reference to the famous Forrest Gump quote: 'Life is like a box of chocolates. You never know what you're gonna get.' As in Forrest Gump's life, so it is in R&I: you never know what sort of gains you are going to get.

When the world arrived at the Rio Games, there would be much interest in the international R&I competition. Who had arrived with the optimal bike design? New Zealand would arrive with carbon wheels manufactured by a company who made America's Cup yachts. The American women were on bikes that really challenged the norm; 'Project 2016', their bike design project, had elected to switch their cranksets from the right to the left side of the bike, and they apparently made significant aero-drag gains because of it. The GB team arrived with their own advances, too, and there was much interest in the small, aerodynamic ribs sewn into their skinsuits. Yet their real major gains had already been made at home. Remember, these were not the smart equipment Games; they were the smart training Games.

During 2014/15, British Cycling set about replacing the large number of coaches and management personnel who had left after London 2012. The most essential hiring of all, arguably, was Emma Barton, even if her job title was the rather unprepossessing 'Performance Support Project Co-ordinator'. She is a Scot who had been working with the Australian team. Shane Sutton, then the technical director of British Cycling, approached her at the Commonwealth Games in Glasgow in the summer of 2014 and, by Christmas time, she was in Manchester working for him. When she started, at the top of her in-tray was a project the importance of which Sutton quickly made very clear. 'The project had been brainstormed before I arrived,' Barton recalls. 'Shane's brief was: bring it together, don't miss a trick.' This is the project that would soon deliver the Chip Van. British Cycling preferred to call it the 'Performance Analysis Caravan', but the Chip Van was how it became known. Its influence would be vast.

In its inexorable battle against aero-drag, British Cycling had tended to use two tools, the wind tunnel and the computer. Initially, both had delivered ground-breaking gains, but a wind tunnel had its limitations: it was expensive, it couldn't replicate the bends of a velodrome, you can't get the four riders of a team pursuit team in a wind tunnel, and the most aerodynamically optimal position you can find in a tunnel might just not be a practical one at which to maintain world record speeds in an Olympic final. And computational fluid dynamics had clear limitations too: real life is often nothing like what it looks like on a laptop.

The Chip Van theory was this: what if you could have live feedback in the velodrome, like having a permanent wind tunnel in the work-place? This is what Barton was instructed to pull off in the Manchester velodrome where the GB team trained.

In short, she put in a timing system under the track and a camera system above, and the two of them would be connected. Where would they be connected? In the van. The caravan was situated at the top of the bend inside the track and every piece of relevant data would feed live into the computers within it. If your speed increased or your power dropped or the aerodynamics between riders in a pursuit team changed, for instance, then, in the van, you could call up the figures and the pictures simultaneously so you could see what was working and what wasn't – how low the head should be, for instance, or how tucked in the elbows, or the best positions for different speeds at different points on the track.

With the van, aerodynamics was now no longer a one-size-fits-all science – every rider is marginally differently built and therefore aero-dynamically marginally different. The van allowed each coach and individual rider to learn what they hadn't seen before: what exactly works best. In the words of Paul Barratt, one of the biomechanists charged with translating all the data into information: 'It is like a guided discovery, or a constant stream of mini-experiments.'

Every coach will tell you that it is one thing to instruct an athlete what to do, but altogether more convincing if they can see it with their own eyes. This is what the Chip Van delivered, after every lap of every effort every day. And because it was live, and didn't require a post-training analysis session, the riders could watch what worked and then go and practise it so that it became ingrained into muscle memory.

Why did the men's team sprint team break the Olympic record on Day Six in Rio? And why did the women's team pursuit team break the world record? For lots of reasons, all based around athletes and coaches. Yet, according to Sutton: 'That particular coaching tool was the number one thing. That was what made most of the difference.'

In the autumn of 2015, Glenn Hunter, head of R&I at the English Institute of Sport, travelled to Aigle, Switzerland, to the headquarters of the UCI, the world cycling federation, to request a change to the rule regarding the angle of a bicycle's saddle. The UCI's rules dictated that saddles should be pretty much horizontal and that the biggest downward tilt could be a mere 2.5 degrees. Hunter was campaigning for an extra 6.5 degrees. He wanted it to go all the way to nine

Why? As he explained to the UCI: it was medical evidence, uncomfortable medical evidence. That is why his mission was called 'Project Ouch'. Bikes can create saddle sores – every rider knows that. If you are an Olympic track rider, pushing your body to the limit in its most aerodynamic position, then due to the G-forces on the apex of the velodrome bend, 3–5 times your body weight will come down through approximately one square centimetre of saddle. That is a recipe for saddle sores, both for men and women. And the word 'sores', here, is a whopping understatement; this is chronic pain on a level that can break an Olympic campaign.

So, yes, the UCI changed the ruling. Its rule-makers understood that marginally tilting a saddle would reduce the pressure and thus reduce the threat of saddle sores. The new, permissible tilt was nine degrees. Job done.

In the 'smart training Olympics', this was a masterstroke. A survey of the GB riders had shown that 100 per cent of them were affected by saddle sores in training. It was either the amount of time they had been able to train that was affected, or the effort they could put into holding the aerodynamic, yet uncomfortable, position. Or both. Fifty per cent said that it affected them in competition. One female rider said that she got the symptoms at a competition and was unable to train for four weeks afterwards. If you are losing that much training time and quality training, then it can only affect your Olympic hopes detrimentally. If GB were now suddenly saving that much missed time, then, conversely, it raised their chances.

The UCI rule was not just for GB, of course. Any other international team who had read the UCI rule update could now use the nine-degree tilt too. But how many of them understood the benefits it would bring? How many of them had awaited it and now exploited it quite so keenly as the GB team did?

The point is that you can't train smart if you can't train. You can't use the Chip Van if you can't train. That is why GB's success on the track, which started on Day Six, continued peerlessly all the way to the end of the track programme on Day 11. It consisted of six golds out of ten, plus four silvers and a bronze. And it proved that if you can work out how to train longer, better and smarter than your competitors, then you can sustain your competitive advantage.

Chapter learnings by Chelsea Warr

There is a temptation to believe that you know all the answers yourself – but don't be so constrained. This chapter is about actively embracing others and their knowledge. And this doesn't just apply to sport. Whatever your industry, bring in new people from outside to look at old issues. That is so much better than trying to solve the same problem over and over yourself and not really getting anywhere.

Accept mistakes. To sustain success, you need to learn faster than the opposition. Therefore, you've got to innovate but you must have an acceptance of making mistakes.

Value curiosity Find people either in sports or external/other industries who are incredibly curious. The 'curious people' who will often ask the annoying or difficult questions are actually your greatest assets for future performance breakthroughs.

Never lose sight of the outcome. With innovation, it's easy to get diverted when trying to solve problems. The bottom line is: if it doesn't make the boat go faster then don't bother.

18

How to build a cohort of winners

BOXING, MOTOWN, DUTCH SPEED SKATERS

In 2010, when Anthony Joshua was on parole for cannabis possession and intent to supply, one of the many concerns for GB Boxing was the workload being demanded of him on his long stints of unpaid community service. Joshua was given a lot of fences to paint. The trouble, of course, is that if you paint too many fences with one arm, then you exercise the one and ignore the other – and boxers, clearly, need a balance, they have to keep both hands up, not just one, not just the painting hand. The result was that clear and simple instructions went out from GB Boxing to Joshua: if you don't want to mess up your life even more, then discipline yourself and alternate your painting hand.

This was not Joshua's first brush (apologies!) with the law, but it would be his last. Within two years, he was Olympic champion; within six, he had turned pro and had won one of the world heavyweight title belts. This is a storyline that chimes with many young boxers and is a cliché only because it is regularly proven true: boxing keeps young men in the gym and out of jail.

'I certainly had a couple of court appearances, making character references for a couple of the lads,' says Dan Salcedo, who now works as a coach in triathlon but came there from boxing, where one of his roles was working closely with the Olympic wannabes as their lifestyle adviser. 'That was pretty much par for the course.'

In the GB Boxing squad, they have a rule: two strikes and you are out. And, yes, there have been a couple who have used up their two strikes, generally for petty theft, and lost their place in the squad.

That is all background, but worth bearing in mind when you walk through the double doors into the gym in Sheffield where the GB squad train.

Even in its design, this place is intended as a place where young people can aspire. There are three Olympic-sized boxing rings in here, the middle one purchased from London 2012 after the Games – it is the very ring in which Joshua won his gold. And around the walls, there are framed pictures of every GB boxer who has ever won an Olympic medal. In other words, if you come here, this is what you should be aiming at too.

That is just how it looks. But it feels that way too. At any one time, six or seven mini coaching sessions are underway, either in the three rings or alongside them. On one patch of canvas, you can be working out with Richie Woodall, one of those with his own framed picture on the wall (bronze, Seoul Olympics, 1988). Ten yards away, you can be working out with Rob McCracken, the performance director. McCracken once fought for the WBC middleweight crown, so he knows what it is like to be in a big fight. He also trained Carl Froch, the four-time super-middleweight world champion, which shows – as if the three GB golds in the London Olympics did not make it clear enough – that he knows what it is like to train champions too.

The pace is fast. Sessions are timed. There is no chatting by the water-cooler. The place is efficient, business-like. There is an emphasis here on the quality of each session. You are not just going through the motions you went through yesterday; every training session is a learning opportunity. The athletes work hard and fast. Afterwards they will often re-watch their training session on the iBoxer video facility; then, after warming down, they leave. And then the next cohort arrives. When

McCracken started, the whole squad would work out together; one of the many changes he made was to stagger training through the day. Staggered training means fewer athletes in at any one time, which in turn means far more one-to-one coaching. It is all so purposeful, and that is how the athletes operate.

If I had to describe what a winning environment looks like, I'd be describing this boxing gym.

Ask anyone how and why this room feels this way and the first answer they will give is Rob McCracken. That is Salcedo's first answer too. He extrapolates: 'When Rob came, in 2009, he treated the boys like human beings. Up to that point, that hadn't been the case. The philosophical default before was: they were bad people. Rob treated them as good people; that was the fundamental. It was: we expect the best of you, we expect the right behaviour from you. The boys generally come in here with nothing. That is very often how boxing is. Rob's philosophy was: however they come to us, they leave as better people. These are boys who've got into trouble at school, boys who people always thought the worst of. Now they have people expecting the best of them.'

It worked for Joshua; the Rio Olympians came to learn that it could work for them too.

When you are considered good enough to join the GB Boxing Olympic squad, you move into the accommodation at Darnell, ten minutes' walk from the gym. The block of flats here, plus four houses, can accommodate up to 38 people. It is when you move in there that you see how the other Olympians live. It is a lifestyle with expectations: you keep your room clean and tidy, you are in your room getting ready for bed by around 10pm, you are up and being weighed-in at 7am, and you are expected to eat well. Two coaches live at the bottom of the block, in Flat 14, so they know exactly who is conforming and who isn't.

Of course, no one expects you to know how to eat well, or not on arrival, anyway. This is why Mark Ellison, the nutritionist, hands out polystyrene food boxes to each athlete, with their every meal perfectly measured out. As they get close to competition, Ellison says, 'they stick to it like glue'. Ellison has worked with Andy Murray, Jessica Ennis-Hill and Manchester United, but he says the boxers present a different challenge: 'Some will never have been in the kitchen before, some are male stereotypes. "No, I'm not going in the kitchen, that's women's work." The same with their tastes: you get some who have never been exposed to fruit and vegetables. Often it's: "Why do I need to change? I am national champion." Some are like the fussiest children. You find yourself going: "All I am going to do is put this grape in your mouth; you can spit it out if you like."'

No one wants them to be completely dependent on polystyrene food parcels, so Ellison gives them cooking classes too. 'We can go to the flats to do it,' he says, 'do a class there and watch the football and have a laugh.' And that way they learn how to cook an omelette.

This way, the new generation learn the behaviours expected of an Olympic prospect. The management hand down the lessons via a kind of oral history too: they tell them how Luke Campbell, another London gold-medallist, was always first in and last out of the gym; they tell them of Fred Evans, a London silver-medallist, and how his Olympic campaign was turbo-charged in the 18 months before the Games when his attitude to training was transformed. And when they tell the Anthony Joshua story, they weave in the recollection that he was the athlete who never stopped asking questions. A lot of new recruits don't do that, they have never been encouraged to have inquisitive minds, but if it worked for Joshua, they surmise, then maybe it can work for them too.

In the gym, you can see how they work as a team too. My visit to their gym is six months before Rio and it is striking. Boxing is as individual as a sport can be: when you are in the ring, no one can help you; your achievements and successes are yours and yours alone. Yet this group are clearly stronger together. They feed off each other's successes and spur each other on. This was Qais Ashfaq, from Leeds, who would go to Rio as the GB bantamweight: 'I've been here six years. I've trained with Luke Campbell, Anthony Joshua, the lot. You learn from them and that's what makes you better. Champions breed champions, and we've seen that as the years have gone on.'

Six years ago, when Ashfaq arrived in the programme, it was at the same time as three others, one of whom is Joe Cordina, who would go to Rio as the GB lightweight. 'In the house,' Ashfaq says, 'we are like family After every training session, we'll talk to each other about what we did wrong. In the gym, if I am sparring, they'll be watching and giving me tips. We know how good we are, we trust each other's judgement. That's the bond you build.'

Bob Dillon, one of the coaches, looks around the gym with pride. 'There is so much passion in this room for each other,' he says. Given that he's 58 years old and spends four nights a week living in Flat 14, you'd have thought that he would be sick of the sight of them all, but the opposite is true. 'The bond is great,' he says. 'It's great living with them. You eat together, cook together. Everybody cares about everybody.'

And he is absolutely convinced that this all works: 'Every time we get a new generation through, there is something about them, they are just a little bit bigger and stronger than the last ones. They are excited, there is a buzz about them; no one is afraid. Whenever we go to a tournament, we are fear free. Cuba, Russia, Ukraine – we are up there with them. Back in the day, they'd not even acknowledge you. Now, when we walk in, I see the Russians looking at us, like: who have they brought?'

'In 1959, songwriter and producer Berry Gordy launched a small, independent record company using $800 he borrowed from family members.' This is the opening sentence of Sydney Finkelstein's *Superbosses*, in which he describes one of the all-time great winning environments. One of the first acts that Gordy signed was William 'Smokey' Robinson, whose song 'Shop Around' would become the first hit of what we know today as the Motown label, one of the all-time giants of the music industry. Gordy didn't just talent-spot the likes of Marvin Gaye, Stevie Wonder, The Supremes, The Four Tops and The Jackson 5, he developed them as one big team. He would have weekly meetings for what he described as 'quality control and product evaluation'. He would train up his talent on their social skills, stage presence, even table manners. Each individual artist or group was in pursuit of their own success, so arguably they were all in competition with each other, yet Gordy developed a culture in which they were not working against each other, but were supporting each other. As Duke Fakir, of The Four Tops, explained in an interview in *Vanity Fair*: 'We were friends; we played basketball together, we played cards together, we ate together. It wasn't like: if I got a hit, somebody else ain't going to get one. Because one after the other, you kept getting hits, and more hits.'

The term Finkelstein uses to describe success built this way is 'The Cohort Effect' – it's not just me winning, or you winning, it's everyone building on each other's victories to create even more success. He quotes a Paul McCartney interview in *The New Yorker* when he described the simple, creative tension between him and John Lennon: 'If I did something good, he'd want to do something better. It's just the way we worked.'

The Cohort Effect worked brilliantly too, according to Finkelstein, on *Saturday Night Live*, the iconic NBC comedy sketch show, created by executive producer Lorne Michaels in 1975, that became a foundation stone of modern comedy for the next 40 years. *SNL* would launch careers in comedy the way Motown did in music: from Bill Murray and John Belushi at the beginning, to the Chris Rocks and Tina Feys of today. Writers and performers in the seventies and eighties recalled the 'high-octane atmosphere'. Every week, the team would write and produce a show. 'It was simple,' recalled writer/actress/comedienne Rachel Dratch, 'either write good sketches with funny characters, or sit on the sidelines watching each week's show.' So there was high pressure, intense collaboration and strong emotional bonds. According to Finkelstein, 'Michaels wanted a sense of family to prevail, but he also specifically encouraged competition by hiring more cast members than could perform regularly on the show. The result was intense but subtle jostling each week.' In other words, he created an environment where competition and collaboration worked hand in hand, where the wittiest writers and artists he could find would push themselves to a place where they were actually pushing forward the art of comedy.

'For all employees of superbosses,' Finkelstein writes, 'the burden is on them to prove they are worthy of the temple in which they work.' In other words, create a temple and you have the environment for success.

It was only when Tom Daley left Plymouth that he understood the nature of the temple he had left behind. For most of his life, his training under coach Andy Banks had been alongside Tonia Couch and Sarah Barrow. Couch and Barrow's success as a pair, in the 10 metre synchro, won them the European title in 2012, European silver in 2013 and fifth place at London 2012. Five years older than Daley, their relationship with him morphed from being older sisters, in the early days, to best friends in the present. They were his training partners and his family.

In 2014, though, Daley felt he needed a change. Not from Banks or Couch or Barrow, but something different, a different stimulus, a different voice, probably not a voice in Plymouth. He teamed up with Jane Figueiredo, a Zimbabwean, in what seemed like an ideal partnership. Her coaching CV was long on success; she had run the programme at the University of Houston and had taken a number of Russian female divers to the Olympic podium. Daley and Figueiredo would work together at the London Aquatics Centre – the 2012 Olympic pool. It would be one-to-one and thus elite and intense.

Except Daley didn't like it that way. He missed the team. As a diver, he may have been, by and large, a solo artist; in training to perform, however, he found he was missing the team, the collaboration, the mutual support. It was as simple as this: can we bring in someone else? It wasn't what Figueiredo wanted to hear, but she couldn't pretend she wasn't hearing it. So Daley was soon joined by Georgia Ward, a 2015 European synchro champion, and Emily Boyd, an Australian.

'When it was him and I, we got so much done,' Figueiredo will tell you, with a smile of resignation. 'We still get a lot done, but it is more fun now because of the other girls. He grew up with people around. For me, I prefer one on one. He was probably: "I hope someone else comes." I was: "I hope no one comes!" I love the focus. There are pros and cons to both.'

It isn't just the blend of competition and collaboration that builds a temple, but that certainly helps, and that was what helped Gerard Kemkers build one of the great temples of recent sporting achievement. Kemkers is a former speed skater from Groningen in Holland, a nation where speed skating is deep in the blood, the second biggest sport in the land. Kemkers won a bronze in the 1988 Calgary Games and then went into coaching. He would coach two of the all-time greats, Ireen Wust and Sven Kramer, a star pair who were expected to dominate at the Vancouver Olympics. For Kemkers, though, Vancouver was a personal disaster.

In Vancouver, Wust did win one gold medal, which Kemkers acknowledges was lucky because 'she was not at her best'. And Kramer won one too. So, on the face of it, not a bad haul. It was no secret, though, that the two Dutch galacticos could and should have done better, most obviously in the men's 10,000 metres, which Kramer dominated and in which he actually crossed the line first with a time that beat the Olympic record. As Kramer crossed the finish line, he threw his arms aloft in celebration, but very quickly he realised that something was up. What was up was his disqualification. Midway through the race, he had skated in the wrong lane – which is a disqualification offence. And it was his coach, Kemkers, who had told him, in error, which lane he should be in. It was entirely the coach's mistake; he had cost his athlete a gold medal. He described it afterwards as 'the worst moment of my career'. Overall in the Vancouver speed skating Holland had to settle for a mere three golds out of 12. Kemkers said: 'My world collapsed.'

On their return home, the first question was whether Kemkers would keep his job as their coach. He did. Just. This is how he saw it: 'I think I failed and my team failed in Vancouver. With the team I had, the budget that we ran, the ambition we have, I believe that we didn't meet our standards. So I never considered stopping after Vancouver.'

The second question, which he asked himself, was: am I getting their preparation right? For the Vancouver campaign, Kemkers had taken the concept of performance and individualised training to the extreme. 'I wanted the athletes to have the best opportunity to get the best out of themselves,' he explains, 'and I thought individual programmes connected to their specific events were the way to go. In fact, I discovered after Vancouver that I completely lost my team with that strategy. I had all my athletes all standing on their own island. The big lesson was that even with individual athletes, the strength still lies within the team setting, working together. You cannot completely individualise, you have to work it so that your athletes can work as a team.

'Look at the question another way: how do you select a football team? Do your best 11 skaters make the best team? That was the question I started asking myself. So I started looking at forming my team differently. So we built this team in a way that Sven and Irene would take advantage of. In skating, we were not used to looking beyond performances, but for the Sochi cycle, I started scouting skaters on personality: what type of person are you? Do you fit?'

Kemkers took this approach to the point where he persuaded a retired professional skater back out of retirement and on to the team, merely to perform the role of training partner. That way, for a whole season leading up to the Sochi Olympics, four years after Vancouver, there was an athlete on the group who was entirely free of performance stress and who had the kind of personality to transfer this temperament to the rest of the group. Certainly stress and pressure goes with the role of being a world's-best skater in Holland. 'Getting Ireen and Sven ready for Sochi, with their status as cult heroes, was not an easy job,' Kemkers says. 'If you are heroes like them, you experience different types of pressure and performance stress.'

For the Sochi Games, Kemkers was not only the personal coach to Wust and Kramer, plus Koen Verweij and a Pole, Konrad Niedzwiedzki, but also head coach of the whole Dutch team. And their success was so comprehensive that it drew squeals of dissatisfaction from their opponents. Kramer won two golds and a silver, Wust two golds and three silvers; Verweij also won gold as one of Kramer's teammates in the team pursuit; and in that team pursuit, Niedzwiedzki was in the Polish team that got bronze. Overall, of the 12 golds in the 12 speed skating events, Holland won eight, and of the 36 total medals on offer, Holland departed with 23.

A lot of that was down to an altered team environment.

Eight out of 12 golds is about as dominant as any team in any Olympic sport. It bears comparison with the Jamaican sprinters in Rio (five out of six), the Chinese divers in Beijing and Rio (seven out of eight) and the British track cyclists in London (seven out of ten). Perhaps not surprisingly, then, by the time the speed skating had finished in Sochi, Simon Timson, the performance director at UK Sport, had been in touch with Kemkers to ask the necessary questions: how did you do it? And: what can we learn?

In March 2015, a year after Sochi, a small group of GB coaches from across the different Olympic sports went on a UK Sport 'Talent Tour' which included a visit to Kemkers in Holland. These tours are precious experiences; they take British coaches right inside the temples of successful medal factories. The value is all in the learning. The questions are clear: what is it about this place that makes champions? What is it that makes yours the winning environment?

Two years earlier, another Talent Tour had made a stop-off at that other very different, very elite winning environment, in England, in Surrey: the Yehudi Menuhin School. They were by no means alone in having come here looking for answers: Chelsea FC had been there, too, with the same questions. How do you best develop elite children? How do *you* do it?

Best answer: give them the perfect environment.

Best example? In the late nineties/early noughties, Nicola Benedetti was a child at the school and, in the words of Nicolas Chisholm, who was her headmaster, she was 'the most extraordinary youngster, very self-possessed even at a young age. When she was on stage the audience just listened right from the word go.' Two years above her was another outstanding talent, another violinist, Alina Ibragimova, from Polevskoy in Russia, who was 'very similarly talented'.

Chisholm gesticulates with his hands, to suggest that they were climbing uphill together. 'They were both like this all the way through,' he says. 'When you're bringing all these talents together, they learn as much from each other as they do from their teachers. Having that competition, which of course has its ups and its downs but also spurs each other on in a very positive way, and having someone to work with as well as against, can be really helpful.'

Didn't they compete to be top dog? Chisholm: 'One of the things that we were trying desperately not to encourage was anything that reinforced that.'

Judging by an interview Benedetti gave, after she had left the school, these efforts worked. Benedetti recalled how she would spend weekends away from school at Ibragimova's parents' house in Wimbledon: 'I looked up to Alina. She was more advanced than me; I'd ask her technical advice.'

This is Chisholm again: 'Children are competitive anyway and they are jealous of each other. One of my big things that I would say regularly was: "Everyone has got different levels of talent and different talents." Nicola and Alina are prime examples. Alina would be playing Mozart beautifully and I don't see Nicola playing Mozart. It's just a different style. To compare each other, either favourably or, as most youngsters do – unfavourably – is a mistake.'

At the Yehudi Menuhin School, therefore, they are so intent on unpicking any sense of pecking order among young musicians, they won't even allow children to get used to where they sit in an orchestra. No-where is comparison and pecking order more implied than when only one violinist can be your lead. And are you front or back, second violins or third? You get used to your sense of worth if you are eternally a third violin. So the positions are rotated. No one is allowed to settle into top position or bottom. Everybody is encouraged to aspire.

As a cohort effect, it works pretty well. Ninety-five per cent of the pupils become musicians. For Benedetti and Ibragimova, the creative/collaborative/competitive dynamic seemed to work rather well too. In December 1998, aged 11 and 13, they played Bach's double violin concerto in Paris at the opening ceremony of UNESCO's fiftieth anniversary of the Universal Declaration of Human Rights. When she was 16, Benedetti won the BBC's Young Musician of the Year competition. Six years later, Ibragimova won the Royal Philharmonic Society's prestigious Young Artist Award. In 2013, Benedetti was awarded an MBE for services to music; three years later, Ibragimova followed suit.

Here is an easy conclusion: the Yehudi Menuhin School had such high success rates because it selected the right pupils; likewise Berry Gordy selected the right musicians, and Lorne Michaels was just brilliant at recognising talented funny people. In other words, they all got their Talent ID right. Correct, but only up to a point. In theory, Talent ID is wonderful; in actuality, any model that places too much emphasis on it is flawed. Pretty much every study of the draft system in US professional sports reaches that same answer – and the draft is about as Talent ID'd a system as you will find anywhere in the world.

Every year, the top college athletes in the NFL and NBA are catwalked before the professional franchises for the draft. The way the draft works is that it allows the franchises to take turns to pick a player from the catwalk; clearly, those believed to be the most talented kids will be picked in the first round. If you are picked in the seventh and eight rounds, then the opposite is true. Of course, at the time, the first-round picks are the ones that cause all the excitement; however, the internet is now overloaded with lists of 'Worst Ever First Draft Picks'.

Being a 'first draft' is a guarantee of nothing. Some statistical analysis shows that third- to seventh-round picks outperform the first and second drafts. If Talent ID-to-success was linear, for instance, then, in the NFL draft in 2000, the New England Patriots would have picked Tom Brady first – yes, the same Tom Brady who would go on to help the Patriots win five Super Bowls, who would be four times Super Bowl MVP and would become regarded as one of the greatest quarterbacks of all time. But in 2000, he wasn't the player the Patriots picked in the first round, he was the guy that every single franchise turned a blind eye to until they went for him in the sixth.

The big joke, here, is on the Portland Trail Blazers. In 1984, they were second in line in the draft for the best young basketball players in the country. They picked a high school sensation called Sam Bowie, who would remain on their payroll for five disappointing years, during which time he played a meagre 139 games. If talent-spotting was straightforward, they wouldn't have picked Bowie at all, they'd have gone for the guy who was picked third, straight after him, by the Chicago Bulls. That was Michael Jordan.

Likewise, in 1998, the Indianapolis Colts were presented with a delicious problem. They had the first pick of the talent coming into the NFL and there were two stand-out college quarterbacks on the catwalk. Which one should they pick? Would they go for Ryan Leaf, who had just led Washington State to their first Conference title in 67 years? Or would they pick Peyton Manning, who had been doing a handy job at the University of Tennessee? One future superstar or the other? For all their analysis, they struggled to split the two, so they got their eight scouts to vote and they were split four and four. But they ended up going for Manning, which seemed the right answer. San Diego Chargers, who had second pick, went straight for Leaf.

In retrospect, Manning versus Leaf reads like this: Manning, two Super Bowls, 15 seasons, five times MVP, one of the greatest quarterbacks of all time; Leaf, four seasons, three of them with the Chargers before they shifted him out, then drugs, burglary, prison and attempted suicide. In his rookie season, Leaf completed one pass out of 15. In three seasons, Leaf started just 14 games and his touchdown to interception ratio stank: 13 touchdowns to 33 interceptions. His legacy in the game is to be stuck in those lists of Worst Draft Picks, often at the top. He comes second (behind Bowie) in ESPN's list of 100 Worst Draft Picks Ever. 'Thank you Ryan Leaf,' is the ESPN commentary. 'Thank you for destroying a franchise.'

It is one thing being anointed as a kid with a golden future; it is quite another when you don't live up to it.

What Yehudi Menuhin, Gordy, Michaels and the New England Patriots have in common is not so much the ability to spot the golden future, but the capacity to develop it. In the Sheffield boxing gym, this is exactly how McCracken sees his role too. He is very clear on this: 'If you have ability and you're dedicated and you're a boxer and you come to GB Boxing, I'd like to think you're given every chance to fulfil your potential. If you buy into it – and not all buy into it – then you've got every chance.'

Over the four Olympic Games up to Athens in 2004, before they had Sheffield and that winning environment, GB boxers won a total of three medals. They have won three or more in each of the three Olympics since. In Rio, they were actually disappointed to hit the bottom end of their target range and come back with only three. Now that is a cohort working well.

Chapter learnings from Simon Timson

Great environments are highly aspirational, infectious and promote quality, whilst poor ones can be toxic and demoralising. The best performance environments are usually created by a group of like-minded and passionate people. Boxing's leader, Rob McCracken, has been notably successful using simple yet powerful principles including:

Provide high levels of individual support. Create time and opportunity to focus all your effort on meeting the specific development needs of the person in front of you.

Proactively foster a culture of interdependence. Kindle a Cohort Effect firstly by educating new members about the team's history and culture – this can create a sense of belonging. Celebrate success so people can share one another's achievements; use your successes as motivation to push further the boundaries of performance.

Select your team on cultural fit just as much as talent. The capacity to embrace the environment's culture and traditions can be as important as raw potential. Look for new recruits who are prepared to buy in to the organisation's ethic.

Make high-performance behaviours a way of life. For instance, by accommodating the players in those houses together, keeping tidy rooms, having cooking classes, boxing conditioned high-performance behaviours.

Epilogue

Carry on sustaining

On Sunday 21 August, just a few hours before the Rio Olympics closing ceremony, Joe Joyce, the British super-heavyweight boxer, became the last name added to the statistics of success. He lost the final gold-medal bout to the Frenchman, Tony Yoka, a decision which many at ringside found questionable. Nevertheless, his became the 23rd silver medal, to complete the overall medal tally of 67. Two better than London 2012. Most of them would travel home the next day on a British Airways flight called the 'VictoRIOus'. An extra 77 bottles of champagne were loaded for the flight. There is no record of any of them coming back anything other than empty.

Four weeks later, similar scenes were played out. The last medallists were swimmers Bethany Firth and JJ Applegate, gold and silver in the 200m medley (SM14 class), which took the total to 143 – 27 better than London 2012. The British Paralympic team returned home on the same plane, same refreshments. Similar success.

Overall, this was a mission far more successfully accomplished than anyone had dared imagine. Every other Olympic host nation had peaked at their home Games and then dipped at the next. These two GB teams had proved that success can be sustained.

And, yes, that's all very well. However, no one takes time to pause for breath before asking: what's next? At the moment, Rio is the summit of GB's Olympic achievements. But does GB now dip? Does success now drop off? We could, after all, be reflecting one day on Rio as GB's golden era, an era that came and went. The alternative is that success is sustained further. It goes on and on. Yet as with all matters related to sport and 67 Olympic medals, success is only achieved if it is planned for.

So how do you carry on sustaining?

The danger ahead is all too clear. Modern western society does not develop athletes in the quantity that it once did. You do not need the best coaches in the UK to tell you that the raw material walking through the doors into their gyms and swimming pools is not what it was 10–15 years ago, that there has been a generational shift, that the smartphone/ PlayStation age just does not have the same motor skills as those who grew up playing outside instead.

No, you don't need to be a top coach to know that, but here are three of them anyway. This is Andy Banks, Tom Daley's original diving coach: 'You get a lot of what I would call motor morons coming into the pool. They haven't run round the streets and played with their mates, they've stayed at home and they've sat in front of the computer, so consequently they're pretty damn rubbish at what we want them to do.'

And this is Paul Hall, Louis Smith's coach: 'I've seen a change even in a generation. A lot of the kids we see nowadays are not as tough. I think the fact that we've got such a good life and it's so easy in terms of money and holidays and cars that there's no real sense of adventure any more – it becomes very hard to find kids with the right sort of qualities. That's one of the challenges that we have in gymnastics and I think in all of sport, really. It's finding kids that are tough enough to cope with that competitive nature. They all want to be Olympic champions, but most of the kids struggle with the hard work and the effort and the repetitions.'

And this is Mel Marshall, Adam Peaty's coach: 'A lot of them haven't got a killer instinct now. Comfort is breeding. Life's much easier now.

You don't even have to go out to get things any more, you can get them delivered.'

It's not just in the UK, though. Every nation has its own challenges. The potential of China, for instance, is pretty scary. But how long can the wheels keep turning? In the modern world of social media, and set against the politics of a softer, more commercial Chinese communism, will the Chinese kids carry on as they are, so disciplined, so obedient, sent away to sports schools, sometimes from the age of six, and not seeing their parents week to week? Will they still be willing conveyor belt products? What will they be like eight years from now? Can the old Chinese hard-work dogma possibly survive?

Jane Figueiredo, Tom Daley's current coach, has seen an answer right before her very eyes. Between 1996 and 2012 she coached Russian girls: Yuliya Pakhalina (one gold, three silvers, one bronze), Vera Ilina (one gold, one silver), and Anastasia Pozdiakova (one silver). 'The most beautiful diver, most talented of the three,' she says, 'was the one I had at the end, Anastasia.' So, why was she least successful? 'The other two had grown up in sports schools and the sports system, where you go away from home to training camps from the age of seven. But then, Russia changed so much. You had a different mentality; that Soviet work ethic just disappeared.'

To sustain success beyond Rio, then, it would be helpful to see into the future? Yes, and that is what the leaders of British sport have been thinking too: if we could glimpse the future, then we could better prepare for it. Or, to put it another way: we'd have a better chance of continuing on this cycle of success if we knew what success would look like. Or, at least, if we thought we knew.

So why not try finding out?

In early 2015, then, that is exactly what they did. The Talent Lab created what it called its 'Futures Lab' and sent out invitations asking people to join. 'Help us shape the future of elite sport in Great Britain' was the headline. They sent the invitations to leaders far and wide: in the military, in the worlds of genetics and genomics, neuroscience, pharmaceuticals, healthcare and medicine, Silicon Valley, business, academics, society and culture analysts, sociologists, entrepreneurs, music and reality TV, business analysis. Oh yes, and sport too. And they gave a taster of the kind of questions they would like to debate:

- What factors will shape the world of elite sport by 2024?
- Where will be the limits of athletic performance?
- How will we be managing athlete health?
- How will our successful leaders and coaches operate?
- How will our industry be interfacing with technology and big data?

By April, the Futures Lab had 92 different willing leaders, from a vast range of specialisms, who were invited to a series of different 'Hackathons'. The message was simple: come on down, join us in peering into the future, hack away at what it might look like. In other words: allow us to hoover your brains.

First, there were four Hackathons at the Bailbrook House Hotel in Bath, on four different themes: leadership in 2024, coaching elite athletes in 2024, athletic performance and health in 2024, technology and data in 2024.

On 26 April, I attend another of these myself, just outside Guildford. Again there is a cast of around 60 people from an extraordinarily wide range of specialisms, people from medicine, from science, from sportswear, from music, from social media. We talk about sport being, increasingly, an entertainment form – what does that mean for the Olympics and Paralympics? We talk about ethics in sport and we ask ourselves about emerging nations: do they have ethically lower standards that threaten the fabric of world sport? We talk about solo sport. Sport was always about competition, person v person and team v team, but increasingly, in the modern world, it is about bettering oneself. Soon, you'll be able to have a virtual superstar athlete, a Jessica Ennis-Hill hologram or a Jason Kenny, training in your living room with you. Is sport less and less a social event? And, we ask ourselves, can't we finally give sport more meaning by connecting it better with healthcare? In Finland, which used to have the worst record of cardio-vascular problems in Europe, extraordinary improvements have been made and sport has been at the heart of it. We discuss gene therapy. Can predictive genomics be used in the future, and is it ethical; and isn't it inevitable that China will embrace it, and if that is the case, surely we should too? We discuss mental health and how, for sporting lives played out in the theatre of social media, this is a growing concern. We discuss training and injury issues: how can we better predict an injury? For some reason, too, we discuss a behavioural study about the re-use of hotel bath towels. But that is the point – let the discussion roam. There is no definitive destination.

If future generations are the gaming generations then, yes, you can dismiss them as motor morons, or alternatively you can work with them. And the latter option is already working very well, thank you.

Back in 2008, Nissan wondered out loud about the fact that a career as a racing driver is only available to a privileged few. First you have to have someone put you in a go-kart, then you have to be funded in go-karting, and that's before the real finance even kicks in to take you into cars. So if we fish around with a net for a few talented kids who fit that profile and we're lucky, we'll scrape in a few. On the other hand, there are millions of kids racing karts and cars every day on their Xboxes and their PlayStations. Why don't we find some of them?

This was the birth of the idea that virtual athletes could become real athletes. Nissan launched a talent search, via PlayStation's most popular driving game at the time, Gran Turismo. They found out who were the best young virtual reality drivers in the world and set about turning them into real drivers, and they were so successful, they started to do it annually. There are over 100 million PlayStation users worldwide and approximately a million of them will apply each year to compete in Nissan's driving competition. Nissan then go through the full talent search and talent confirmation process. The numbers are whittled down fast: some 200 of the best of the million applicants are invited to a week-long training camp at a Formula 1 circuit, in Europe, Asia or the United States, and the very cream of these are then drafted on to the Driver Development Programme, a two-month residential at Silverstone where they are provided with psychology, nutrition, strength and conditioning and lifestyle support. The selectors do not just want those who are good with a steering wheel; what they are looking for is a toughness, a willingness to learn, the ability to perform under pressure and a determination to win. In the first seven years of the Nissan GT Academy, 21 PlayStation fanatics had completed the transformation to becoming professional racing drivers.

If the transfer can work in a sport as complicated as motor racing, then why not in Olympic sports too? Most obviously shooting and archery. The barriers preventing entry into motor racing were demolished by the Nissan Academy. The main barrier into shooting is the kit – a gun – and yet, for PlayStation users, a gun is the weapon of choice.

The message is not lost on the guardians of GB's Olympic sports. They have done their due diligence. They have visited the Nissan Academy. Some of the great future Olympians will, at this very moment, be honing their Olympic skills on their console.

Sometimes it is not about chasing the future; it can be about improving the past.

For a few years now, Paul Thompson, the women's head coach in rowing, has been concerned about the number of girls coming through. He was worried about future Olympic teams. He couldn't see where the Helen Glovers and Heather Stannings of the future were going to come from. The evidence was there before him. In 2012, for instance, one junior GB team had only three girls on it – out of a possible 18.

Why? Gender bias in rowing remains a huge problem. Not at the top; the number of girls recruited through Talent ID matches the number of boys. However, the numbers coming through the standard production line – the clubs – is embarrassing, in some years as low as a third.

This is Thompson's damning view: 'We've got a nineteenth-century club structure in the twentieth-first-century.'

Thompson decided to do some research of his own. He started emailing as many former top-level female rowers, who had competed at Olympics or world championships, and asked them two questions. One: what was the catalyst that made you come up to the national squad? Two: if you were in the sport now, what would you do?

There was one answer common to Question One. The catalyst was that a significant senior figure went out of their way to tell them: 'You're really good, you have potential to be even better.' While that may sound encouraging, it is also concerning. It tells us that success in women's rowing has been a largely random thing. It has required a random intervention. And you wonder: how many potentially world-class rowers never won an Olympic medal because no one ever tapped them on the shoulder?

There was also an answer common to Question Two: 'Take Royal out of everything.'

Here we come to the nub of it. The Henley Royal Regatta is the real driver in rowing in the UK. Club coaches get paid bonuses for their performances there and while the number of events at Henley Royal Regatta is weighted 4:1, men to women, what Henley is actually driving is a gender imbalance. At the 2016 Royal Regatta, there were 16 men's events and four women's. There were three men's intermediate events and two men's events for students but nothing for women in either category. Even the 'Ladies' Challenge Plate' is a men's event. Yes, there is also a Henley Women's Regatta which is held a fortnight before the Royal regatta, but it is not called Royal, it has a different, shorter course and, most significantly, nothing of the kudos.

None of this was lost on Caryn Davies, a double US gold-medallist, who rowed the women's Boat Race in 2015 in Oxford's dark blue. What she found 'surprised' her. 'The biggest difference is in facilities,' she says. 'The Oxford boathouse is designed to be a men's boathouse. The women's facilities are an afterthought. Contrast that with the US: the women's rowing programmes here are often better funded than the men's. In England, attitudes are changing; it is facilities that are going to be the slowest to change rather than attitudes.'

It is not Thompson's job to change attitudes, but he is doing his bit. He has tried to wage a little war online, and started up a Facebook page, Women On Water. By accessing the community, he is trying to maximise the chances of talented female rowers getting a tap on the shoulder.

There is a broader point. The future does not look good unless you spot the trouble ahead, identify the weaknesses and mend them.

So what does the future of sport look like? When the hackathons were complete and the feedback was sifted and assessed, this is where we got to.

- It's going to be a lot more about athletes. Not so much my country or the higher order or the greater calling, but me, it's going to be about me, The Athlete PLC, the future star, my brand, my identity. Instant self-gratification. Not so much Team GB as Team me.

- With that comes more and more and more social media. Elite sportspeople will be playing out their lives as characters on Twitter, Snapchat, wherever social media goes. That brings pressure. It's difficult to say there's been an increase in mental health problems, or if we are just more aware. But sustained success means more support around mental health. When sports were asked, 'What's the number one thing we need to be brilliant at?' – they said: 'After we've found an athlete, don't get sick, don't get injured. If you can help us do that, more athletes will make it.' Mental health is big in the new world of Me.

- It's going to be about hi-tech training environments, simulated training experiences, holograms. Soon enough, the GB hockey goalkeeper will be able to stand in front of a hologram of her Dutch opponent, and then the Aussie opponent, and she'll spend hours and hours in this simulator while they fire shots at her. The best nations will be the ones who get there first.

- It's going to be about hi-tech athlete welfare. One day soon, you'll be walking into training and you'll be infra-red beamed which will tell us: your recovery status, weight, body fat, sleep, etc. Everything will be instrumented. Rather than the coach saying, 'How are you feeling today?' we'll have the stats up on the wall, saying, 'Sorry, you're not training today, go into the sleep pod for two hours.' Again, who gets there first?

- With hi-tech welfare, decisions may be more scientifically and evidence-based and increasingly taken out of the hands of the coach. Good coaching, therefore, will increasingly be about high emotional intelligence. So much of the coach's old intellectual property is now online; if you want a gold-medal-winning programme for rowing, you can literally tap it out from the internet. Coaches will be less about information and more about understanding and emotional connection.

- It's going to be about entertainment: sport as entertainment. By the time the next Tom Daley comes along, maybe we'll be voting on whether he wins gold like we vote for the winners of *The X Factor*. What does that mean? That we have to be more agile, see things through a lens of commercialisation, not just a performance perspective.

Some fundamentals won't shift. However the world changes, to win a medal, you'll need a brilliant athlete with a really good genetic and psychological make-up, they'll have to practise a lot and they can't get sick, they can't get injured. Yet there are some other learnings we have already.

- Trauma is good. The coaching of the next generation will come with a better understanding of the value of placing obstacles in the development journey and how to engineer a pathway so that when the first big hurdle comes up, they have the skills to deal with it.
- Big data will rule. The Intelligence Unit at UK Sport is set to grow. The Moneyball specialists are on their way. We will understand better and better exactly what it takes to win.

Yes, there is a lot of knowledge here. Yes, there has been a lot of forward thinking. However, one of the themes repeated throughout the book is this: we never know enough, we will never have all the answers. As soon as we think we know enough, as soon as we think we have all the answers, then we are on the road to self-destruction.

So, in order to be true to those concepts, here is a challenge. Nearly 100 industry leaders signed up to take part in the Futures Lab, but there are more than 100 people who have the answers. There are probably hundreds of thousands of them. And it would be churlish of UK's Olympic leaders if they didn't want to hear from them. So this, dear reader, is the challenge: why don't you join the Futures Lab too?

Here are five starter questions that need answering:

1. GB succeeded in doing what no one thought possible at the Rio Olympics and beat China. Is it conceivable they can take on the USA – and how?
2. What will be the future global trends and megatrends in 2024 that will shape the world of elite sport?
3. Which emerging technologies have the potential to revolutionise athletes' training and performance, and how?
4. How could the UK's high-performance system reduce its reliance on public sector funding? What are the alternative business models?
5. Where are the future GB medallists that no one has yet spotted?

If you want to help shape the Olympic future by answering those questions, here is the link where UK Sport would like to hear from you: www.uksport.gov.uk/talentlab. Join the conversation. Come on in to the Talent Lab.

There is, of course, another way to sustaining success; it is the single most long-term effective way, and, despite the success of recent Olympics, it is one that has eluded the British system. It is straightforward: if you widen the base of the pyramid by creating greater participation at school and grassroots level, then you automatically expand your talent pool.

Why does the UK invest £347m over four years into elite Olympic and Paralympic sport? The idea is that, by creating Olympic heroes, you are inspiring a new generation to participate; you are creating a shop window for sport and persuading others to come on in. That is fine, but as a theory it would be far more effective if it overlapped with a more concerted investment programme into school sport, facilities, coaching and opportunity at the grassroots. At the moment, the shop window of Olympic sport in the UK looks brilliant, but there is not enough going on in the shop itself. That is a problem for government and has been for decades.

UK Sport, though, is all about the elite end, the shop window. And even there, after 67 Olympic medals, there is a feeling that the shop window is not yet full enough. There are areas in Olympic competition where GB continues to fail. In rowing, for instance, they cannot get a quad to win a medal; in athletics, the search went out for some female throwers and was unsuccessful. Sophie Hitchon, a 25-year-old hammer-thrower from Burnley, did win a bronze in Rio, but she seemed the exception that proved the rule: yes, we can make female throwers – so why can't we make a few more? Also on the shopping list: middle-distance runners. Why are none of them on the medals board? Kelly Holmes was over a decade ago. And there is no apparent reason why GB can crack it in some sports, but not with both genders.

Since 2000, when there was first a women's modern pentathlon event at the Olympics, GB women have won five medals and GB men none. Similarly, GB doesn't do particularly well in judo, but the four medals since 1988 have all been hung around women's necks.

In a rare, relaxed moment, UK Sport performance director Simon Timson sat back in his chair and dreamily contemplated his future: 'My retirement plan is to settle in at Bath and produce an Olympic high jump champion. Go round the schools, find the kids with the tallest parents, coach them really well. Come on, we've got tall people. It shouldn't be that hard.'

So, yes, the story of Great Britain at the Olympics since 1996 is one of sustained success. No, the Talent Lab hasn't found a solution to everything. The search continues.

Owen Slot would like to thank:

Over 100 people were interviewed for this book. Many more than that helped to bring these stories to life. Inevitably, there will be people whose names should have been included here, and apologies to them. Many thanks to: Mark England, Bill Sweeney, Mike Hay, Tim Hollingsworth, Chris Spice, Mel Marshall, Nigel Redman, Phil Gallagher, Jane Figueiredo, Tom Daley, Andy Banks, Ian Yates, Mark Wood, Helen Glover, Heather Stanning, David Tanner, Paul Stannard, Paul Thompson, Peter Shakespear, Nicolas Chisholm, Karen Daly, Floyd Woodrow, Gary Hall, Paul Buxton, Jack Laugher, Lew Hardy, Paul Hall, Scott Hann, Max Whitlock, Martin Reddin, Eddie van Hoof, Danny Kerry, Steve Peters, Dan Hunt, Rebecca Romero, Giselle Mather, Paula Dunn, Hannah McLeod, Alex Danson, Steve Scott, Steve Headington, John Wood, Steven Seligmann, Matt Parker, Dave Brailsford, Ed Clancy, Wilma Shakespear, David James, Hazel Shaw, Gethin Watts, Toni Minichiello, Mark Nicholls, Alistair Brownlee, Jonny Brownlee, Keith Brownlee, Malcolm Brown, Jack Maitland, Dan Salcedo, Oyvind Sandbakk, Alex Stacey, Kirsty Drawer, Dave Henson, Jayne Kavanagh, Jayne Ellis, Georgina Sharples, Katie Jones, Katherine Grainger, James Bell, Katie Warriner, Giles Scott, Clarissa Farr, Scott Drawer, Tony Purnell, Peter Bentley, Emma Barton, Shane Sutton,

Glenn Hunter, Lee Murgatroyd, Rob McCracken, Mark Ellison, Bob Dillon, Gerard Kemkers, Matt Holt, Graham Taylor, John Norfolk, Sam Timmermans, Mark Wood, Natalie Dunman, Scott Field, Caroline Searle, Emma Kennedy, Scott Dougal, Tim Peake, Gemma Field, Dave Richards, Craig Mortimer-Zhika, Susie Oakley, Clive Woodward, Will Harwood.

On a personal note, thank you to: David Luxton, for your support, Andrew Goodfellow for backing this project, and most of all to Juliet for your love, support and incredible patience.

Simon Timson would like to thank:

British Olympic and Paralympic sport has been on a long journey of evolution to the peaks achieved in Rio. Sustaining success, realising our aspiration to be more successful in Rio than London took huge passion, unique expertise and unwavering commitment from thousands of athletes, coaches, practitioners, and leaders over the last 20 years. Hundreds of them contributed to this book, and supported me on my to journey to Rio. Doubtless, there will be some I should mention here, apologies to those I haven't. Many thanks to: Chelsea Warr, Liz Nicholl, Rod Carr, Jasmina Lazarevic, Vanessa Wilson, Nigel Walker, Mark England, Penny Briscoe, Tim Hollingsworth, Bill Sweeney, Lew Hardy, James Bell, Floyd Woodrow.

Performance Directors play a crucial role setting the strategy for their sports, and managing the inevitable bumps in the road along the way. Their footprint is evident throughout the book, and I would like to thank a number that have given me particular support over the years including Sir David Tanner, John Derbyshire, John Anderson, Hugh Morris, Andi Schmid and Tony Wallington. Thanks also to John Harris for all his wisdom and guidance over the last 15 years as my professional mentor.

UK Sport leads from the front, I would like to thank the entire organisation, and my former team in the Performance Directorate in particular for their vision, drive and energy that helped sustain success and facilitate so many of the achievements highlighted in this book.

On a personal note, my family deserve the greatest thanks of all for the support and sacrifices they have made to enable me to be part of the journey to Rio and writing this book: my Mum and Dad for giving me such a great education and grounding in life; my wife, Jo, for being with me through all the highs and lows of leading a high-performance system along the road to Rio and giving me the belief we could realise the ambition; my children, Josh and Ame, for always providing love and perspective - invaluable at the most challenge times - hopefully they'll draw some inspiration from these stories one day.

Chelsea Warr would like to thank:

The British Government for their unwavering and continuing belief in us; the National Lottery and everyone who plays it; The DCMS and Nick Pontefract; the BOA/BPA; the English Institute of Sport and Home Country Sports Councils for their technical performance support and ensuring our athletes and coaches are the best prepared in the world; the performance directors and WCP teams, who dedicate their lives to helping athletes achieve their dreams.

Liz Nicholl – the backbone of the HP system since it originated and instrumental in the HP systems transformation. She is the wise guardian of the system who shows unwavering dedication, resilience and extraordinary commitment to doing what's right to support our athletes. A woman of huge integrity who role-models it every day.

Sue Campbell – the catalyst for change. She had the ambition to see GB develop into a sporting super-power and has inspired the nation and future generations.

Peter Keen – undoubtedly GB's most intelligent HP architect. Pete made sense of how to get us on a path to winning, for which we will be forever grateful.

Wilma Shakespear who always challenged me, 'Why Not?'

The talented, enormously dedicated and expert UK Sport Team; our competitors, who push us in our quest for continual improvement and excellence; the Great British public, who support Team GB and Paralympics GB and buy those lotto tickets.

And finally, my mum and dad and the whole Warr family – especially my four-year-old niece, who I hope will read this book when she's old enough and be inspired to know that if you really want to achieve something in life, you can – with hard work, dedication and a sprinkling of courage.